BIRDS OF THE PALEARCTIC
PASSERINES

BIRDS OF THE PALEARCTIC
PASSERINES

Text and illustrations by Norman Arlott

Collins

I would like to dedicate this book to ten special children:
Robert, Thomas, Andrew, Kimberley, Rebecca,
Leah, Dylan, Louise, Kassie and Owen.

HarperCollins Publishers Ltd
77–85 Fulham Palace Road
Hammersmith
London W6 8JB

The Collins website address is:
www.collins.co.uk

Collins is a registered trademark of
HarperCollins Publishers Ltd

First published 2007

11 10 09 08 07

10 9 8 7 6 5 4 3 2 1

A catalogue record for this book is available from the British Library.

ISBN-10 0 00 714705 8
ISBN-13 978 0 00 714705 2

Edited and designed by D & N Publishing, Hungerford, Berkshire

Reproduction by Colourscan, Singapore
Printed and bound in Singapore by Imago

CONTENTS

ACKNOWLEDGEMENTS

Bird books take a relatively short time to paint and write, but the knowledge that enables them to be completed is gained over many, many years. I can remember my passion started when I was a very young boy bird-nesting (now, quite rightly, frowned upon) with my father. That passion has since been enhanced by being fortunate enough to be in the field with, and to be inspired by, some well-known and not so well-known 'birders'. In particular, I must mention the following, who have encouraged me and allowed me to pick their brains over the years: the late John G. Williams, the late Eric Hosking, the late Crispin Fisher, Robert Gillmor, Basil Parsons, Brian Leflay and Moss Taylor. This book could not have gone ahead without the help of the staff at the British Museum at Tring, especially Mark Adams and Robert Prys-Jones. I was also given special help by Keith Betton, Kees Roselaar and Richard Sale; the latter took on the vast task of preparing the distribution maps. David Price-Goodfellow deserves special praise for his skill, and patience, in putting together the various component parts of this book. Without publishers there would not be a book, so it gives me great pleasure to thank everyone at HarperCollins, particularly Myles Archibald, Emily Pitcher and Helen Brocklehurst. Last, but definitely not least, I must thank friends and family who have had to put up with my various mood changes whilst trying to sort out some of the more difficult aspects of putting this book together, of whom my wife Marie probably endured more than most.

Jay (*Garrulus glandarius*) variation across the region.

INTRODUCTION

When originally encouraged to take on this project I knew that I wanted it to do two things: to be a reminder of birds already seen and to be a helpful nudge towards what to look for when searching for new birds. I did not want to produce just a coloured checklist or the ultimate field guide – size alone meant that the latter, with the restriction on the amount of text and number of plates, was not possible anyway. I decided that most of the text in this book would be based on the type of notes I make before embarking on a field trip to a new area; hopefully they will, along with the illustrations, help to identify most birds that will be encountered. Obviously, the use of more in-depth tomes will be required for some of the trickier species (*see* Further Reading).

I also decided, owing to the great number of species involved, to split the book into two volumes: non-passerines and passerines. Rightly or wrongly, and for many reasons that do not need explanation here, I decided to produce the passerine volume first.

Hopefully within these pages I have been able to add to the pleasure of anticipation or memory, and perhaps even add some extra piece of knowledge about the birds of this vast region.

Yellow Wagtail (*Motacilla flava*) variation across the region.

AREA AND SPECIES COVERED

When deciding on the species to include in this guide, the biggest problem came when trying to define the Palearctic area. Having looked at various compilations I could find no reason not to follow the excellently argued and put together checklist by Mark Beaman. I have used his area of delineation (there is not room here to duplicate his explanations for where the Palearctic boundaries should be placed; *see* map) and his species list, only adding species that have appeared in the area since his book was published. I hope that any new additions, from mid-2005 on, will be incorporated into expected future updates. I have also had to tweak the established order a little to aid plate composition – hopefully this will not cause too much aggravation.

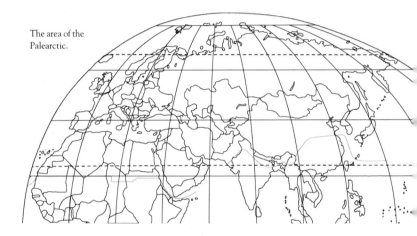

The area of the Palearctic.

Every species of the region, and most major subspecies, have been depicted in breeding plumage, and in non-breeding plumage when it differs significantly. To keep the book to a manageable size, no juvenile plumages have been illustrated, although, when necessary, a short passage in 'Field Notes' has been included.

The abbreviations and symbols used on the plates are as follows:
♂ = Male.
♀ = Female.
br = Breeding.
n-br = Non-breeding.
nom = Nominate race.

NOMENCLATURE

I have headlined the English names that I believe are those used by most birding persons, which means I have in many cases reverted to 'old school' names rather than some of the more modern interpretations, e.g. Jay rather than the long-winded Eurasian Jay. Most of these 'new' names, along with others that are well known, are included in parentheses.

IDENTIFICATION

It is hoped that the illustrations will be all that is needed to identify a specific bird, but quite obviously with some of the trickier 'little brown jobs' more information is needed, hence the need for Field Notes, Song, Call and Habitat.

FIELD NOTES: Because of the need to keep text to a minimum, this section does not mention those aspects of a bird that should be obvious from the illustrations, e.g. wing-bars, bill shape, etc. It is used mainly to point to a bird's habits or to mention facets of identification hidden in a standing or perched bird.

SONG: A bird's song is probably the first sign of its presence, especially in the breeding season. The descriptions are shown in *italics*. Where space has allowed I have included different interpretations of the same song. Although it is difficult to produce an accurate reproduction of a bird song in the written word, this, and the call section, are worth studying in order to get a feel for what is often the most important area of bird identification.

CALL: The common calls are described and shown in *italics*. This is a very important area of bird identification, especially in the non-breeding season when most birds do not give their full song. The call may be vital in helping to locate and identify small, fast-moving, semi-hidden birds, so they are well worth learning.

HABITAT: The distribution maps should be consulted in conjunction with this section. The main habitat preferences mentioned are those in which a species breeds; also included are wintering habitats if appropriate.

RACES: This informaton is included to show distinct variations. It will be noticed that many of the depicted races have been, or are about to be, considered as full species. General areas of occurrence are given.

Singing male Subalpine Warbler (*Sylvia cantillans*).

11

BIRD TOPOGRAPHY

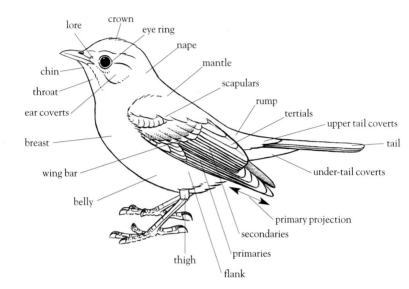

lore
crown
eye ring
nape
mantle
scapulars
rump
tertials
upper tail coverts
tail
chin
throat
ear coverts
breast
wing bar
belly
thigh
primaries
flank
secondaries
primary projection
under-tail coverts

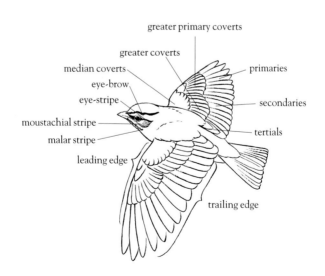

greater primary coverts
greater coverts
median coverts
eye-brow
eye-stripe
moustachial stripe
malar stripe
leading edge
primaries
secondaries
tertials
trailing edge

SPECIES DESCRIPTIONS

AND COLOUR PLATES

1 TYRANT FLYCATCHERS, PITTAS, CUCKOO-SHRIKES AND MINIVETS

1 EASTERN PHOEBE *Sayornis phoebe* 18cm (Vagrant) FIELD NOTES: Frequent fly-catching sallies from a prominent perch. Persistently wags and spreads tail. SONG: Distinctive *fee-be*. CALL: Sharp *chip*. HABITAT: In native North America: woodland, woodland edge, farmland, stream sides, farm and suburban buildings.

2 ACADIAN FLYCATCHER *Empidonax virescens* 15cm (Vagrant) FIELD NOTES: Makes darting fly-catching sallies, usually from deep shade below tree canopy; wags tail when perched. SONG: Explosive *wee-see*. CALL: Thin *peet*. HABITAT: In native North America: deep shade in deciduous wooded swamps.

3 HOODED PITTA *Pitta sordida* 19cm (Vagrant) FIELD NOTES: Ground feeder, often perches on vines or branches when singing. SONG: Loud *whew-whew*. CALL: When alarmed, *skyew*. HABITAT: In native India and SE Asia: various forest types, from broadleaved evergreen to bamboo.

4 FAIRY PITTA *Pitta nympha* 20cm FIELD NOTES: Ground feeder. SONG: Clear whistled *kwah-he kwa-wu*. CALL: *kriah*. HABITAT: Mostly in moist lowland forest with thick undergrowth but can be found in lighter deciduous forest or scrub jungle, especially in China.

5 BLACK-WINGED CUCKOO-SHRIKE *Coracina melaschistos* 24cm FIELD NOTES: Arboreal, singly or pairs, works through branches, often hovering in front of leaves to feed on insects, when white patch under each wing may be conspicuous. SONG/CALL: Slow, descending, 3- or 4-note whistle *twii-twii-weeo-weeow*. HABITAT: Open woodland up to 2000m.

6 LONG-TAILED MINIVET *Pericrocotus ethologus* 20cm FIELD NOTES: Gregarious. Large flocks, 20–40 plus, fly chattering from treetop to treetop where they feed among the branches, often hovering in front of leaves to hawk insects. SONG: Distinctive double-whistled *pi-ru*. CALL: *djib-djib* and a tit-like chatter, possibly used as a contact call as flocks move along treetops. HABITAT: Open forests mainly at 1000–2000m.

7 GREY-CHINNED MINIVET *Pericrocotus solaris* 17cm FIELD NOTES: Forages in small, noisy, flocks. SONG: Soft *tzee-zip*. CALL: Soft *trip* or stronger *trii-ti*. HABITAT: Montane forests.

8 SMALL MINIVET *Pericrocotus cinnamomeus pallidus* 15cm (Vagrant) FIELD NOTES: Flits about in small flocks. SONG/CALL: Constantly repeated thin, drawn-out *tswee-swee*. HABITAT (race *P. c. pallidus*): In native Pakistan: foothill forests, scrub jungle, acacia and subtropical dry forests. Altitudinal wanderer to region.

9 ASHY MINIVET *Pericrocotus divaricatus* 20cm FIELD NOTES: Forms small flocks to feed on insects in tree canopy. Shows large white underwing patches in flight. SONG/CALL: Jangling metallic trill, often uttered in flight. HABITAT: Deciduous woodland and forest edge.

10 RYUKYU MINIVET *Pericrocotus tegimae* 20cm (Often regarded as subspecies of Ashy Minivet) FIELD NOTES: As Ashy Minivet? SONG/CALL: As Ashy Minivet? HABITAT: As Ashy Minivet?

2 LARKS

1 SINGING BUSH LARK *Mirafra cantillans* 14cm FIELD NOTES: Song-flight like Skylark, but at less elevation. SONG: In flight or from a prominent perch, various repetitive short phrases ending in a buzzing trill; often includes mimicry. CALL: *chirrup*, usually uttered when alarmed. HABITAT: Open areas of short grass with bushes.

2 DUNN'S LARK *Eremalauda dunni* 14–15cm FIELD NOTES: Forms small, nomadic flocks in non-breeding season. SONG: Rapid series of chirping and dry notes, given from a low perch or in flight. CALL: Loud *chee-ooo* when flushed. Flight calls varied, *chiup-chiup*, *too-weet* or a thin *prrp*. HABITAT: Flat, gravelly or sandy desert or semi-desert. RACES: *E. d. eremodites* (fig 2b) Middle East.

3 KORDOFAN BUSH LARK *Mirafra cordofanica* 15cm FIELD NOTES: High (100m), long-lasting song-flight. SONG/CALL: Much like Singing Bush Lark with a variation of whistles and trills, but less repetitive. HABITAT: Arid desert or semi-desert with sparse grass and scattered bushes.

4 BLACK-CROWNED SPARROW-LARK *Eremopterix nigriceps* 12cm FIELD NOTES: In winter forms flocks of 20–50, occasionally more. SONG: Repeated *wit-ti-weee*, or similar, given during a low, drifting, wing-fluttering song-flight or from a bush or rock. CALL: Sparrow-like *tchip* or a *zree* when alarmed. HABITAT: Arid or semiarid areas with scattered low bushes or trees.

5 CHESTNUT-HEADED SPARROW-LARK *Eremopterix signata* 12cm (Vagrant) FIELD NOTES: Outside breeding season forms flocks of 40 or so. SONG: Simple twittering given from low perch or in flight. CALL: Sharp *chip-up*. HABITAT: In native NE Africa: semiarid or arid grassy plains.

6 BAR-TAILED DESERT LARK *Ammomanes cincturus arenicolor* 14cm FIELD NOTES: Nomadic, non-breeding flocks perform wader-like twists and turns in flight. SONG: Repeated, thin, rhythmic note interspersed with louder *see-oo-lee*. Often given during aerial display. CALL: Harsh *bshee*, a nasal *chup* and a thin *peeyu*. HABITAT: Stone or sandy desert, semiarid savannah.

7 DESERT LARK *Ammomanes deserti* 15–17cm FIELD NOTES: Can be confiding. SONG: Repeated, far-carrying, 2- or 3-syllable phrase *trreooee*, given from ground or flight. CALL: Variable, *chu* or *chee-lu*, which becomes a rapid twitter when excited. HABITAT: Rocky hill-slopes near escarpments in desert or semi-desert. RACES: *A. d. payni* (fig 7b) Morocco, SW Algeria; *A. d. annae* (fig 7c) N Jordan. Other races occur, their colour usually matching their habitat.

8 HOOPOE LARK *Alaemon alaudipes* 18–20cm FIELD NOTES: Confiding. In flight, black and white wing pattern is striking. SONG: Characteristic desert sound, given during acrobatic display-flight: melodious piping notes, starting slowly, accelerating as bird climbs, a short trill at peak of ascent, reverting to piping notes, lowering in tone and speed, during descent. CALL: Buzzing *zeee*. HABITAT: Desert, semi-desert, rolling dunes with or without sparse vegetation.

9 DUPONT'S LARK *Chersophilus duponti* 17cm FIELD NOTES: A skulker, often runs off when encountered. SONG: Twittering and buzzing notes, given from ground or during towering song-flight. CALL: Fluting *hoo-hee*, *pu-chee* or *coo-chic*; a short *tsii* when alarmed. HABITAT: Open arid or semiarid flat land with low scrub or tufted grass. Outside breeding season often frequents cereal fields. RACES: *C. d. margaritae* (fig 9b) Algeria, Tunisia, N Libya, NW Egypt.

10 HORNED LARK (SHORE LARK) *Eremophila alpestris flava* 16–19cm FIELD NOTES: Small winter flocks often include buntings and finches. SONG: From perch or flight, simple rippling trills followed by a short chatter. CALL: Various, including a short *eeh* or double *eeh-ti*; also a harsher *tsrr*. HABITAT: *E. a. flava* breeds on dry tundra and winters on salt marshes, beaches and stubble-fields. RACES: Many races occur throughout the region, varying mainly in intensity of upperpart and head colour. *E. a. albigula.* (fig 10b) Turkmenistan, NE Iran east to Tien Shan.

11 TEMMINCK'S LARK *Eremophila bilopha* 15cm FIELD NOTES: Often confiding. Loose flocks include other lark species. SONG: In flight or from ground, similar to, but quieter than, Horned Lark, monotonous warbling and twittering interspersed with short whistles. CALL: Loud *tsip* or *sweep*, or *see-oo*. HABITAT: Barren, flat stony desert or semi-desert with sparse vegetation.

3 LARKS

1 THICK-BILLED LARK *Ramphocoris clotbey* 17cm FIELD NOTES: When feeling threatened will often run, rather than fly. Forms large winter flocks. SONG: Quiet medley of tinkling and warbling notes, given from the ground or in flight. CALL: Far-carrying *coo-ee*, a quiet *shree*, in flight a sharp *prit*. HABITAT: Breeds in flat stony desert with scattered low vegetation, sometimes in more vegetated areas. In winter often spreads to more cultivated areas and arid coastal plains.

2 CALANDRA LARK *Melanocorypha calandra* 18–20cm FIELD NOTES: Underwing looks blackish with distinct white trailing edge; white-sided tail. Sociable. SONG: Skylark-like but louder and more complex with harsher, stronger notes, usually given in flight. CALL: *treeh*, *trip-trip* or a harsher *tshrreeep*. HABITAT: Grass plains, open cultivation, wasteland and steppe.

3 TIBETAN LARK *Melanocorypha maxima* 21–22cm FIELD NOTES: In flight shows white trailing edge to wing and much white in tail. SONG: Given from flight or perch, a mix of slow-flowing phrases interspersed with grating notes and mimicry of other birds. Continuous or split into short strophes. CALL: Loud whistles when disturbed, also low grating notes. HABITAT: High-altitude grassy or marshy lakeside or riverside areas.

4 BIMACULATED LARK *Melanocorypha bimaculata* 16–18cm FIELD NOTES: In flight, underwing greyish, white-tipped tail. SONG: Like Calandra Lark but with fewer harsh notes, given in flight or perched. CALL: *churrup*, *chup* or a liquid *plip*. HABITAT: Mostly stony sparsely grassed plateaux in hilly or mountainous areas, also in dry grass areas on plains.

5 MONGOLIAN LARK *Melanocorypha mongolica* 18cm FIELD NOTES: In flight shows a very wide white trailing edge to wing. SONG: Sustained twittering, mixed with dry notes, much like Bimaculated Lark. CALL: Various harsh, high-pitched, rolling notes. HABITAT: Prefers dry grassland, but also found in damper areas and rocky uplands.

6 WHITE-WINGED LARK *Melanocorypha leucoptera* 18cm FIELD NOTES: Wing with broad white trailing edge. Forms large flocks in winter. SONG: Skylark-like though sweeter, higher pitched and jerkier, given in flight or from ground. CALL: Harsh *tcher-ee*, a tinny *wed* and a twittering *drrit-drrit*. HABITAT: Natural steppe, dry heath; also cultivated areas in winter.

7 BLACK LARK *Melanocorypha yeltoniensis* 20cm FIELD NOTES: Fresh-plumage male has pale fringes, giving bird a scaly look. Worn females becomes darker above, including head, often blotched darker below. SONG: Like Skylark but with shorter frantic phrases, higher pitched and including mimicry, given in display-flight or from low perch. CALL: Short, harsh notes similar to Calandra Lark. HABITAT: Grassy and shrubby steppe often by lakes; also cultivation edge in winter.

8 SKYLARK (EURASIAN OR COMMON SKYLARK) *Alauda arvensis* 16–18cm
FIELD NOTES: Forms winter flocks, often with other ground feeders, e.g. pipits, finches, buntings. SONG: Various, lengthy, warbling and trilling phrases mixed with mimicry and the odd call note, from high display-flight or low perch. CALL: When flushed a liquid *chirrip* or dryer, short notes such as *prrylh* or *preet*. HABITAT: Various grassy areas, e.g. cultivated fields, moorland and alpine pastures; disperses in winter to include salt marshes and coastal beaches. RACES: *A. a. dulcivox* (fig 8b) SE Russia, C Asia; *A. a. japonica* (Japanese Skylark) (fig 8c) Japan. Other races occur throughout region, grading from darkish brown to greyish.

9 ORIENTAL SKYLARK *Alauda gulgula* 16cm FIELD NOTES: More secretive than Skylark, keeping to cover and flying only a short distance when flushed. SONG: Much like Skylark, but weaker than, Skylark, given in similar display-flight or from low perch. CALL: Distinctive buzzy *baz-baz* or *baz-terr*; also *twip*. HABITAT: Dry upland grassland, coastal marshes, edges of lakes, rivers and paddies; also less often in large forest clearings.

10 RASO LARK *Alauda razae* 14cm FIELD NOTES: The only lark on Raso Island. SONG: Skylark-like but less complicated, with longer gaps between phrases, delivered in flight or on ground. CALL: Weak versions of those of Skylark. HABITAT: Mostly on flat, decaying, lava plain with sand patches that support low vegetation; disperses to other areas in non-breeding season.

4 LARKS

1 SHORT-TOED LARK *Calandrella brachydactyla* 15cm FIELD NOTES: Crouched feeding posture. Large flocks out of breeding season. SONG: Mainly given in flight, contains accelerating simple notes, several hesitant notes, finished off with long series of repeated bubbling phrases. CALL: *chirrup, dreet* or *trilp*. HABITAT: Dry plains, dry cultivation, semi-desert. RACES: *C. b. dukhunensis* (Rufous Short-toed Lark) (fig1b) Tibet, C China.

2 LESSER SHORT-TOED LARK *Calandrella rufescens apetzii* 14cm FIELD NOTES: Shows more primary projection than Short-toed Lark. Low, circling display-flight with slow wing-beats. SONG: Richer, more varied and faster paced than Short-toed Lark. CALL: Dry, buzzing *prrit* or *chirrick*. HABITAT: Dry plains, steppe and cultivation, saline flats, semi-desert. RACES: *C. r. minor* (fig 2b) N Africa, Middle East.

3 BLANFORD'S LARK *Calandrella blanfordi eremica* 14cm FIELD NOTES: Often considered a race of Short-toed Lark; actions similar. SONG: Given in flight, *chew-chew-chew-chew* with call notes and more fluid phrases added. CALL: *peeeep, pit-wit-wit*, a soft *tsru* and a *drelit-drelit* in flight. HABITAT: High, open, bare or grassed areas, stony with or without bushes. Lower areas in winter.

4 SAND LARK *Calandrella raytal* 13cm FIELD NOTES: Actions much like Short-toed Lark. Noticeably short-tailed. SONG: Usually in flight, short with disjointed, dry rattling phrases. CALL: Dry *churrp* or *che-chir*. HABITAT: Dry, sandy, coastal and river sandbanks, also salty mudflats.

5 HUME'S SHORT-TOED LARK *Calandrella acutirostris* 14cm FIELD NOTES: Beware, very similar to greyish races of Short-toed Lark. Small winter flocks rarely contain other lark species. SONG: Monotonous series of faint disjointed notes, given mainly in flight. CALL: Sharp *trree* or rattled *drreep*. HABITAT: High sandy or gravelly areas with sparse vegetation.

6 ASIAN SHORT-TOED LARK *Calandrella cheleensis* 14cm FIELD NOTES: Often regarded as a race of Lesser Short-toed Lark; actions similar. SONG: Given mainly in flight, simple and flowing, including a long *tije-tije-tije-tije-tije…* and mimicry. CALL: Lapland Bunting-like percussive rattle and a ringing *ut-ut-ut*. HABITAT: Arid steppe, semi-desert, salt and soda plains with scattered scrubby vegetation; in winter disperses to take in wet meadows and fields. RACES: *C. c. leucophaea* (fig 6b) Turkey east to Kazakhstan.

7 WOODLARK *Lullula arborea* 15cm FIELD NOTES: Readily perches on trees, bushes or wires. SONG: Beautiful, starts slowly then quickens with a repeated *lee - lee-lee-leeleeleeleelululululul…ee-lu-ee-lu-ee-luee-lu-eelululululu…*. CALL: Soft *tlwee-tleww* or feeble *dudulee*. HABITAT: Open forest, heathland, young plantations, and open country with trees; in winter, often found in more open cultivation, e.g. stubble-fields.

8 THEKLA LARK *Galerida theklae* 17cm FIELD NOTES: Underwing greyish. Perches more readily on bushes than Crested Lark. SONG: Prolonged loud fluting, interspersed with short whistles, trills and mimicry, often from a low perch. CALL: *tu-telli-tew-tille-tee*. HABITAT: Mainly rocky slopes with bushes, mountain-slopes, dry steppe; less often on lowland cultivation. RACES: *G. t. carolinae* (fig 8b) N Africa.

9 CRESTED LARK *Galerida cristata* 18cm FIELD NOTES: Underwing tinged rusty. SONG: Given in flight, less so from ground, a mix of sweet fluty warbling phrases, call notes and mimicry. CALL: *treeleepuu* or *vu-tee-vuu*. HABITAT: Fields, wasteland, open industrial sites, dry steppe and semi-desert. RACES: *G. c. magna* (fig 9b) Kazakhstan east to N China. Many other races throughout the region, the birds' colour often reflecting habitat colour.

5 MARTINS AND TREE SWALLOW

1 PLAIN SAND MARTIN *Riparia paludicola mauritanica* 12cm FIELD NOTES: Weak fluttering flight can recall a small bat. SONG: Soft twittering often uttered in flight. CALL: Low *chrrr* or a harsh *sveeh*. HABITAT: Near rivers, streams, lakes and sandpits. Often roosts in reed-beds.

2 SAND MARTIN *Riparia riparia* 12cm FIELD NOTES: Rapid, light flight. Highly gregarious. SONG: Broken twittering phrases. CALL: Harsh *tschr* or *brrtt*. HABITAT: Various watercourses or sandpits where vertical banks are available for nesting. Often roosts in reed-beds. On migration, in open areas, e.g. grassland and farmland. RACES: *R. r. diluta* (Pale Sand Martin) (fig 2b) Nepal, Kazakhstan. Often treated as a full species.

3 BANDED MARTIN *Riparia cincta* 17cm (Vagrant) FIELD NOTES: Noticeably large. Often solitary. Flight slow and sluggish compared with Sand Martin. SONG: Subdued squeaky warbling or a louder chattering. CALL: Short *chip*. HABITAT: In native Africa: marshland, rivers and grassland. Roosts in reed-beds.

4 TREE SWALLOW *Tachycineta bicolor* 15cm (Vagrant) FIELD NOTES: Flight light, often straight and direct with sudden dips or turns to catch food. SONG: Repeated *weeet-triit-weeet*, rounded off with a liquid twitter. CALL: Sharp *cheet* or *chi-veet*, and a *duli-duli-duli* contact call. HABITAT: In native N America: open woodlands usually near water. Roosts in marshes or trees.

5 PURPLE MARTIN *Progne subis* 19cm (Vagrant) FIELD NOTES: Feeds high up, to 50m plus. Often flies in circles with a gliding then rapid-flapping flight; less mobile than most European martins. SONG: Highly vocal, male has a gurgling croak, female a chortle; various other sub-songs. CALL: *cher*, *zweet* and *zwrack* when alarmed. HABITAT: In native N America: forest edge, semi-open areas, usually near water and around human habitation. Roosts in trees or on buildings.

6 HOUSE MARTIN *Delichon urbicum* 13cm FIELD NOTES: Less twisting flight than Swallow, more gliding and soaring, often at great height. SONG: Soft, rapid twittering interspersed with a dry rattling. CALL: Abrupt *prrt* or longer *pri-pit*. HABITAT: Buildings in towns, villages and farms, also cliff-faces. Feeds in various open areas.

7 NEPAL HOUSE MARTIN *Delichon nipalensis* 13cm FIELD NOTES: Fast flight. Highly gregarious. SONG/CALL: Mostly silent, sometimes a high-pitched *chi-i* flight call. HABITAT: Wooded mountain ridges with cliffs and river valleys, also around mountain villages.

8 ASIAN HOUSE MARTIN *Delichon dasypus* 13cm FIELD NOTES: Flight slow and fluttering. Highly gregarious. SONG/CALL: Similar to House Martin. HABITAT: Gorges, valleys, villages in hilly or mountain areas; also sea-cliffs and caves.

9 ROCK MARTIN *Ptyonoprogne fuligula obsoleta* 13cm FIELD NOTES: Flight slow. Pale spots on spread tail. SONG: Low twitter. CALL: High-pitched *twee* or rapid *chir-chir-chir*. HABITAT: Cliffs, gorges, ravines in dry country, also some desert towns. RACES: *P. f. spatzi* (fig 9b) SC Algeria. Other races occur, varying in intensity of colour.

10 CRAG MARTIN (EURASIAN CRAG MARTIN) *Ptyonoprogne rupestris* 15cm FIELD NOTES: Powerful agile flight. Pale spots on spread tail. SONG: Quiet, throaty, rapid twitter. CALL: *prrit* or *chwit*. HABITAT: Cliffs, gorges, buildings in hills or mountains. Outside breeding season often around coastal buildings and sea-cliffs.

6 SWALLOWS

1 SWALLOW (BARN SWALLOW) *Hirundo rustica* 18cm FIELD NOTES: Agile, fast flier that twists and turns to catch flying insects. Juvenile has much shorter tail streamers. SONG: Melodious twittering interspersed with a grating rattle, given in flight or perched. CALL: *vit-vit* or a sharper *flitt-flitt* or *chir-chir* when alarmed. HABITAT: Mainly open country where buildings are available for nesting. RACES: *H. r. savignii* (fig 1b) NE Africa.

2 PACIFIC SWALLOW *Hirundo tahitica nameyei* 13cm FIELD NOTES: Fast flight with glides and frequent swerving and banking. SONG: Twittering *twsit-twsit-twsit*. CALL: *tit-see*. HABITAT: Coastal cliffs, open country, forested hills and human habitations near water.

3 ETHIOPIAN SWALLOW *Hirundo aethiopica* 13cm (Vagrant) FIELD NOTES: Low-flying fast flight, with few glides. SONG: Melodious weak twittering. CALL: Repeated *cheep* or *chi* and *preut* when alarmed. HABITAT: In native Africa: open areas, open woodland, coastal cliffs and human habitations.

4 WIRE-TAILED SWALLOW *Hirundo smithii* 14–21cm FIELD NOTES: Flight fast, often low over water. Immatures have brownish crown and lack fine tail filaments SONG: Twittering *chrrickweet-chrrickweet*. CALL: *chit-chit* or *pwee*; when alarmed, *chichip-chichip*. HABITAT: Grassland, open woodland, cultivation and human habitation, all usually near water.

5 RED-RUMPED SWALLOW *Cecropis daurica* 16–17cm FIELD NOTES: Flight slow and graceful, much gliding and soaring. Juvenile, which can look like House Martin, duller with shorter tail streamers and buffy rump. SONG: Twittering, shorter and quieter than Swallow. CALL: A contact *djuit*, an aggressive *krr*; territorial mewing. HABITAT: Open hilly country, valleys and gorges where cliffs, caves, old buildings or bridges can be used for nest sites. RACES: *C. d. japonica* (fig 5b) NE and E China, Korea, Japan; *C. d. rufula* (fig 5c) SW and S Europe, N Africa east to Asia.

6 LESSER STRIPED SWALLOW *Cecropis abyssinica* 15–19cm (Vagrant) FIELD NOTES: Flight erratic with much fluttering and gliding, although can be swift and direct. Immature birds have much shorter tail streamers. SONG: *chip-chip-chwip-kreek-kree-kree-kreep-chwip-kreee*, more vigorous and squeaky than Swallow. CALL: *tee-tee-tee*. HABITAT: In native Africa: forest edge, open woodland, grassland, savannah and around villages and towns.

7 AMERICAN CLIFF SWALLOW *Petrochelidon pyrrhonota* 14cm (Vagrant) FIELD NOTES: Glides and soars more like Red-rumped Swallow than other hirundines. SONG: Rapid squeaky twittering. CALL: *chur* or *purr* when alarmed. HABITAT: In native N America: open areas, farms and towns.

8 INDIAN CLIFF SWALLOW *Petrochelidon fluvicola* 12cm (Vagrant) FIELD NOTES: Weak, fluttering flight. SONG: Twittering. CALL: Sharp *trr-trr*. HABITAT: In native India: open country, foothills, cultivation and human habitation, often near water.

7 PIPITS

1 RICHARD'S PIPIT *Anthus richardi* 17–20cm FIELD NOTES: Undulating, powerful flight with long dips. Often stands very upright with neck stretched. SONG: Simple grinding *chee-chee-chee-chee-chia-chia-chia*, given during circling display-flight. CALL: Harsh *schreep* or longer *sherreeep* given as bird rises from ground; also a short *chup*. HABITAT: Wet meadows, moist grassland, and large open areas in forest. In winter, various grassy habitats and stubble-fields.

2 BLYTH'S PIPIT *Anthus godlewskii* 16cm FIELD NOTES: Very similar to Richard's Pipit. Walks a little more horizontally. SONG: *zreet-zreet-zreet zreet*, followed by a high-pitched *zrit-zrit-zrit-zrit* and ending in a rapid *zre-zre-zre-zre*, given in wing-fluttering display-flight. CALL: *chip-chip*, a nasal *psheeu* or a *bzrp* when alarmed. HABITAT: Dry grassy steppe, rocky hills and mountainsides with or without sparse grass. Winters in various grassy areas, much as Richard's Pipit.

3 UPLAND PIPIT *Anthus sylvanus* 17cm FIELD NOTES: When agitated stands upright, often on a rock, and flicks tail; otherwise creeps around in low vegetation. SONG: Repeated *seetyu-seetyu* or *tyu-see-tyu-ee*; also a more monotonous *weeeeee-tct-weeeeeee-tch* or *wichee-wiche-wichee*, rendered from a prominent perch or less often in flight. CALL: Sparrow-like *chirp*, not often used. HABITAT: Steep rocky and grassy slopes with scattered bushes and boulders; abandoned terrace cultivation and clearings in open pine forest.

4 TAWNY PIPIT *Anthus campestris* 17cm FIELD NOTES: Frequently pumps tail, especially when agitated. Juveniles can be similar to Richard's Pipit but with darker lores. SONG: Usually delivered in undulating display-flight is a monotonous repeated *tsirliih-tsirliih-tsirliih… tsirliih-tsirliih-tsirliih*. CALL: Weak *chilp* or *chirleep*. HABITAT: Open dry areas, e.g. sandy heaths, sand dunes and grassland with dwarf shrubs or trees.

5 LONG-BILLED PIPIT *Anthus similis* 17cm FIELD NOTES: Flicking tail action rather than the pumping of Tawny Pipit. Usually less upright carriage than Tawny Pipit. SONG: Far-carrying series of monotonous unmusical well-spaced phrases, *tjup-threee-tjup-tjup-threee* or *chreep-shreep-chew-ee*, delivered from perch or during fluttering, slow, display-flight. CALL: *chupp* or *chevlee*. HABITAT: Rocky hillsides and gorges with grasses and scrub. Lower plains in winter.

6 BERTHELOT'S PIPIT *Anthus berthelotii* 14cm FIELD NOTES: Often confiding. When wary prefers to run rather than fly away. SONG: Given from a perch or during undulating display-flight: series of cheerful energetic notes *tschilp-tschilp-tschilp-tschilp* or *tsiree-tsiree-tsiree-tsiree*. CALL: *tsri* or soft *chup*. HABITAT: Various dry open areas from sea-level to 2000m.

7 PADDYFIELD PIPIT *Anthus rufulus* 15cm FIELD NOTES: Much as Richard's Pipit. SONG: Like Richard's Pipit but faster and higher pitched. CALL: Hard *chep* or *chep-chep*. HABITAT: Open short grassland, savannah woodland, paddies, stubble-fields, roadsides and wetland edge. Altitudinal wanderer to the region.

8 RED-THROATED PIPIT *Anthus cervinus* 14cm FIELD NOTES: Rufous areas on head can be much less intense (female) or lacking altogether. SONG: Series of variable notes followed by thin rattling and buzzing notes, usually during display-flight. CALL: Short *tew* or longer, high-pitched *pseeeeu*. HABITAT: Marshy tundra. On migration, open, often damp, areas, e.g. meadows, paddies, coastal flats and grassy lake or river edges.

9 PECHORA PIPIT *Anthus gustavi* 15cm FIELD NOTES: Mouse-like skulker; if flushed, flies, often without calling, a short distance before dropping into cover. SONG: Usually given in a long lark-like hovering display-flight; distinctive with short buzzy or clear notes, alternated with drawn-out very fast buzzy rattles. CALL: *tsip* or a repeated *tsip-tsip-tsip-tsip*. HABITAT: Wet shrubby tundra, marshes with tall sedge or reeds; during migration, wet meadows, edges of marshes and paddies. RACES: *A. g. menzbieri* (Menzbier's Pipit) (fig 9b) Isolated area in NE China and SE Russia. Sometimes considered a full species.

8 PIPITS

1 OLIVE-BACKED PIPIT *Anthus hodgsoni* 14cm FIELD NOTES: Western race has a much plainer mantle. Actions similar to Tree Pipit. SONG: Given from a treetop perch or during display-flight; Tree Pipit-like but weaker and more varied, lacking the *swee-urr-swee-urr* ending. CALL: A drawn-out thin *tseez* much like Tree Pipit; *tsit* when alarmed. HABITAT: Mixed dense forest, more open lowland forest in winter.

2 TREE PIPIT *Anthus trivalis* 15cm FIELD NOTES: Walks with a slower, more deliberate gait than Meadow Pipit. Quite secretive, when flushed usually takes cover in a bush or tree. SONG: Given from treetop or during display-flight, consists of trills and repeated notes: *zit-zit-zit-zit-cha-cha-cha-surrrrrrrrrrr-siiiia-tvet-tvet-tvet-siva-siivi-siiiiha-swee-ur-swee-urr-swee-urr*; order of phrases may change but the end phrase generally remains the same. CALL: Hoarse, thin *tzeez* and a *seet-seet-seet* when alarmed. HABITAT: Woodland, woodland edge and heathland, or grassland with developing scrub and trees.

3 MEADOW PIPIT *Anthus pratensis* 15cm FIELD NOTES: Overall colour varies (mainly due to wear) from that shown, to paler olive-buff above and whiter below. Often perches on low wires after flushing. SONG: Given mainly during a display-flight that ends in a parachuting descent, consists of a series of accelerating *seep-seep-seep-seep* notes that gain in pitch, mixed with longer *tseut* phrases and ending in a long trill. CALL: Squeaky *seep* or *seep-seep-seep*. HABITAT: Wide variety of open grassland from coast to alpine meadows; heathland and moorland. In winter often found on lakesides and beaches feeding among strandline debris.

4 ROSY PIPIT *Anthus roseatus* 16cm FIELD NOTES: Actions similar to Water Pipit. SONG: Mainly during display-flight, starts with a monotonous *tree-tree-tree…* as bird rises, combined with single drawn-out notes, leading to pleasant *tsuli-tsuli-tsuli* during descent. CALL: Thin single or double *tseep*. HABITAT: Above tree line on alpine meadows and grassy slopes with scattered boulders and scrub. On migration, wetter locations, e.g. marsh and lake edges, paddies, etc.

5 ROCK PIPIT *Anthus petrosus* 16cm FIELD NOTES: Usually relatively confiding, flying only a short distance when flushed. SONG: Series of sharp repeated notes with various theme changes, usually rendered during display-flight: *zru-zru-zru-zru-zru-zre-zre-zre-zre-zre-zre-zre-sui-sui-sui-sui-zre-zre….* CALL: *weest*, usually repeated several times but not as rapidly as Meadow Pipit. HABITAT: Rocky coasts. In winter, occasionally inland by lake and river sides.

6 WATER PIPIT *Anthus spinoletta* 16cm FIELD NOTES: Usually more wary than Rock Pipit, flying some distance when flushed. More liable to perch on trees than Rock Pipit. SONG: Very similar to Rock Pipit's but with the addition of a buzzing *zeeer-zeeeer-zeeeer* phrase. CALL: Sharp *peezp*. HABITAT: Mountain slopes with short grass and scattered boulders and bushes, usually above the tree line. On migration and in winter, spreads to freshwater areas, e.g. sewage-farms, lakesides, marshes and wet meadows; rarely found on seashores.

7 BUFF-BELLIED PIPIT (AMERICAN PIPIT) *Anthus rubescens* 16cm FIELD NOTES: Actions much like Water Pipit, although tends to have quicker, lighter gait and more often found in flocks. SONG: Given from perch or display-flight: a series of fast, high notes repeated in phrases, e.g. *chwee-chwee, tsip-tsip-tsiru, treeu-treeu-treeu* or *pleetrr-pleetrr-pleetrr*. CALL: High *sipit, sip* or *tsweep*, or *si-si-si-si-si* when flushed. HABITAT: Rocky alpine and subalpine tundra. In winter prefers moist grassland, marshland and various other wetland edges. RACES: *A. r. japonicus* (fig 7b) NE and C Russia. Although *japonicus* is probably the only race found in the region, there is a school of thought that considers the race found in NE Siberia to be the nominate *rubescens*.

8 GOLDEN PIPIT *Tmetothylacus tenellus* 15cm (Vagrant) FIELD NOTES: In flight, male appears all yellow with black wing-tips. SONG/CALL: Not likely to be heard in the region; a series of flute-like whistles interspersed with a hurried, grating warbling, given during fluttering display-flight, otherwise silent. HABITAT: In native E Africa: dry acacia bush, open savannah and scrubby grassland.

9 WAGTAILS

1 FOREST WAGTAIL *Dendronanthus indicus* 16cm FIELD NOTES: Sways tail and rear body from side to side. Runs or walks rapidly; when flushed flies into tree canopy. SONG: Repeated high-pitched squeaky disyllabic note, *zlic-zheee - zlic-zheee - zlic-zheee - zlic-zheee - zlic-zheee*. CALL: Hard, shrill *pick* or *pick-pick*. HABITAT: Deciduous and evergreen broadleaved forest, mixed forest and, less often, pure pine forest.

2 YELLOW WAGTAIL *Motacilla flava* 16cm FIELD NOTES: Nominate race often referred to as Blue-headed Wagtail. Regularly perches on bushes, telephone wires, fence posts, etc. In winter and on migration very gregarious. SONG: Simple, repeated, harsh *tsre-tsree - tsre-tweeo* or *tsre - tsre - tsre*; single call-like notes mixed in: *tsre, psweo* or *tsrriep*. CALL: Loud *pseet*, a longer *swee-eep*; variations occur among the many races, southern races having a harsher *tsreep, shreep* or similar. HABITAT: Grassy areas, e.g. meadows, cornfields, grazed marshes, tundra, moist steppe and large openings in many forest types. On migration and winter spreads to almost any open habitat. RACES: M. f. iberiae (Spanish Wagtail) (fig 2b) Iberia, SW France, NW Africa; M. f. tschutschensis (Alaskan Yellow Wagtail)(fig 2c) NE Siberia; M. f. thunbergi (Grey-headed Wagtail)(fig 2d) Scandinavia east to NW Siberia; M. f. feldegg (Black-headed Wagtail) (fig 2e) SE Europe, Turkey east to Iran; M. f. cinereocapilla (Ashy-headed Wagtail) (fig 2f) Italy (including Sardinia, Sicily), Slovenia; M. f. lutea (Yellow-headed Wagtail) (fig 2g) SW Russia, N Kazakhstan; M. f. leucocephala (White-headed Wagtail) (fig 2h) NW Mongolia, NW China; M. f. taivana (Green-headed Wagtail) (fig 2i) SE Siberia, N Japan; M. f. flavissima (Yellow Wagtail) (fig 2j) Britain and adjacent coastal areas from France to Norway.

3 CITRINE WAGTAIL *Motacilla citreola* 17cm FIELD NOTES: Actions much as Yellow Wagtail. SONG: Like Yellow Wagtail but usually more varied: *tzreeep - tchip-tchip… tzreeep… tzreeep… tzreep-tcheree-tche-tche… tzreeep… tcherewe-tche-tche*. CALL: Sharp *tzreep, tcheep* or *tchreet*. HABITAT: As Yellow Wagtail, but in arctic tundra said to prefer denser scrub.

4 GREY WAGTAIL *Motacilla cinerea* 19cm FIELD NOTES: Constantly pumps rear body and tail. Often perches in trees or bushes overhanging water. SONG: Series of short, sharp notes, *ziss-ziss-ziss-ziss*, often with added phrase of higher notes *si-si-si-siu*. CALL: High-pitched *zit-zit*, rapidly repeated when alarmed. HABITAT: Mainly fast-flowing hill streams and rivers in open and wooded areas. In winter, spreads to various water-edge places.

5 JAPANESE WAGTAIL *Motacilla grandis* 21cm FIELD NOTES: Actions as White Wagtail. SONG: Series of simple notes and phrases, e.g. *chzeeo… birzzchle-birzzchle… chzleeo… birzzchle… birzzchelou… chzleeo-pzchy… chzleeo-pzh-ly-birz… birzzchle-pzchy… chzleeo-pzchly-birzz….* CALL: Harsh, shrill, single or repeated *bzzr, tzzr* or *tzreh*. HABITAT: Mainly edges of streams, rivers, lakes and ponds; in winter spreads to wider variety of habitats.

6 AFRICAN PIED WAGTAIL *Motacilla aguimp* 20cm FIELD NOTES: Actions as White Wagtail. SONG: Simple and monotonous to rich and varied *tchuu-tchuu… tchuu-tchuu-tchee… tchuu-tchuu-tcherewe… tchu-tchu-wee… tchu-tchu-wee… tchuu-tchuu- tchu-tche…*; complex nasal buzzing and rattled notes often added. CALL: Loud metallic *tzink, tzchip* or similar. HABITAT: Lake shores, sandbanks, riversides and around human habitations.

7 WHITE WAGTAIL *Motacilla alba* 17cm FIELD NOTES: Walks with nodding head while wagging tail up and down. Agile insect feeder using running, jumping or acrobatic short fluttering flights to capture prey. Often perches on bushes, trees, fences, buildings, telephone wires, etc. SONG: Single repeated note, *tchelee, psiwip, psilili* or similar, or a complex twittering interspersed with call notes. CALL: *tslee-wee, tslee-vit* or similar, often repeated. HABITAT: Various, e.g. farmland, seashore, waterside, tundra, mountainside and human habitations. RACES: M. a. personata (Masked Wagtail) (fig 7b) C and SW Asia; M. a. subpersonata (Moroccan Wagtail) (fig 7c) Morocco; M. a. ocularis (Swinhoe's Pied Wagtail) (fig 7d) N and NE Siberia; M. a. leucopsis (Chinese White Wagtail) (fig 7e) C and E China, SE Russia; M. a. lugens (Black-backed Wagtail) (fig 7f) SE Russia, Korea, Japan; M. a. alboides (Hodgson's Wagtail) (fig 7g) S China; M. a. yarrelli (Pied Wagtail) (fig 7h) Britain, Ireland.

10 FINCHBILLS AND BULBULS

1 CRESTED FINCHBILL *Spizixos canifrons* 22cm FIELD NOTES: Juvenile crest shorter and greener than adult. Often in small parties. SONG: Mainly a long bubbling trill *purr-purr-prruit-prruit-prruit….* CALL: *pri-pri-pri-prrrr* when excited or alarmed. HABITAT: Open woodland, clearings, scrub and gardens.

2 COLLARED FINCHBILL *Spizixos semitorques* 22cm FIELD NOTES: Juvenile head and upperparts much browner than adult. Usually in small groups, often fly-catches for insects. SONG/CALL: Hurried whistles *ji-de-shi-shei - ji-de-shi-shei - shi-shei.* HABITAT: Up to 3000m in forest clearings and edges, undergrowth and bamboo.

3 CHINESE BULBUL *Pycnonotus sinensis* 19cm FIELD NOTES: Juvenile lacks pale head markings of adult. Sometimes fly-catches from a perch. Gregarious, attracted to fruiting trees. SONG/CALL: Consists of noisy chattering chirps, simple phrases and non-musical calls. HABITAT: Forest edge, scrub, gardens and mangroves.

4 WHITE-CHEEKED BULBUL *Pycnonotus leucogenys* 20cm FIELD NOTES: Can be very confiding. Usually in small parties; restless, constantly flicks tail and wings when foraging, and often bows and postures while perched on bush top. SONG: Often transcribed as *tea for two* or *take me with you.* CALL: When agitated a *pit-pit, pit-lo* or a chattering *pit-pit-it-it- it* or *pititititit.* HABITAT: Hillsides with scattered wild fruit bushes, open scrub, hedgerows and around human habitations.

5 WHITE-EARED BULBUL *Pycnonotus leucotis* 20cm FIELD NOTES: Often treated as a subspecies of White-cheeked Bulbul, so actions and habits similar. SONG/CALL: As White-cheeked Bulbul. HABITAT: Coastal mangroves, otherwise much as White-cheeked Bulbul.

6 RED-VENTED BULBUL *Pycnonotus cafer* 20cm FIELD NOTES: Noisy and flock-loving. In flight shows pale rump. SONG: Cheery, often transcribed as *be-care-ful.* CALL: When alarmed, a sharp, loud, repeated *peep*; also a chattering *peep-a-peep-a-lo,* a rapid *pititititit* and a slower *peet-wit-wit-wit wit.* HABITAT: Gardens, orchards, cultivation, scrub and sometimes around buildings.

7 RED-WHISKERED BULBUL *Pycnonotus jocosus* 20cm FIELD NOTES: Juvenile lacks red ear-patch and has browner head with shorter crest and paler pinkish undertail. SONG: Lively, varied musical phrases, e.g. *wit-ti-waet - queep-kwil-ya - queek-kay.* CALL: Rolling *proop.* HABITAT: Possibly established in some Gulf States? Favours gardens, orchards and cultivated areas.

8 WHITE-SPECTACLED BULBUL (YELLOW-VENTED BULBUL) *Pycnonotus xanthopygus* 20cm FIELD NOTES: Often confiding, sometimes gathers in noisy loose groups. SONG: Variable fluty, bubbling, repeated phrases, *whee-too-too* or similar. CALL: Sharp scolding *weck* or a harsh *tscheck*; also a strong, sharp *wit-wit-wit, teewit* or *tew.* HABITAT: Gardens, palm groves, bush and various fruit-growing plantations.

9 COMMON BULBUL *Pycnonotus barbatus* 20cm FIELD NOTES: Bold. Gregarious in non-breeding season, forming loose flocks. SONG: Fluty phrases, e.g. *huit-huit-hwitera-hwitera, vigouro-vigouro, wee-te-treeou* or *tree-ou - tree-ou - tree-ou - tree-ou.* CALL: Loud repeated *tit-tit-tit* or a more casual *chahr-chahr-chahr.* HABITAT: Gardens, cultivation and watercourses in mountains and oases.

10 BLACK BULBUL *Hypsipetes leucocephalus psaroides* 22cm FIELD NOTES: In non-breeding season often forms large foraging flocks that feed in the treetops, frequently launching fly-catching sallies from highest branches. SONG: Variable, a discordant series of notes *trip-wi-tit-i-whi,* with other higher notes added. CALL: Drawn-out, whistled, mewing *hwiiii* or *hwieeer* and an abrupt nasal *ber-ber-bic-ber - ber.* HABITAT: Broadleaved evergreen and deciduous forest from 500 to 3000m; lower in winter.

11 BROWN-EARED BULBUL *Hypsipetes amaurotis* 27cm FIELD NOTES: Sociable, noisy, often attracted to garden feeders. In non-breeding season roams in quite sizeable flocks. In flight, shows pale chestnut underwing. SONG/CALL: Loud, fluty *peet-peet-pii-yieyo.* HABITAT: Deciduous woodland, plantations, parks and gardens.

11 WAXWINGS, DIPPERS, WREN, CATBIRD, THRASHER AND MOCKINGBIRD

1 **CEDAR WAXWING** *Bombycilla cedrorum* 18cm (Vagrant) FIELD NOTES: Juvenile duller and streaked below. Highly gregarious. SONG/CALL: High-pitched whistled hiss, less buzzy than Waxwing. HABITAT: In native N America: open deciduous or coniferous woodland, orchards, etc. Wanders in winter, often feeding on berry-bearing trees and bushes in town parks and gardens.

2 **JAPANESE WAXWING** *Bombycilla japonica* 16cm FIELD NOTES: Crest held erect more often than Waxwing. Gregarious. SONG/CALL: High-pitched, lisping *hee-hee-hee*. HABITAT: Cedar and larch forest. Wanderers in winter can be found feeding on berry bushes and trees, from mountain woodland to suburban parks.

3 **WAXWING (BOHEMIAN WAXWING)** *Bombycilla garrulus* 18cm FIELD NOTES: Juvenile duller than adult, with shorter crest and lacking black throat. Starling-like flight. Very gregarious. SONG: Series of quiet trilled phrases. CALL: A ringing *sirrrr*. HABITAT: Coniferous forest, sometimes mixed with birch. In winter spreads to wide variety of woodland, including hedgerows, parkland and gardens, in search of berries.

4 **GREY HYPOCOLIUS** *Hypocolius ampelinus* 23cm FIELD NOTES: Usually in small parties. SONG/CALL: Various mewing and whistling notes, a low, harsh *chirr*, and a continuous *kirrrkirrrkirrr…*, often given during display-flight. HABITAT: Semi-desert with scrub, palm groves, trees and gardens.

5 **DIPPER (WHITE-THROATED DIPPER)** *Cinclus cinclus* 18cm FIELD NOTES: Swims, also walks underwater feeding on stream or river bottom. Bobs whole body while perched. Juvenile grey above with paler scalloping and mottling, below grey, scalloped and mottled darker, throat white. SONG: A sustained rippling warble. CALL: Loud rasping *zink* or *zrets*. HABITAT: Fast-flowing rivers and streams, chiefly in upland areas. Sometimes visits lower areas in winter. RACES: *C. c. gularis* (fig 5b) Scotland, Wales, N and W England.

6 **BROWN DIPPER** *Cinclus pallasii* 18cm FIELD NOTES: Actions as Dipper. Juvenile greyish brown with pale grey scalloping and mottling. SONG: Short and rich, more musical than Dipper. CALL: Shrill *dzchit-dzchit*. HABITAT: Fast-flowing mountain and upland streams and rivers. Sometimes lower areas in winter.

7 **WREN (WINTER WREN)** *Troglodytes troglodytes* 10cm FIELD NOTES: Restless, feeding mouse-like amongst low herbage, showing itself only in fleeting glimpses. Often more prominent when singing from exposed branch or telephone wire. SONG: Very loud for such a small bird, mixture of trills and rattling warbles ending in a longer, dry, rattling trill. CALL: Harsh, often repeated, *tek*. When alarmed, a rapid chittering. HABITAT: Very varied, virtually wherever there is low cover, from coast to moorland, even above tree line in a few areas.

8 **GREY CATBIRD** *Dumetella carolinensis* 20cm (Vagrant) FIELD NOTES: Skulks in thick cover. SONG: Sweet varied phrases interspersed with harsher notes and mewing. CALL: Cat-like mewing, also an explosive *kak-kak-kak*. HABITAT: In native N America: dense, low thickets alongside streams, roads, woodland edge, garden shrubbery, etc.

9 **BROWN THRASHER** *Toxostoma rufum* 28cm (Vagrant) FIELD NOTES: Rather shy. Forages in leaf litter under bushes and trees. SONG: Has been transcribed as like a telephone conversation, *hello - hello - yes-yes - who is this - who is this - I should say - I should say - how's that - how's that*; also a quieter low warble. CALL: Loud *tschek* or *chip*. HABITAT: In native N America: bushy woods, shelterbelts, copses, suburban shrubberies, small trees in open areas.

10 **NORTHERN MOCKINGBIRD** *Mimus polyglottos* 26cm (Vagrant) FIELD NOTES: In flight shows large white wing-patches. Forages mostly on ground, usually on short grass, e.g. lawns. SONG: Highly variable phrases, each repeated 3 or more times. Often mimics other birds, animals or even piano notes! CALL: Loud *tchack*. HABITAT: In native N America: thickets, copses, shelterbelts and garden shrubbery.

12 ACCENTORS

1 DUNNOCK (HEDGE ACCENTOR) *Prunella modularis* 14.5cm FIELD NOTES: Wing twitching makes it appear nervous as it creeps, mouse-like, in undergrowth. Juvenile like a dull adult with dark streaking below. SONG: Slow, weak jangling. CALL: *seep* or *seeh*, also a quieter *ti-ti-ti*. HABITAT: Gardens, open woodland, heath, spruce and juniper forest; in south of range, more a tree-line species.

2 JAPANESE ACCENTOR *Prunella rubida* 14cm FIELD NOTES: Never far from cover. SONG/CALL: High-pitched slow trill, sounding much like a squeaky bicycle wheel. HABITAT: Dwarf pines and birch up to tree line on high mountains; in winter, at lower elevations.

3 KOSLOV'S ACCENTOR *Prunella koslowi* 15cm FIELD NOTES: Much as Dunnock? SONG/CALL: Unrecorded? HABITAT: Juniper scrub and grassland on dry mountain slopes; in winter, arid scrub in sandy desert.

4 BLACK-THROATED ACCENTOR *Prunella atrogularis* 15cm FIELD NOTES: Actions much like Dunnock. SONG: Like Dunnock but thinner and drier with occasional buzzing notes. CALL: *zee-zee-zee-zee*. HABITAT: Stunted spruce shrubs, dense thickets and scrub of the subalpine zone.

5 SIBERIAN ACCENTOR *Prunella montanella* 15cm FIELD NOTES: Actions Dunnock-like. Juvenile duller, supercilium paler. SONG: Very like Dunnock, more melodious than Black-throated Accentor. CALL: Ringing *tsee-ree-see*. HABITAT: Stunted birch and coniferous woodland and waterside thickets, mainly of willow. From lowland to mountain tree line.

6 RADDE'S ACCENTOR *Prunella ocularis* 15.5cm FIELD NOTES: Dunnock-like. Juvenile duller. SONG: Gentle, sweet twittering or trembling, quite similar to that of Dunnock. CALL: Slurred *tseer*. HABITAT: Low scrub in dry, rocky mountains; moves to slightly lower areas in winter.

7 BROWN ACCENTOR *Prunella fulvescens* 15cm FIELD NOTES: Quiet Dunnock-like feeding actions. SONG: Short, low warble. CALL: *ziet-ziet-ziet*. HABITAT: Open alpine mountain slopes with scrub; lower in winter, often around mountain camps and villages.

8 ARABIAN ACCENTOR *Prunella fagani* 15cm FIELD NOTES: Actions as Dunnock. SONG: A short, fast *drsi-drsi-drsi-dy-dy-dy*, often with a scratchy ending; also a more trilling *dri-drrriii-tyi-driivivivi*. CALL: Very like Dunnock. HABITAT: Bushy areas in rocky mountains.

9 RUFOUS-BREASTED ACCENTOR *Prunella strophiata* 16cm FIELD NOTES: Very similar to Dunnock. SONG: Wren-like, but not so loud, interspersed with occasional harsh notes. CALL: High-pitched *tirr-r-rit*. HABITAT: Forest and scrub near tree line. More open, lower areas in winter.

10 ROBIN ACCENTOR *Prunella rubeculoides* 16cm FIELD NOTES: Gregarious in winter. Confiding. In summer more in cover. SONG: Sweet and short, chirping *si-tsi-si-tsi - tze-e-you*. CALL: As Rufous-breasted Accentor but sharper and more metallic; *zieh-zieh* when alarmed. HABITAT: Rhododendron and willow scrub, grassy meadows. In winter, often around upland villages.

11 MAROON-BACKED ACCENTOR *Prunella immaculata* 14cm FIELD NOTES: Secretive, keeps to cover. SONG: Unrecorded. CALL: Metallic *zieh-dzit*. HABITAT: Damp undergrowth in coniferous and rhododendron forest. Winters in more open scrub.

12 ALTAI ACCENTOR *Prunella himalayana* 15.5cm FIELD NOTES: Gregarious, often in mixed flocks with other accentors and mountain finches. SONG: Sweet trilling warble. CALL: Finch-like *tee-tee*. HABITAT: Rocky alpine meadows.

13 ALPINE ACCENTOR *Prunella collaris* 16cm FIELD NOTES: Like Dunnock though often more upright. Gregarious in winter. SONG: Dunnock-like, but lower pitched and more musical. Often in short song-flight. CALL: Rolling *chirrup* or *chirrriririp*, or a sharp *pyrrt* and a Linnet-like *tjew-tjew-tjew*. HABITAT: Rocky mountain slopes with sparse vegetation, areas around mountain huts and rocky crags above the tree line. Often descends in winter.

13 ROBINS, SHORTWINGS, BLUETHROAT AND NIGHTINGALES

1 RUFOUS BUSH ROBIN (RUFOUS-TAILED SCRUB ROBIN) *Cercotrichas galactotes* 16cm FIELD NOTES: Spreads and cocks tail. SONG: Rich and varied ringing notes. CALL: A hard *tek-tek* or a sibilant *tseeet*. HABITAT: Semi-arid scrub country, scrub-lined watercourses, orange groves, parks and gardens. RACES: *C. g. syriacus* (fig 1b) SE Europe, Turkey and Middle East.

2 BLACK BUSH ROBIN (BLACK SCRUB ROBIN) *Cercotrichas podobe* 19cm FIELD NOTES: Tail often cocked and spread over back. SONG: Series of melodious whistles occasionally interspersed with harsher *tew-ti-heat* notes. CALL: A hoarse squeak or a liquid chatter. HABITAT: Flat or rolling sandy plains with dry scrub; bushy oases and gardens.

3 GOULD'S SHORTWING *Brachypteryx stellata* 13cm FIELD NOTES: Mouse-like as it feeds in tangled roots and fallen branches. SONG: *tssiu - tssiu - tssiu - tssiu-tssiu - tsitsitsiu....* High-pitched and piercing. CALL: *tik-tik*. HABITAT: Rhododendron, bamboo, juniper and subalpine forest.

4 RUSTY-BELLIED SHORTWING *Brachypteryx hyperythra* 13cm FIELD NOTES: Skulks in thick undergrowth. SONG: Starts with 2 spaced notes, e.g. *tu-tiu*, leading into fast warble of slurred notes. CALL: Not recorded. HABITAT: Dense thickets and undergrowth, from 1100 to 3000m.

5 WHITE-BROWED SHORTWING *Brachypteryx montana curalis* 13cm FIELD NOTES: Behaves much like Robin. SONG: Starts slowly with a few single notes, then speeds to a plaintive babble and ends abruptly. CALL: A quick *tek*; *tt-tt-tt-tt* when alarmed. HABITAT: Damp shady forests of oak and rhododendron with undergrowth; dense brush in ravines or near streams.

6 ROBIN (EUROPEAN ROBIN) *Erithacus rubecula* 14cm FIELD NOTES: Wary, but can become quite confiding. SONG: Melodic warbling and trilling phrases, usually beginning with a few high-pitched drawn-out notes. CALL: A hard *tick* or, *tick-tick-tick-tick....* Also a plaintive *seeh*. HABITAT: Woodland, hedgerows, parks and gardens. RACES: *E. r. superbus* (Tenerife Robin) (fig 6b) Gran Canaria, Tenerife.

7 JAPANESE ROBIN *Erithacus akahige* 14cm FIELD NOTES: Keeps to dense undergrowth. Cocks tail. SONG: Distinctive, repeated *tsee - chararararararar* or similar. CALL: A thin *tsip*. HABITAT: Undergrowth in deciduous or mixed high-elevation forest.

8 RYUKYU ROBIN *Erithacus komadori* 14cm FIELD NOTES: Actions similar to others in genus. SONG: Like Japanese Robin but weaker with more variation. CALL: Penetrating *tsee* and a harsh *kwrick*. HABITAT: Thick forest.

9 RUFOUS-TAILED ROBIN *Luscinia sibilans* 13cm FIELD NOTES: Shivers tail. Skulks on or near ground. SONG: Repeated accelerating trill, falling in pitch towards end. CALL: *chirp* or *chirrup*. HABITAT: Dense shady forest undergrowth.

10 BLUETHROAT (RED-SPOTTED BLUETHROAT) *Luscinia svecica* 14cm FIELD NOTES: Chestnut tail-bases 'flash', as bird flits into cover. SONG: Vigorous, includes bell-like *ting-ting-ting* and a throaty *torr-torr-torr-torr*. Mimics birds, insects,, etc. CALL: *tacc-tacc*, a croaky *turrc-turrc* and a plaintive *hweet*. HABITAT: Bushy areas on tundra, damp forest edge, riverine thickets, hill and mountain scrub. RACES: *L. s. cyanecula* (White-spotted Bluethroat) (fig 10b) Belgium, E France east to W Russia; *L. s. magna* (fig 10c) Caucasus.

11 THRUSH NIGHTINGALE *Luscinia luscinia* 16cm FIELD NOTES: Skulking. SONG: Far-carrying clicking and bell-like phrases, often beginning with sharp whistles interspersed with rasping notes. CALL: Harsh *errrr* and a piercing *whip*. HABITAT: Dense, damp undergrowth in deciduous woodland, waterside thickets, thickly wooded parks and gardens.

12 NIGHTINGALE *Luscinia megarhynchos* 16cm FIELD NOTES: Extreme skulker. SONG: Loud, melodic phrases mixed with trills and rattles, most striking being a fluting *pew-pew-pew-pew- pew...* and rapid, low *jug-jug-jug-jug....* CALL: A deep *grrrrr*, a thin *seeeee*, a hard *tacc-tacc* and a harsh *tucc-tucc*. HABITAT: Thick undergrowth in deciduous woodland, dense thickets.

14 RUBYTHROATS AND ROBINS

1 SIBERIAN RUBYTHROAT *Luscinia calliope* 15cm FIELD NOTES: Shy, often more exposed when singing. Cocks tail. SONG: Loud, rich and varied sustained warbling, interspersed with harsher notes. CALL: *chak-chak* and a falling whistle, *ee-uk*. HABITAT: Bird cherry, willow or birch thickets; forest edge, riverine scrub and bushy areas in damp meadows.

2 WHITE-TAILED RUBYTHROAT (HIMALAYAN RUBYTHROAT) *Luscinia pectoralis* 15cm FIELD NOTES: Secretive. Cocks tail. Often more exposed when singing. SONG: Loud, shrill, complex series of undulating warbling trills and twitters. CALL: *tchuk* or *it-it*, a sparrow-like *tchink* and a *siiii-siiii* when alarmed. HABITAT: Scrub and bushes in subalpine forest or above tree line. Lower areas in winter. RACES: *L. p. tschebaiewi* (fig 2b) SW China.

3 FIRETHROAT *Luscinia pectardens* 14cm FIELD NOTES: Flicks tail. Skulks in thick cover. SONG: Loud, long, sweet and varied, each note repeated several times, also including some mimicry and harsh notes. CALL: *tok*. HABITAT: Broadleaved forest, bamboo, dense scrub.

4 RUFOUS-HEADED ROBIN *Luscinia ruficeps* 15cm FIELD NOTES: Skulks, usually on ground, in thick cover. Cocks tail. SONG: Rich, powerful, melodious phrases preceded by single note, *ti-chulululu - ti-chewtchewtchew - tititichewtchewtchew....* CALL: A deep *tuc* or *toc*. HABITAT: Dense scrubby subalpine forest.

5 BLACK-THROATED ROBIN (BLACKTHROAT) *Luscinia obscura* 14cm FIELD NOTES: Flicks tail. Skulks in thickets. SONG: Simple phrases, each repeated after short intervals: *drree - drree - dree-drree - drreeedreee - huti-huti - huti-huti - huti-huti*. May also include short trills and warbles. CALL: A series of *tup* notes. HABITAT: Bamboo thickets in coniferous forest.

6 INDIAN BLUE ROBIN *Luscinia brunnea* 14cm FIELD NOTES: Flicks wings and tail. Skulks in thick cover. SONG: A few thin introductory whistles followed by a short, sweet jumble of hurried phrases. CALL: When alarmed, a hard *tuk-tuk*; also a high *tsee* punctuated with *chr-r*. HABITAT: Dense undergrowth in oak or coniferous forest.

7 SIBERIAN BLUE ROBIN *Luscinia cyane* 14cm FIELD NOTES: Shivers tail. Skulks in cover. SONG: Rapid, loud *tri-tri-tri-tri - tjuree-tiu-tiu-tiu-tiu*, usually introduced with a few *sit* notes. CALL: When alarmed a *chuck-chuck-chuck*, also a subdued *tak* and louder *se-ic*. HABITAT: Coniferous and mixed forest with dense shrubs and undergrowth.

8 WHITE -THROATED ROBIN *Irania gutturalis* 17cm FIELD NOTES: Skulks in ground cover. SONG: Loud, clear, bell-like notes interspersed with harsher notes. Given from perch or in flight, as bird glides down hillside with wings and tail fully spread. CALL: A loud *tji-thyt* or a soft *teck*. HABITAT: Stony, scrubby hillsides and valleys. On migration, also in dense lowland scrub.

9 RUFOUS-BREASTED BUSH ROBIN *Tarsiger hyperythrus* 13.5cm FIELD NOTES: On or close to ground, where it often adopts an upright stance. Can be quite tame. SONG: A lisping warble *zeew - zee - zwee - zwee....* CALL: A low *duk-duk-duk-tseak*. HABITAT: Rhododendrons, bushes and streamside vegetation.

10 RED-FLANKED BLUETAIL (ORANGE-FLANKED BUSH ROBIN) *Tarsiger cyanurus* 14cm FIELD NOTES: Cover-loving, but not an intense skulker. SONG: *tetee-teeleee-tititi*; ending trails away. CALL: *tic-tic*; also a soft *huit* and guttural *kerrr*. HABITAT: Moist mixed and coniferous forest with undergrowth. On migration, all types of woodland, orchards or gardens.

11 WHITE-BROWED BUSH ROBIN *Tarsiger indicus* 15cm FIELD NOTES: Fairly tame. On or near ground in dense undergrowth. SONG: Rapidly repeated, sharp, rising and falling *shri-de- de-dew... shri-de-de-dew*. CALL: *tiutiut*. HABITAT: Mixed subalpine forest.

12 GOLDEN BUSH ROBIN *Tarsiger chrysaeus* 15cm FIELD NOTES: Cocks tail. In thick undergrowth. SONG: A wispy *tse-tse-tse-tse-tse-chu-r-r* or similar. CALL: Croaky *trrr* and a scolding *chirik-chirik*. HABITAT: Coniferous forest with dense rhododendrons; scrub above tree line; and thickets on boulder-covered alpine slopes.

15 REDSTARTS

1 WHITE-CAPPED REDSTART *Chaimarrornis leucocephalus* 19cm FIELD NOTES: Sits on rocks in or close to water, continuously flicking tail. SONG: Weak, undulating whistle. CALL: Plaintive *tseeit-tseeit*. HABITAT: Mountain streams and rivers; moves down river in winter.

2 PLUMBEOUS REDSTART *Rhyacornis fuliginosus* 14cm FIELD NOTES: Flicks tail as it flits from rock to rock. SONG: Rapid jingle, *stree-tree-tree-treeh*. CALL: Sharp *ziet-ziet* or a threatening *kree*. HABITAT: Fast-flowing streams and rivers, 1000–4300m.

3 EVERSMANN'S REDSTART (RUFOUS-BACKED REDSTART) *Phoenicurus erythronota* 15cm FIELD NOTES: Flicks tail up and down. Drops from rock or twig to pick up insects, returning to same perch or one nearby. SONG: Loud and lively. CALL: Whistled *few-eet* and a croaking *gre-er*. HABITAT: Subalpine conifer forests. Winters on plains in woodlands and arid scrub.

4 PRZEVALSKI'S REDSTART (ALASHAN REDSTART) *Phoenicurus alaschanicus* 15cm FIELD NOTES: Often treated as a subspecies of Eversmann's Redstart; actions similar. SONG/CALL: As Eversmann's Redstart? HABITAT: Montane conifer forest, dense bushes and rocky slopes.

5 BLACK REDSTART *Phoenicurus ochruros* 15cm FIELD NOTES: Shivers tail. SONG: Rapid warble interspersed with a rattle, ending in a rushed burst of ringing notes. CALL: *tsip*, a *tucc-tucc* and, when alarmed, a *tititicc*. HABITAT: Rocky hills, towns, villages and industrial areas. In winter, coastal areas, including golf courses in Spain. RACES: *P. o. phoenicuroides* (fig 5b) S Russia, W China, Mongolia; *P. o. gibraltariensis* (fig 5c) W and C Europe, including N Spain, Sicily, Greece and N Africa east to Latvia; *P. o. rufiventris* (fig 5d) C Asia.

6 REDSTART (COMMON REDSTART) *Phoenicurus phoenicurus* 15cm FIELD NOTES: Shivers tail. Usually sits in cover; shows itself when dropping to feed on ground. SONG: Variable; *hooeet* followed by a weak melancholic warbling. CALL: *hooeet*, also *tek*, often combined. HABITAT: Deciduous and mixed forest, orchards, parks and gardens. On migration can be in any woods and scrub. RACES: *P. p. samamisicus* (fig 6b) Crimea to S Turkey.

7 DAURIAN REDSTART *Phoenicurus auroreus* 15cm FIELD NOTES: Shivers tail. Feeds in trees and bushes, often similar to flycatcher. SONG: Series of cheerful, whistled notes. CALL: *wheep* and a soft *tac-tac*, preceded by series of soft whistles. HABITAT: Subalpine forest scrub; in winter moves to bushy lowlands and cultivation.

8 HODGSON'S REDSTART *Phoenicurus hodgsoni* 15cm FIELD NOTES: Often hunts in trees, like flycatcher. SONG: Short and tinny, lacking in modulation. CALL: *prit* and *trr* or *tschrrr* when alarmed. HABITAT: Scrub and grassy areas in open forest, often near rivers or streams.

9 BLUE-FRONTED REDSTART *Phoenicurus frontalis* 15cm FIELD NOTES: Flicks tail up and down. Descends to ground, from branch or rock, to catch insects. SONG: Similar to Black Redstart but less wheezy. CALL: *tic* and, when alarmed, a repeated soft *ee-tit - ti-tit*. HABITAT: Alpine zone at or above the tree line, in dwarf rhododendrons, juniper and birch, and on boulder-strewn slopes.

10 MOUSSIER'S REDSTART *Phoenicurus moussieri* 13cm FIELD NOTES: Perches in open, with actions much like Stonechat. SONG: Short scratchy warble. CALL: A thin *wheet*, *hiip-hiip* or *psew*. HABITAT: Dry stony or grassy hills or mountains with scrub; coastal forest and thickets. Moves to lower, often desert, areas in winter.

11 WHITE-THROATED REDSTART *Phoenicurus schisticeps* 15cm FIELD NOTES: Often feeds in flycatcher-like manner. Restless. SONG: Undescribed. CALL: Drawn-out *zieh* followed by a rattling note. HABITAT: Thick scrub in subalpine conifer forests. Descends in winter.

12 GÜLDENSTÄDT'S REDSTART (WHITE-WINGED REDSTART) *Phoenicurus erythrogaster* 18cm FIELD NOTES: In display-flight, quivers wings showing large white wing-patch; otherwise rather shy. SONG: A series of clear notes, followed by burst of short, wheezy notes. CALL: *tik* or harder *tek*. HABITAT: High-altitude boulder-strewn slopes, rocky meadows often near water. Forced lower during severe weather.

16 REDSTARTS, ROBINS, GRANDALA, COCHOA AND FORKTAILS

1 BLUE-CAPPED REDSTART *Phoenicurus coeruleocephalus* 15cm FIELD NOTES: Shakes tail, other actions much as others of genus. SONG: A loud, fast, high-pitched ringing. CALL: *tik-tik* or a piping *tit-tit-tit* when alarmed. HABITAT: Open montane forests with rocky slopes. Winters in lower-altitude open forest and scrubby areas.

2 INDIAN ROBIN *Saxicoloides fulicata cambaiensis* 16cm FIELD NOTES: Hops or runs on ground, with tail often carried erect or well over back. Can be very confiding. SONG: A short, cheery warble, consisting of 4 or more shrill whistles that merge into each other. CALL: A repeated *wheech* or a harsh *chu-r - chu-r*. HABITAT: Dry stony foothills with scrub, cultivation and often near habitation.

3 WHITE-TAILED ROBIN *Myiomela leucura* 18cm FIELD NOTES: Shy bird of dark thickets. When perched often spreads tail showing white tail-bases. White neck-spot usually concealed. SONG: Clear, liquid, separated phrases *te-tle-i-at- we-i…tl-yei-ya-we-i….* CALL: A low *tuc*. HABITAT: Dense undergrowth in montane forest.

4 WHITE-BELLIED REDSTART *Hodgsonius phaenicuroides* 19cm FIELD NOTES: Shy and retiring. Tail often held vertically and spread, especially when singing. SONG: Loud, 3-note, whistled phrase, often written as *he-did-so.* CALL: *chuck* or, when alarmed, *tsiep-tsiep-tk-tk* or *tck-tck-sie.* HABITAT: Dense low scrub and vegetation above tree line. Various montane forests, coniferous, rhododendron, broadleaved evergreen, bamboo, etc.

5 GRANDALA *Grandala coelicolor* 22cm FIELD NOTES: Posture like rock thrush. Winter flocks act much like Common Starling, wheeling around before dropping into trees to rest. SONG: Subdued *tju-u tiu-u ti-tu tji-u.* CALL: *tji-u.* HABITAT: Alpine meadows, bare rocky areas above tree line, open forests.

6 PURPLE COCHOA *Cochoa purpurea* 28cm FIELD NOTES: Secretive; generally arboreal, feeding in fruiting trees, but often forages on ground. SONG: Flute-like *peeeee* or *peeee-you-peeee.* CALL: Thin *sit* or *tssri.* HABITAT: Dense, humid, broadleaved evergreen forest.

7 LITTLE FORKTAIL *Enicurus scouleri* 13cm FIELD NOTES: Active. Constantly wags tail up and down, also rapidly opens and closes it in a scissor-like movement. Juvenile browner, lacking white forehead. SONG/CALL: Loud, thin *ts-youeee.* HABITAT: Mountain rivers, streams and waterfalls.

8 SPOTTED FORKTAIL *Enicurus maculatus* 27cm FIELD NOTES: Superficially wagtail-like, although tail swayed up and down rather than wagged. Juvenile browner, lacking white forehead. SONG/CALL: A sharp, creaky *cheek-chik-chik-chik-chik*, also a shrill, rasping *kreee* or *tseek.* HABITAT: Mountain forest streams.

9 WHITE-CROWNED FORKTAIL *Enicurus leschenaulti* 28cm FIELD NOTES: Restless feeder, constantly spreading tail. Juvenile browner, lacking white cap. SONG: Series of elaborate, very high-pitched whistles. CALL: Harsh, shrill *tssee* or *tsee-chit-chit-chit.* HABITAT: Rivers and streams in mountain forests.

10 ORIENTAL MAGPIE ROBIN *Copsychus saularis* 20cm FIELD NOTES: Confiding. Usually conspicuous but can become more secretive in non-breeding season. SONG: Varied, musical, warbling, alternating with churrs and sliding whistles. CALL: Clear rising whistle; when alarmed, a harsh *che-e-e-e-h.* HABITAT: Parks, gardens, groves, open forests, mangroves, etc. Altitudinal wanderer to region.

17 STONECHATS AND ANTEATER CHAT

1 STOLICZKA'S BUSHCHAT (WHITE-BROWED BUSHCHAT) *Saxicola macrorhyncha* 15cm (Vagrant) FIELD NOTES: In flight, white tail-base pattern looks very like that of wheatear. Actions typical of the genus, *see* Stonechat. SONG: Unrecorded. CALL: Sharp *chip-chip*. HABITAT: Sandy, semi-desert scrubland.

2 FUERTEVENTURA STONECHAT (CANARY ISLAND STONECHAT) *Saxicola dacotiae* 13cm FIELD NOTES: Actions as Stonechat. SONG: Scratchy *bic-bizee-bizeeu*, similar to Stonechat. CALL: *chut*, a little sharper than Stonechat. HABITAT: Arid rocky ground with scattered scrub; generally avoids open plains.

3 WHINCHAT *Saxicola rubetra* 13cm FIELD NOTES: Usually perches less upright than Stonechat, with less wing and tail flicking. SONG: Short, scratchy series of warbling phrases. CALL: *tek-tek* or *whuk-tek-tek*. HABITAT: Open country with scattered bushes, including heathland, upland pastures, hillsides, young conifer plantations, etc.

4 STONECHAT (COMMON STONECHAT) *Saxicola torquatus rubicola* 13cm FIELD NOTES: Sits atop prominent perch, flicking wings and tail, dropping to the ground to pick up food and then returning to same perch or one nearby. At times feeds aerially, much like a flycatcher. SONG: Thin, scratchy warble, more variable and richer when given during short song-flight. CALL: *chak* or *wheet*, often combined as *wheet-tak-tak*. HABITAT: From bushy coastal cliffs to heathland, moorland, steppe and scrubby mountainsides. RACES: *S. t. maurus* (Siberian Stonechat) (fig 4b) From NE Russia eastwards; *S. t. variegatus* (fig 4c) Volga steppes to E Caucasus.

5 HODGSON'S BUSHCHAT (WHITE-THROATED BUSHCHAT) *Saxicola insignis* 15cm FIELD NOTES: Actions much as others of genus, although may feed more on the ground than some. SONG: Unrecorded. CALL: Metallic *tek-tek*. HABITAT: Alpine and subalpine meadows with bushes. On migration, more diverse, often found on open grassland and in reeds and other riverside vegetation, etc.

6 PIED STONECHAT *Saxicola caprata rossorum* 13.5cm FIELD NOTES: Actions similar to Stonechat. SONG: Brisk and whistling *chip-chepee-chewee-chu*. CALL: Repeated, plaintive *chep - chep-hee* or *chek-chek-trweet*, also a scolding *chuh* when very alarmed. HABITAT: Low scrub on stony hillsides. Moist areas with thickets, reed-beds, willows and other waterside bushes; also cultivation, orchards and gardens.

7 GREY BUSHCHAT *Saxicola ferrea* 15cm FIELD NOTES: Actions much as others of genus, although tends to use favourite perches for quite lengthy periods. SONG: Short, feeble trill ending with a rolling whistle, transcribed as *tirirririri-swirrr*. CALL: *prrei* or, if alarmed, a repeated *zee-chunk* or *tic-tic-brzeeee*. HABITAT: Open scrub-covered hillsides, forest fringe, forest glades and terraced cultivation; in winter, cultivation and grassland, especially near water, also parks and gardens.

8 NORTHERN ANTEATER CHAT *Myrmecocichla aethiops* 18cm (Vagrant) FIELD NOTES: Often perches on fence posts, bushes, wires or buildings. Ground feeder. In flight, shows the usually hidden white wing-patch. SONG: Prolonged mixture of trills, thin whistles and *tsicking* notes. CALL: Various piping and whistling notes. HABITAT: In native Africa: open country and semi-desert with scattered trees and bushes. Around buildings, and along roadsides and tracks.

18 WHEATEARS

1 RED-BREASTED WHEATEAR *Oenanthe bottae* 17cm FIELD NOTES: In flight shows white rump and white outer tail bases. Distinctive downward tail-wagging. SONG: Often uttered in low flight, consists of fluty and scratchy notes. CALL: *tjeet* when alarmed. HABITAT: Open hillsides with sparse vegetation, and high-plateau cultivation.

2 ISABELLINE WHEATEAR *Oenanthe isabellina* 17cm FIELD NOTES: In flight shows white rump and white outer tail bases. Often very upright stance. Jerky, emphatic tail-wagging. SONG: Sometimes given in short display-flight: loud, varied croaks and whistles, often interspersed with mimicry of other bird songs. CALL: Piped *weep* or *dweet*, high-pitched *wheet-whit* and a quiet *tcheep* or *cheep*. HABITAT: Plains and plateaus with sparse vegetation; typically, border between natural steppe and semi-desert.

3 WHEATEAR (NORTHERN WHEATEAR) *Oenanthe oenanthe* 14.5–15.5cm FIELD NOTES: In flight shows white rump and white outer tail bases. Flicks wings and tail. SONG: Sometimes given in display-flight: a brief scratchy warble interspersed with 'chacking', creaking and fluty notes. CALL: Hard *chak* and a *wheet*, often combined as *wheet-chak-chak*. HABITAT: Various, including tundra, moorland, rocky alpine meadows, closely grazed heath and downs, coastal islands, sand dunes and walled fields. On passage, even wider forms of open areas, especially with managed grass, e.g. golf courses. RACES: *O. o. seebohmi* (Seebohm's Wheatear) (fig 3b) NW Africa.

4 BLACK-EARED WHEATEAR *Oenanthe hispanica* 14.5cm FIELD NOTES: In flight shows white rump and white outer tail bases, the latter often white to near tail-tip. Often perches on bushes, trees or overhead wires. Both races have pale-throated morph (figs 4b, 4d). SONG: From perch or display-flight, consists of rich, cheerful, rapid warbling, including some buzzy and scratchy notes as well as some mimicry. CALL: Clicked *zack-zack* or *chep-chep*. HABITAT: Steppe with rocky outcrops, rocky hill- and mountainsides; open, arid, lightly wooded country. RACES: *O. h. melanoleuca* (figs 4c, 4d) S Italy, Yugoslavia, east to the Caspian and Iran.

5 DESERT WHEATEAR *Oenanthe deserti* 14–15cm FIELD NOTES: In flight shows white rump and mainly black tail. Wary, often perches on low vegetation. SONG: Usually rendered from a bush top, a descending, plaintive *swee-you* or *sweerer-you*, occasionally interspersed with rattles or trills. CALL: Low *chuck*, a whistled *peeeeoo* and a lark-like *trrr*. HABITAT: Dry steppe and desert fringe with sparse vegetation, barren wastes, and dry wadis.

6 RED-RUMPED WHEATEAR *Oenanthe moesta* 16cm FIELD NOTES: In flight shows ochre/rufous rump and small rufous area on outer tail bases. Rump can wear and become very pale buff or off-white. SONG: A sweet, throaty warbling, interspersed with whistles. CALL: Dull *trrrp* and a short *k-wik*. HABITAT: Flat, stony semi-desert or desert with scattered shrubs and an abundance of rodent burrows in which to nest.

7 RED-TAILED WHEATEAR (CHESTNUT-RUMPED OR PERSIAN WHEATEAR) *Oenanthe xanthprymna* 14.5cm FIELD NOTES: In flight shows chestnut rump and black tail with small white area on outer tail bases. Race *chrysopygia* has white area of tail replaced with chestnut. Often perches on bushes, flicks wings, spreads tail. SONG: Short throaty warble, *see - wat-shew - eeper* or *wee-chu-chree*. CALL: Low *chek-chek*, *zvee*, *zvee-tuk* and a soft *thrrr-thrrr-thrrr*. HABITAT: Arid rocky hill- and mountainsides with scattered boulders and sparse vegetation. RACES: *O. x. chrysopygia* (Rufous-tailed Wheatear) (fig 7b) NE Turkey, N Iran eastward. Winters in Arabian Peninsula, S Iraq, S Iran. Regarded by some authors as a full species.

1

2 n-br

br

3 ♂ n-br

3b ♂

♀ br

♂ br

3

♀

4c ♀

♂ ♂

4d ♂ br

4c ♂ br

♂

4

♀

5

♂

6

♀

♂

7

♀

♂

7b

NA

19 WHEATEARS

1 FINSCH'S WHEATEAR *Oenanthe finschii* 15cm FIELD NOTES: In flight shows extensive white rump and large white outer tail bases. On landing, cocks tail then spreads and lowers it slowly. SONG: Often given during descending zigzag display-flight; a variable warble interspersed with some chattering or whistling phrases. CALL: Harsh *chak-chak*. HABITAT: Rocky steppe, barren ravines and semi-desert with scattered scrubby vegetation.

2 PIED WHEATEAR *Oenanthe pleschanka* 15cm FIELD NOTES: In flight shows a white rump and white outer tail bases, the latter sometimes white to near tail-tip. Often feeds shrike-like, swooping after insect prey, then returning to same or nearby perch. There is a pale-throated morph, *vittata* (fig 2b). SONG: Often given during high circling display-flight, a repetition of a 2- or 3-note, buzzy, trilling phrase combined with much mimicry. CALL: A harsh *zack-zack* or *chep-chep*, also a wagtail-like *psyiep*. HABITAT: Stony hill- or mountainsides with bushes or small trees, also high-plateau grassland with scattered boulders.

3 CYPRUS WHEATEAR *Oenanthe cypriaca* 14cm FIELD NOTES: Rump, tail pattern and actions similar to Pied Wheatear. SONG: Cicada-like purring, *bizz-bizz-bizz-bizz…*. CALL: Harsh *zack-zack*. HABITAT: Much as Pied Wheatear.

4 EASTERN PIED WHEATEAR *Oenanthe picata* 15cm FIELD NOTES: In flight shows white rump and white outer tail bases. Three colour morphs occur: *picata*, *opistholeuca* (fig 4b) and *capistrata* (fig 4c). SONG: Scratchy, consisting of low-pitched *chott* notes, whistles, chirrups and trills, given from a prominent perch or flight. CALL: Loud *chek-chek*. HABITAT: Arid boulder-covered hill country with scattered vegetation, fallow fields, ruins and around habitations.

5 ARABIAN WHEATEAR *Oenanthe lugentoides* 14cm FIELD NOTES: Rump, tail pattern and actions similar to Mourning Wheatear, with which it is often thought to be conspecific. SONG: Short bubbling phrases, also a musical *to-too-too*. CALL: *chuck-a-do* and a rasping, often repeated, *kaak*, which is frequently combined with a high-pitched *seek*. HABITAT: Rocky hill- and mountainsides with sparse vegetation, less frequently in areas with bushes or trees or thick juniper scrub near cultivation.

6 MOURNING WHEATEAR *Oenanthe lugens* 14cm FIELD NOTES: In flight shows white rump and extensive white outer tail bases. A dark morph occurs in the basalt deserts of Jordan and Syria. SONG: A pleasing warble often combined with call notes. CALL: Quiet *chack-chack*, also a harsh *zeeb*. HABITAT: Gorges, rocky wadis and rolling hills with sparse vegetation in semiarid and desert areas. RACES: *O. l. halophila* (fig 6b) NW Africa.

7 HUME'S WHEATEAR *Oenanthe alboniger* 17cm FIELD NOTES: Extensive white rump and white outer tail bases. Often perches on bushes. SONG: Loud, cheerful, rising *chew-de-dew-twit* or similar. CALL: Whistled *triki-treek* or *trooti-trooti-tree* and a harsh *chack-chack*. HABITAT: Cliffs, ravines, rocky outcrops and hills, generally with sparse vegetation.

8 BLACK WHEATEAR *Oenanthe leucura* 18cm FIELD NOTES: Wary. In flight shows white rump and extensive white outer tail bases. SONG: Melodious *chokereu-keu-keke*, or similar. CALL: Plaintive *pee-pee-pee* and a scolding *chak*. HABITAT: Steep rocky areas, ravines, sea cliffs, ruins, etc., with sparse vegetation or scattered trees and scrub.

9 HOODED WHEATEAR *Oenanthe monacha* 17.5cm FIELD NOTES: Usually wary. In flight shows extensive white rump and tail. Makes prolonged aerial pursuits of flying insects. SONG: Sweet medley of whistles and thrush-like notes. CALL: Harsh *zack* or a low *wit-wit*. HABITAT: Barren cliffs and ravines in hot, arid, desolate areas.

10 WHITE-CROWNED BLACK WHEATEAR *Oenanthe leucopyga* 17cm FIELD NOTES: Usually wary. In flight shows white rump and extensive white on outer tail. SONG: Very variable, combining warbles, discordant notes and much mimicry of birds and mammals. CALL: A grating *dzik* and a far-carrying *hwee-weet*. HABITAT: Some of the most desolate desert mountain areas, including ravines, wadis, rocky hill areas and around settlements.

♀ pale-throated

♀ dark-throated

2b

1

♀

2

♂

♂

♀

3

♂

4

♀

4c

♂

4b

♀

5

♂

♀

6b

♂

6

♂

7

♀

8

♂

9

♀

♂

♂

10

1st summer

NA

20 CHATS, ROCK THRUSHES AND WHISTLING THRUSH

1 FAMILIAR CHAT *Cercomela familiaris* 15cm (Vagrant) FIELD NOTES: Feeding methods much as Blackstart. Frequently flicks wings and trembles tail. In flight shows rufous rump and extensive rufous on outer tail feathers. SONG: Random series of soft whistles and quiet chattering notes. CALL: Scolding *whee-chuck-chuck* and a shrill *swiiip-swiiip-swiiip*. HABITAT: In native Africa: areas of rocky ground in scrub or light woodland.

2 BLACKSTART *Cercomela melanura* 15cm FIELD NOTES: Active, feeds by fly-catching or dropping onto insects from a low perch. On alighting, frequently half-spreads wings, and fans and downward-flexes tail. SONG: Repeated mellow *chee-yu-chee-yu* or *cheee-yu-chee*. CALL: Piping *cher-u*, a weak *chirp* and, in alarm, a short *tzeetch-eetch*. HABITAT: Scrub in semi-desert, desert, foothills, wadis and isolated buildings and settlements.

3 LITTLE ROCK THRUSH *Monticola rufocinereus* 15cm FIELD NOTES: Usually feeds by dropping onto insects from a bush or tree perch, or by making fly-catching sallies. Quivers tail when perched. SONG: Scratchy notes interspersed with low- and high-pitched fluty notes, *tryyh-rrr-tvi-rirp-tschak-tshak*. CALL: Soft *tyyt* or *trrrt* when alarmed. HABITAT: Rocky slopes, cliffs and gorges in highland regions, always with some trees and bushes.

4 ROCK THRUSH (RUFOUS-TAILED ROCK THRUSH) *Monticola saxatilis* 20cm FIELD NOTES: Usually wary. Drops onto prey from rock, tree or other perch, occasionally makes fly-catching sallies. Frequently wags tail. SONG: Sometimes rendered during display-flight: a series of soft, clear, melodic phrases, can recall Blackbird. CALL: Low *chak-chak* and a clear *diu*. HABITAT: Rocky hill- and mountainsides, usually with stunted trees or bushes, also ruins and buildings. From 500m upward; on passage often in open lowland.

5 BLUE-CAPPED ROCK THRUSH *Monticola cinclorhynchus* 17cm FIELD NOTES: Mainly arboreal, picks insects off trunks and branches, also feeds on ground amongst leaf litter. Wags tail slowly up and down. SONG: Delivered from topmost branch of a pine or fir, also during display-flight: thrush-like *tew-li-di - tew-li-di - tew-li-di* or *tra-trr-treee-treea....* CALL: Various, including short, rich *fi-ya*, a sharp, rising *peri-peri* and a clucking *goink-goink*. HABITAT: Open pine and oak forests, and rocky, grass-covered slopes with scattered trees.

6 WHITE-THROATED ROCK THRUSH *Monticola gularis* 18cm FIELD NOTES: Forages in small trees, or on ground. SONG: Melancholic, flute-like, rising whistles combined with *chat-at-at* call and other more complex phrases. CALL: Sharp *tack-tack*, a soft *queck-queck* and, in flight, a thin *tsip*. HABITAT: Open conifer and mixed montane forests, steep, scrub-covered rocky slopes.

7 CHESTNUT-BELLIED ROCK THRUSH *Monticola rufiventris* 24cm FIELD NOTES: Forages mainly on ground, occasionally makes fly-catching sallies from high branches. Wags tail up and down. SONG: Delivered from a treetop: a pleasant warble; also a whistled *fweeeur-fweet*. CALL: *quock* and a jay-like rasp, interspersed with a shrill *tick*. HABITAT: Open moist conifer or oak and rhododendron forest, from 1000 to 3000m.

8 BLUE ROCK THRUSH *Monticola solitarius* 23cm FIELD NOTES: Wary. Drops on prey from low perch or occasionally fly-catches. SONG: Loud, melodic, Blackbird-like warbles and fluty whistles, *tju-sri - tjurr-titi - wuchi - trr-trrt-tri*; may also include some mimicry of other birds. CALL: Deep *chak-chak*, a plaintive *see* and a nuthatch-like *uit-uit*. HABITAT: Rocky hill- and mountainsides, ravines, gorges, sea-cliffs, rocky coasts and buildings and ruins. RACES: M. s. *philippensis* (Red-bellied Rock Thrush) (fig 8b) NE Russia, China, Japan.

9 BLUE WHISTLING THRUSH *Myophonus caeruleus* 30cm FIELD NOTES: Feeding actions much like Blackbird. Often feeds from rocks in strong-flowing streams, picking food from water surface. SONG: Disjointed string of melodious, high-pitched, human-like whistles, sometimes including mimicry. CALL: Far-carrying *tzeet-tze-tze-tzeet* or *tzeet-tzuit-tzuit-tzuit-zuit*, and a shrill *skreee*. HABITAT: Broadleaf evergreen and mixed deciduous forest, often in gorges and ravines.

21 THRUSHES

1 PLAIN-BACKED THRUSH *Zoothera mollissima* 26cm FIELD NOTES: Shy and unapproachable. In flight, from below, shows the striking white underwing patches common to the genus. Mainly a ground feeder. SONG: Variable, rich, musical phrases, *plee-too...ti-ti-ti* or similar. CALL: Thin *chuck* and a rattling alarm, though generally silent. HABITAT: Rocky alpine areas with juniper and dwarf rhododendron. Lower areas in winter.

2 LONG-TAILED THRUSH *Zoothera dixoni* 27cm FIELD NOTES: Secretive. Feeds on ground in thick vegetation in forest or alpine scrub. SONG: Often begins *w-t-it*, then slow, slurred phrases, *wu-ut - cheet-sher - wut-chet-shuur* or similar, interspersed with twitters and *too-ee* or *ee-ee* phrases. CALL: Unrecorded. HABITAT: Dense fir, oak and rhododendron forests on or above the tree line. Also dwarf juniper forest and high-altitude scrub. Lower, thick forests in the winter.

3 SCALY THRUSH *Zoothera dauma* 27cm FIELD NOTES: Usually remains hidden. Mainly a ground feeder, in moist areas of forests. SONG: Repeated slow phrases, e.g. *pur-loo-tree-lay...dur-lee-dur-lee...drr-drr-chew-you-we-eeee*, sometimes interspersed with low squeaks or twitters. CALL: Soft *tsi*, a drawn-out *tzeep* or *seeh* and *chuck - chuck* when alarmed. Generally silent, apparently reluctant to call, even when alarmed? HABITAT: Various forest types, including mature oak, dense spruce in the taiga zone, and montane and sub-montane, with tangled undergrowth. RACES: *Z. d. aurea* (White's Thrush) (fig 3b) N and NE Asia.

4 AMAMI THRUSH *Zoothera major* 28cm FIELD NOTES: Very shy. Little recorded about habits, presumed to be similar to Scaly Thrush. SONG: Series of slow, varied, flute-like notes, rising and falling, e.g. *piri-piri-kyo-kyo* or *chirrup-chewee - cheue - wiow-we-ep - chewee-wiop*. CALL: As Scaly Thrush. HABITAT: Uncut primary forest and selectively cut mature forest.

5 LONG-BILLED THRUSH *Zoothera monticola* 27cm FIELD NOTES: Shy and retiring. Ground feeder in dense forest undergrowth. SONG: Usually given from the top of a tall tree: loud, melancholic series, of up to 3 plaintive whistles, *te-e-uw* or *sew-a-tew-tew* or similar. CALL: A loud *zaaaaaaa* alarm, otherwise generally silent. HABITAT: Thick undergrowth, often with moist mossy areas, in dense, high-altitude fir forests. Winters at lower levels.

6 PIED THRUSH *Zoothera wardii* 22cm FIELD NOTES: Shy when breeding, less so in winter. Forms small migrating flocks. Mostly a ground feeder, but also in trees and bushes when they are in fruit. SONG: A short, repeated, 2-note, warbled phrase, *pie-dee*, sometimes with a rising *zik* ending. CALL: An occasional sharp, spitting *ptz-ptz-ptz-ptz*. HABITAT: High-altitude broadleaved woods and forests. Altitudinal wanderer to the region.

7 SIBERIAN THRUSH *Zoothera sibirica* 22cm FIELD NOTES: Very secretive; often overlooked. Mainly a ground feeder, but will feed on berries and fruit when available. SONG: Rich, whistled phrases, interrupted by long pauses, falteringly or languidly delivered, transcribed as *tvee-tring, tvee-tryu - tvee-kvee* or *tvee-kwi-tring* or similar. CALL: Weak *tseee* and a soft *zit*; a gruff squawk when flushed. HABITAT: Mainly dense alder undergrowth, in the extensive coniferous taiga of lowland Siberia.

8 VARIED THRUSH *Zoothera naevia* 23cm (Vagrant) FIELD NOTES: Shy, feeds low down or on ground, in the dark shaded areas in forests. SONG: Unlikely to be heard in region; vibrant, eerie, melancholic and sustained notes, varying rapidly from high to low pitch, also a buzzing trill. CALL: Weak *chuck*, also a thin *woooeeee*. HABITAT: In native N America: dense coniferous forests with undergrowth of dogwood and wild currant.

Typical underwing
pattern of *Zoothera*
thrushes

22 THRUSHES

1 YEMEN THRUSH *Turdus menachensis* 23cm FIELD NOTES: Shy. Ground feeder in dense scrub. SONG: Series of soft low- and high-pitched phrases, *tissik-tissik-tssechup*, a stuttering trill or soft croaking note. CALL: Quiet *chuk-chuk*, a thin *seep* and a more explosive *chuck-chuck-chuck*. HABITAT: Scrub on steep rocky slopes and hillsides; cultivated wadis and tree-lined terraces.

2 TICKELL'S THRUSH *Turdus unicolor* 21cm FIELD NOTES: Typical actions of the genus. Feeds on ground and in fruiting trees. SONG: Monotonous, rendered as *chellya-chellya-chirrali -cherlya-cherya-cherlya-chellya - chellya-chellya*. CALL: *dew-dew*, *wiw-wiw* or a chuckling *quoit-quoit* or *chuck-chuck*, alarm similar, but harsher, than the latter. HABITAT: Mixed forest with clearings, open broadleaved woodland, willow groves and orchards.

3 RING OUZEL *Turdus torquatus* 26cm FIELD NOTES: Actions like Blackbird but generally more shy. Juvenile breast crescent very faint or lacking. SONG: Several loud, repeated, melancholy, fluty phrases, sometimes rounded off with a rattling chuckle. CALL: Hard *tak-tak-tak*. HABITAT: Mountains, rocky uplands, hilly areas with stunted trees; in the Middle East, often down to sea-level. RACES: *T. t. alpestris* (fig 3b) Mountains of S and C Europe.

4 WHITE-COLLARED BLACKBIRD *Turdus albocinctus* 28cm FIELD NOTES: Generally wary. Feeds in fruiting trees and shrubs and on ground. Juvenile lacks pale collar. Rusty shaft-streaks above, brownish orange mottled with dark spots below. Pale throat with dark malar streak. SONG: Mellow series of descending whistles, *tew-i-tew-u-tew-o* or similar, occasionally with some hissing or squeaking notes. CALL: Throaty *tuck-tuck-tuck*. HABITAT: Various forest types: deciduous, open conifer with good ground cover, mixed and rhododendron scrub above the tree line.

5 BLACKBIRD *Turdus merula* 27cm FIELD NOTES: Usually conspicuous. Feeds on ground and in fruiting bushes and trees. Juvenile like female but mottled with darkish spots below. SONG: Beautiful, clear, rich, fluty notes that merge into short continuous phrases, not repeated phrases like Song Thrush. CALL: Low *chuck-chuck-chuck* or similar, rapidly repeated when alarmed. Also a high, drawn-out *tseee*. HABITAT: Very varied, including all types of forest and woodland, scrub, farmland with hedges, parks and gardens, etc.

6 GREY-WINGED BLACKBIRD *Turdus boulboul* 29cm FIELD NOTES: Generally shy. Feeds much as others of genus and forms small winter flocks, sometimes in the company of White-collared Blackbirds. SONG: Rich and melodious, generally consists of soft opening note followed by 4 high notes descending in tone. CALL: *chuck-chuck*, *chook-chook* and a *churi* contact call. HABITAT: Moist oak and rhododendron forest, evergreen forest, clearings, hillside scrub.

7 AMERICAN ROBIN *Turdus migratorius* 24cm (Vagrant) FIELD NOTES: Similar actions to Blackbird and most others of genus. SONG: Unlikely to be heard in the region: pleasant *cheerily-cheery-cheerily-cheery*. CALL: *tut-tut-tut*, a more excited *kli-kli-kli….* HABITAT: In native N America: forests, woods, meadows, thickets, farms with hedges, parks, gardens, towns and cities.

8 KESSLER'S THRUSH *Turdus kessleri* 28cm FIELD NOTES: Gregarious, even in breeding season. SONG: Rarely heard, said to be a short series of Mistle Thrush-like melancholy phrases. CALL: Soft *squack*, harsher when alarmed, also a soft *dug-dug*, a high *swi-swi-swi-swi* and *chock-chock-chock*. HABITAT: Dwarf juniper and conifers, various scrub types, from 3600 to 4500m.

9 IZU THRUSH *Turdus celaenops* 23cm FIELD NOTES: Actions similar to others of genus. Izu Islands endemic. SONG: Usually a repeated high-pitched rattle, *tche-e-e-e-e - tche-e-e-er* or similar. CALL: Series of dry, grating notes. HABITAT: Deciduous or mixed woods, orchards and large gardens

10 BROWN-HEADED THRUSH *Turdus chrysolaus* 23cm FIELD NOTES: Feeds low down, in or near the cover of bushes. Often forms large flocks in winter. SONG: *tseefee-tseetee-tseetsssyu* or similar trisyllabic phrase that may end with a *tringtstssss*, a rising *wewwikwer-sli* or a dry *z-korrn-korrn-kwer-sli*. CALL: *chuck-chuck-chuck*, a *tsi* or a *tsssup-ssup-sup-sup…* when alarmed. HABITAT: Dry deciduous or mixed woodland with shrubby undergrowth. Winters in fields, scattered woodland, orchards, parks and gardens.

23 THRUSHES

1 CHESTNUT THRUSH *Turdus rubrocanus* 24–28cm FIELD NOTES: Shy, perches in treetops, mainly a ground feeder. In winter often forms small flocks, which may include other thrushes. SONG: Short, warbled phrases repeated up to 8 times, then changing to a Song Thrush-like *yeee-bre - yee-bre - diddiyit-diddiyit-diddiyit - yip-bru - yip-bru*…. CALL: *chuck-chuck-chuck* and, when alarmed, a rapid *kwik-kwik - kwik-kwik*. HABITAT: Conifer and mixed forest with ground cover, 2300–3300m. Lower levels in winter. RACES: *T. r. gouldi* (fig 1b) C China.

2 GREY-SIDED THRUSH *Turdus feae* 23cm FIELD NOTES: Shy. Mainly a ground feeder. Forms winter flocks, which often include Eyebrowed Thrushes. SONG: Little recorded, said to consist of series of repeated, short double- or triple-note phrases, *sit-twee00 - wet-too - chit-to-loo*. CALL: Thin *zeeee*. HABITAT: Montane broadleaved forest, above 1500m, slightly lower in winter.

3 PALE THRUSH *Turdus pallidus* 23cm FIELD NOTES: Shy and wary. Mainly a ground feeder, in undergrowth. In winter forms flocks, which often include Eyebrowed Thrushes, when it may feed more in the open. SONG: Far carrying. Various, repeated, double or triple whistles, *tuvee-tulee - tulee-tevee* or *tve-tveeeu-weet-weet-tveeu-trrrsss* or similar. CALL: *chook, tuck-tuck* and a thin *tsee* or *tsee-ip*; a Blackbird-like *think-think* when alarmed. HABITAT: Dense, mixed montane and sub-montane forests. In winter and during migration, occurs in more open areas, e.g. copses, scrub, orchards, open fields, parks and gardens.

4 GREY-BACKED THRUSH *Turdus hortulorum* 23cm FIELD NOTES: Very shy. Ground feeder amongst leaf litter, also spends long periods in foliage of trees. Forms loose flocks in winter. SONG: Not well documented. Said by some authorities to be superlative, consisting of a series of loud fluty whistles. CALL: Harsh *chack-chack*, a low chuckle and, in alarm, a shrill *cheee*. HABITAT: Dense oakwoods, often near water, and mixed woods of various species. Winters in open woods, bamboo, scrub woodland, etc.

5 EYEBROWED THRUSH *Turdus obscurus* 22cm FIELD NOTES: Wary during breeding season, less so on migration and in winter, often in flocks with other thrushes. Feeds on ground, and in trees and bushes when in fruit. SONG: 2 or 3 mournful phrases, *teveteu - trryutetyute - trrryutetyutyu*, a pause, then a lower twittering, warbling and chattering, interspersed with pauses. CALL: Soft *chuk*, a hard *tack-tack* and a *shree*; also a *dzee* flight call. HABITAT: Dense spruce and fir forests or high-altitude mixed forests. In east of range, frequents birch forests. Winters in open forests, open country, parks and gardens.

6 NAUMANN'S THRUSH *Turdus naumanni* 23cm FIELD NOTES: Mainly a ground feeder; acts much like Fieldfare. Forms flocks in winter, often in association with Black-throated Thrush. SONG: A melodious, fluting, *tvee-tryuuu-tee - tvee-tryuuuu-tvee*, ending in faint trill. CALL: Shrill *cheeh-cheeh*, often repeated, a harsher *ket-ket-ket* and a chuckling *chak-chak*. HABITAT: Open forests and woods. Winters in more open areas, including woodland edge, scrub, stubble-fields, parks and gardens. RACES: *T. n. eunomus* (Dusky Thrush) (fig 6b) N Siberia.

7 RED-THROATED THRUSH *Turdus ruficollis* 24cm FIELD NOTES: Ground feeder; actions like Fieldfare. Forms large winter flocks, often with other thrush species. SONG: Rambling, simple, *chooee - whee-oo-ee - oo. T. r. atrogularis* more hoarse with frequent pauses. CALL: Soft *chuk*, a weak *seep* and a harsh *chak*; also a Blackbird-like chatter. HABITAT: Mainly sparse mountain forest and mossy scrub tundra. *T. r. atrogularis* prefers the undergrowth of dense taiga forests, also subalpine steppe with scattered larch. RACES: *T. r. atrogularis* (Black-throated Thrush) (fig 7b) E Russia east to C Siberia, south to NW China.

8 JAPANESE THRUSH *Turdus cardis* 22cm FIELD NOTES: Usually shy. In winter often joins with flocks of Siberian Thrushes. SONG: Series of repeated fluty trills and whistles, *see-tew - see-tew - see-tew - titupi-tit - seea-tyew - see-a-tyu - se-a- tyu - tilit-tilit-tilit - tyu-tyatyew - tyatyew - tullut-tullut-tillit*…and variants. CALL: Thin *tsweee* or *tsuuu*. HABITAT: Usually dense mixed or deciduous woods and forests on hill- or mountainsides, lower areas in northern Japan.

24 THRUSHES AND AMERICAN THRUSHES

1 MISTLE THRUSH *Turdus viscivorus* 27cm FIELD NOTES: Feeds in open. Undulating flight. White underwing coverts. SONG: Several clear, far-carrying, fluted phrases, e.g. *chuwee - trewuu - tureetruruu - truwutru - truwuwutru…* interspersed with short pauses and some shorter phrases. CALL: Harsh rattle and a *tuck-tuck-tuck*. HABITAT: Various types of woodland, usually with open areas, also hedgerows, parks and gardens. Often moves to more open areas in winter.

2 CHINESE THRUSH *Turdus mupinensis* 23cm FIELD NOTES: Usually in undergrowth, shy. Little known. Cinnamon underwing coverts. SONG: Similar to Song Thrush, although apparently with slower delivery. CALL: Unknown. HABITAT: Mixed or deciduous montane forest plantations and woodland with good undergrowth.

3 SONG THRUSH *Turdus philomelos* 22cm FIELD NOTES: Usually in open, often feeds on snails smashing them on stones. Ochre underwing coverts. SONG: Clear, varied, repeated phrases, e.g. *filip-filip-filip - codidio-codidio - quitquitquit - tittitt-tittitt-tereret-tereret-tereret - kviet-kviet-kviet….* Mimics other birds or mechanical sounds. CALL: *sip* or *zip*, and a loud *chick* when alarmed. HABITAT: Wide variety of open woodland, including parks and gardens, with extensive undergrowth.

4 FIELDFARE *Turdus pilaris* 25cm FIELD NOTES: Bold during breeding season; more wary during winter, when found in large flocks. White underwing coverts. SONG: Series of harsh chattering or warbling notes interspersed with wheezing, squeaky or chuckling notes. CALL: *chack-chack*, a nasal *tseee* and, when alarmed, *chetchetchetje* or *trt-trrrrt-trrt*. HABITAT: Open coniferous, mixed or deciduous forests, parks and gardens. Winters in open areas, including farmland and parks.

5 REDWING *Turdus iliacus* 21cm FIELD NOTES: Rusty underwing coverts. Forms large winter flocks often in the company of other thrushes, especially Fieldfares. SONG: A few short notes, *chirre-cherre-churre* or similar, followed by a prolonged fast, variably pitched twittering. CALL: Thin *seeeh* or *seeip*, also, when alarmed, a rattling *trrrt-trrrt-trrt* or *jip-jip*. HABITAT: Birch woodland, birch and willow scrub, mixed conifer woodland, and locally in parks and gardens.

6 WOOD THRUSH *Hylocichla mustelina* 20cm (Vagrant) FIELD NOTES: Usually shy and retiring. Mainly a ground feeder. SONG: Consists of fluty phrases interspersed with call notes and ending with a soft trill, unlikely to be heard in the region. CALL: *pit-pit-pit* and a low *tuck-tuck*. HABITAT: In native N America: deciduous woodland undergrowth, often near water.

7 GREY-CHEEKED THRUSH *Catharus minimus aliciae* 16cm FIELD NOTES: Shy, usually feeds below mid-tree level in cover. SONG: High pitched, starts slowly *chook-chook…* then *chee-chee*, finishing with a descending *wee-oh-wee-oh….* CALL: *wee-ah*, a sharp *chuck* and a *cheerrr* flight note. HABITAT: Mainly dense conifer forest, also mixed forest with shrubby thickets. RACES: *C. m. bicknelli* (Bicknell's Thrush) (fig 7b) N America. Often considered a full species. Nominate is a vagrant to W Palearctic.

8 HERMIT THRUSH *Catharus guttatus* 16cm (Vagrant) FIELD NOTES: Shy and retiring. Nervous, constantly flicks wings and raises tail. SONG: Similar to Wood Thrush, unlikely to be heard in the region. CALL: Typically a low *chuck*; also a ringing *cheeeee*. HABITAT: In native N America: mixed, or coniferous, forest clearings with shrubby undergrowth, often near streams or bogs.

9 SWAINSON'S THRUSH *Catharus ustulatus* 17cm (Vagrant) FIELD NOTES: Shy and retiring, keeping to cover of trees and undergrowth. SONG: Fluty notes that fade into a squeaky twittering, unlikely to be heard in the region. CALL: Liquid *whit* or a soft *whup*. HABITAT: In native N America: undergrowth in coniferous, deciduous or mixed forests, also woodland thickets, often near streams.

10 VEERY *Catharus fuscescens* 17cm (Vagrant) FIELD NOTES: Secretive. Actions like Hermit Thrush but lacks its wing and tail flicks. SONG: Descending *da-vee-ur - vee-ur - veer - veer*, unlikely to be heard in the region. CALL: Fluted *phew*, *whee-uu* and also a slow, slurred *weee-oo*. HABITAT: In native N America: undergrowth in deciduous or mixed forests, often near streams.

25 BUSH WARBLERS

1 ASIAN STUBTAIL (ASIAN STUBTAIL WARBLER) *Urosphena squameiceps* 10cm
FIELD NOTES: Skulks on ground or in low vegetation. SONG: Insect-like *see-see-see-see-see-see-see…*, louder at the end. CALL: *chip-chip-chip*. HABITAT: Dense undergrowth of coniferous and deciduous forests. More open scrub in winter.

2 JAPANESE BUSH WARBLER *Cettia diphone* 15cm FIELD NOTES: Generally secretive.
SONG: Pulsating whistle followed by *hot-ket-kyot*, then a descending *pe-chew - pe-chew - pe-chew*
CALL: Dry ticking. HABITAT: Dense scrub bamboo and grass thickets, up to 3000m. RACES: C. *d. canturians* (Manchurian Scrub Warbler) (fig 2b) N China. Sometimes considered a full species.

3 BROWNISH-FLANKED BUSH WARBLER *Cettia fortipes* 12cm FIELD NOTES: Skulks, more often heard than seen, hard to flush. SONG: Sustained, rising *weee* followed by explosive *chiwiyou*. CALL: Persistent *tack-tack*. HABITAT: Open forests with thick undergrowth; bamboo thickets. From 1200 to 3300m, lower elevations in winter.

4 CHESTNUT-CROWNED BUSH WARBLER *Cettia major* 13cm FIELD NOTES: Skulking Little recorded. SONG: Single note followed by a 3- or 4-note explosive whistle. CALL: Sharp *peep*. HABITAT: Scrub and forest undergrowth, 1800–4000m. Winters in tall grass and reed-beds at lower elevations.

5 ABERRANT BUSH WARBLER *Cettia flavolivacea* 13cm FIELD NOTES: Skulks in dense foliage, sometimes inquisitive. SONG: *dir - dir-tee - teee-weee*. CALL: A shivering *brrt-brrt* and a *chick*; when alarmed, a harsh grating note. HABITAT: Tall grass, bamboo, scrub and thickets in forests, 1200–4900m. Lower elevations in winter.

6 YELLOWISH-BELLIED BUSH WARBLER *Cettia acanthizoides* 11cm FIELD NOTES: Skulks in thick cover. SONG: Peculiar, 3 or 4 long, drawn-out whistles followed by several fast, repeated *chew-chew* notes. CALL: *tik-tik-tik* and a vibrant *brrr*. HABITAT: Forest undergrowth, dense scrub and bamboo thickets, 1500–4000m. Lower areas in winter.

7 GREY-SIDED BUSH WARBLER *Cettia brunnifrons* 11cm FIELD NOTES: Skulking. Sometimes sings in the open. SONG: Continuous *dzit-su-ze-sizu*, often followed by *bzeeuu-bzeeuu*. CALL: Soft *tsik*. HABITAT: Dense thickets and scrub in subalpine zone. Lower in winter.

8 CETTI'S WARBLER *Cettia cetti* 14cm FIELD NOTES: Skulks, more often heard than seen. Often sings in the open. SONG: Very loud and explosive *pwit-piti-chewit-chewit-chewit*. CALL: Sharp *chip* and a *tsuk*; a Wren-like rattle when alarmed. HABITAT: Various thick cover, near water, or other damp areas.

9 SPOTTED BUSH WARBLER *Bradypterus thoracicus* 12cm FIELD NOTES: Often less shy than others of the genus. SONG: Dry, persistent, low-pitched buzzing. CALL: *tchik-tchit* and an explosive *pwit*. HABITAT: Rhododendron scrub, dwarf juniper, scrub in pastures and low scrub above tree line. RACES: *B. t. davidi* (Père David's Bush Warbler) (fig 9b) SE Russia, N China.

10 LARGE-BILLED BUSH WARBLER *Bradypterus major* 13cm FIELD NOTES: Skulker, very difficult to flush. SONG: Rapid, monotonous reeling. CALL: Quiet *tic* and a grating *trrr*. HABITAT: From 2400 to 3600m in open wasteland, hillside bushes, forest fringe and low scrub jungle. Winters in rank grassland and fields.

11 BROWN BUSH WARBLER *Bradypterus luteoventris* 13cm FIELD NOTES: Skulking, but sings from prominent perch. In winter very secretive. SONG: Little recorded. CALL: A rapid reeling and a *teck-teck*. HABITAT: Grassy and dense weedy areas, 1200–3300m. Lower in winter.

12 CHINESE BUSH WARBLER *Bradypterus tacsanowskius* 13cm FIELD NOTES: Secretive, creeps around in tangled vegetation. SONG: Similar to Spotted Bush Warbler, but lower pitched and with drier buzzing notes. CALL: *chir-chir*. HABITAT: From 2800 to 3600m in riverside forest with dense undergrowth, grassy glades and dry mountain valleys with thick vegetation. Winters in grassland, paddies and reed-beds.

26 PRINIAS, SCRUB WARBLERS, GRASSHOPPER WARBLERS AND CISTICOLA

1 **GRACEFUL PRINIA** *Prinia gracilis fusca* 11cm FIELD NOTES: Twitches tail and wings, the latter often producing a 'snapping' sound, especially in aerial display. SONG: Monotonous repetition of a thin *tzeee-bit* or *zerwit*. CALL: Trilling *bleep* and a flat *jit*. HABITAT: Very varied, from low vegetation in arid areas to grassy swamp, reed-beds, cultivation, gardens, etc. RACES: *P. g. deltae* (fig 1b) Nile delta to W Israel.

2 **PLAIN PRINIA** *Prinia inornata* 13.5cm (Vagrant) FIELD NOTES: Active, though skulking. Performs aerial display, which includes 'wing-snapping'. SONG: Monotonous, insect-like reeling. CALL: Rapid, repeated *chi-up* or *chip*. HABITAT: In native India: various wet areas, reed-beds, paddies, mangroves, coastal salt marshes, etc.

3 **HILL PRINIA** *Prinia atrogularis* 17cm FIELD NOTES: Active, noisy, constantly twitches tail SONG: Monotonous *cho-ee - cho-ee - cho-ee…*, *tze-tze-tze…* or *tulip - tulip - tulip*. CALL: Soft *tp-tp-tp…* and a scolding *churr-churr-churr*. HABITAT: Grass and scrub in sub-montane and montane forests; reed-beds and other waterside vegetation.

4 **STRIATED PRINIA** *Prinia criniger* 17cm FIELD NOTES: Skulking. Sings from bush top or overhead wires. SONG: Wheezy, scraping, like a saw being sharpened on a grindstone. CALL: Sharp *tchack-tchack*. HABITAT: Tall grass and scrub, cultivated hillsides up to 3100m.

5 **SCRUB WARBLER** *Scotocerca inquieta* 11cm FIELD NOTES: Mouse-like actions and usually difficult to see well, but can be quite inquisitive. SONG: Variable, a thin *di-di-di-di-di*, then a descending *di-di-di-de-de* followed by a warbling *toodle-toodle-toodle*. CALL: Various, e.g. *drzip*, a rasping *prrt*, a high *te-he* and a *dri-drrrirr*. HABITAT: Low scrub in semi-desert; on bare stony hillsides and sandy plains. RACES: *S. c. saharae* (fig 5b) Algeria, Tunisia, Libya.

6 **CRICKET WARBLER** *Spiloptila clamans* 11cm FIELD NOTES: Active, often in small family groups. SONG: Usually a lively, rapid, tinkling trill. CALL: Ringing whistle and a sharp *zzt*. HABITAT: Scattered scrub and grass on desert or semi-desert plains.

7 **ZITTING CISTICOLA (FAN-TAILED WARBLER)** *Cisticola juncidis* 10cm FIELD NOTES: Difficult to see well when feeding, much easier when singing, either from exposed perch or undulating song-flight. SONG: Simple, persistently repeated *zit-zit-zit-zit-zit…*. CALL: Usually *chip* or *plip*, also *tsipp-tsipp-tsipp*. HABITAT: Tall grass, reeds, sedges, grassy wasteland, cultivations and salt-marsh vegetation. RACES: *C. j. brunneiceps* (fig 7b) Japan.

8 **CHINESE HILL WARBLER** *Rhopophilus pekinensis* 16cm FIELD NOTES: Active. Frequently runs with tail slightly cocked. Often associates with babblers (some authors feel it belongs in that family). SONG: A sweet *dear-dear-dear-dear*, each first syllable starting high, falling, then rising again before start of second syllable. CALL: A mellow *chee-anh*. HABITAT: Scattered bushes on dry, stony hill- or mountainsides.

9 **PALLAS'S GRASSHOPPER WARBLER** *Locustella certhiola* 14cm FIELD NOTES: Extreme skulking, creeping, mouse-like actions on or near ground. SONG: Hesitant start followed by rapid loud trill. CALL: Rattling *trrrrrrr*, also a sharp *pit*. HABITAT: Varied, from coastal thickets, waterside vegetation and forest clearings to damp meadows between the tree-line and mountain tundra.

10 **LANCEOLATED WARBLER** *Locustella lanceolata* 12cm FIELD NOTES: Difficult to see; actions similar to others of genus. May sing from exposed bush top. SONG: Insect-like reeling, similar to Grasshopper Warbler. CALL: *chi-chirr*, a *pit*, a soft *tak* and a scolding *cheek*. HABITAT: Usually damp grassy or similar areas with scattered scrub or small trees; forest clearings.

11 **GRASSHOPPER WARBLER** *Locustella naevia* 13cm FIELD NOTES: Actions typical of genus. More often heard than seen. SONG: Dry insect-like reeling, which may continue for several minutes. CALL: Sharp *thik*, repeated in alarm, and a quieter *whit*. HABITAT: Scrubby thickets or rank vegetation on heathland, moorland, downland, marshy areas, and low trees of forest edge.

27 GRASSHOPPER WARBLERS AND REED WARBLERS

1 MIDDENDORFF'S GRASSHOPPER WARBLER *Locustella ochotensis* 15cm FIELD NOTES: Skulker, but exposed when singing either from a perch or looping song-flight. SONG/CALL: Short, jarring warbles. Little else recorded. HABITAT: Open thickets in damp grassland, dwarf bamboo, waterside scrub and reed-beds. Winters mainly in reed-beds and mangroves.

2 STYAN'S GRASSHOPPER WARBLER *Locustella pleskei* 15cm FIELD NOTES: Actions similar to Middendorff's Grasshopper Warbler. SONG/CALL: Few details, said to differ from Middendorff's? HABITAT: Open thickets in lush grassland, low vegetation on coastal headlands, exposed fields and hills. Winters in reed-beds and mangroves.

3 RIVER WARBLER *Locustella fluviatilis* 14cm FIELD NOTES: Sings from exposed perch, otherwise shy and elusive. SONG: Rapid, cricket-like *zre-zre-zre-zre-zre…* delivered for long periods. CALL: *tschuck* and a repeated *chick-chick-chick*. HABITAT: Various types of dense bush, usually near water or other damp areas. Not necessarily near water in winter.

4 SAVI'S WARBLER *Locustella luscinioides* 14cm FIELD NOTES: Skulker with mouse-like actions. Sings from exposed perch. SONG: Quiet ticking followed by vibrant, insect-like, buzzy reeling. CALL: Sharp *tchink* and a soft *puitt*. HABITAT: Reed-beds and dense waterside vegetation

5 GRAY'S GRASSHOPPER WARBLER *Locustella fasciolata* 15cm FIELD NOTES: Very secretive, even singing from deep cover. SONG: Usually a soft *chit-chu* then a loud *chit-chit -tu-chi*, followed by a rapid, falling-away *u-chic-toi-tu-tee-chee*. CALL: Trilling *cherr* and a loud *tschrok*. HABITAT: Dense vegetation in steppe, woodland fringe, forest clearings, river valleys and mountain slopes. RACES: *L. f. amnicola* (Sakhalin Grasshopper Warbler) (fig 5b) Japan.

6 JAPANESE SWAMP WARBLER *Locustella pryeri* 13cm FIELD NOTES: Secretive but seen in the open during short circling song-flight. SONG: Low-pitched *djuk-djuk-djuk*. CALL: *chuck*. HABITAT: Mainly reed-beds and coastal grassland.

7 AQUATIC WARBLER *Acrocephalus paludicola* 13cm FIELD NOTES: Shy and retiring. Sings from exposed perch or during short song-flight. SONG: Has been transcribed as *trrr…dew dew-dew…churr…di-di-di*. Less complex and more monotonous than Sedge Warbler. CALL: *tuk* or *chuck*, also *cher-cherr*. HABITAT: Open, waterlogged sedge meadows. On passage uses a wider range of waterside vegetation.

8 SEDGE WARBLER *Acrocephalus schoenobaenus* 13cm FIELD NOTES: Furtive, but often shows well, especially when singing. SONG: Complex, loud medley of harsh and sweet phrases, a typical phrase transcribed as *chit-chit-tuk-tuk-tuk-chit-ter-we-terwee-tit-tit-twee-twee-tit-it-it-it-cherwee…*, etc. CALL: *tuc*, often repeated when alarmed, and a soft *churr*. HABITAT: Dense vegetation, usually near water.

9 MOUSTACHED WARBLER *Acrocephalus melanopogon* 13cm FIELD NOTES: Often feeds on reed debris near water surface. Cocks tail when alarmed. SONG: Starts with a Nightingale-like *lu-lu-lu-lu…* followed by typical *Acrochepalus* phrases, which are thinner and sweeter than Sedge Warbler. CALL: *tak-tak*, *tik* and a rattling *trrrrrrr*. HABITAT: Reed-bed edge and various waterside vegetation.

10 BLACK-BROWED REED WARBLER *Acrocephalus bistrigiceps* 13cm FIELD NOTES: Elusive except when singing from exposed perch. SONG: Typical of genus, sweeter, less scratchy than Reed Warbler. CALL: *tuc*, and a high-pitched *zit*. HABITAT: Mainly wet areas, including reed-beds, meadows, bogs, willow scrub, etc.

11 SPECKLED REED WARBLER *Acrocephalus sorghophilus* 13cm FIELD NOTES: Forages low down in vegetation. Sings from prominent perch. SONG/CALL: No information. HABITAT: Little information; thought to include reed-beds, boggy grassland and rice and millet fields.

28 REED WARBLERS

1 BLUNT-WINGED WARBLER *Acrocephalus concinens* 13cm FIELD NOTES: Usually calls as it forages through vegetation. Sings from exposed perch. SONG: Said to be strident and scratchy. CALL: Vibrant *thrrak* or *tschak*. HABITAT: Mainly waterside vegetation, but uses drier locations in mountain valleys.

2 PADDYFIELD WARBLER *Acrocephalus agricola* 13cm FIELD NOTES: Constant tail-cocking and flicking. SONG: Like Marsh Warbler but less varied. CALL: Variable, includes *chik* and a nasal *cheeer*. HABITAT: Various waterside, or near waterside, vegetation. RACES: *A. a. tangorum* (Manchurian Reed Warbler) (fig 2b) Manchuria and Ussuriland. Possibly a full species.

3 BLYTH'S REED WARBLER *Acrocephalus dumetorum* 13cm FIELD NOTES: Mostly arboreal but also drops to ground to feed. SONG: Various phrases repeated, slowly, often interspersed with the clicking call and mimicry. CALL: Clicking *zeck* and a harsh *tchirr*. HABITAT: Damp deciduous forests, thickets, shrubby areas in river valleys or on hillsides, parks and gardens.

4 MARSH WARBLER *Acrocephalus palustris* 13cm FIELD NOTES: More lethargic, less agile than Reed Warbler. SONG: Liquid, chattering warble of high- and low-pitched notes, trills, fluted notes and much mimicry. CALL: Variable, e.g. *chirr*, *tchak*, *tue*, *tweek* and *wheet-wheet-wheet*. HABITAT: Tall herbaceous vegetation, often near marshy or damp areas.

5 CAPE VERDE WARBLER *Acrocephalus brevipennis* 14cm FIELD NOTES: Elusive, especially out of breeding season. Sings from within cover. SONG: Rich, vibrant rattle of 3–5 notes. CALL: Throaty *pitchow*, sharp *chuk* and a croaking *churr*. HABITAT: Trees, bushes, giant cane, reeds; plantations e.g. sugarcane, banana, coffee.

6 AFRICAN REED WARBLER *Acrocephalus baeticatus* 13cm FIELD NOTES: Actions similar to Reed Warbler. SONG: Like Reed Warbler but slower and clearer. CALL: Short *churr*. HABITAT: Mangroves.

7 REED WARBLER (EUROPEAN REED WARBLER) *Acrocephalus scirpaceus* 13cm FIELD NOTES: Furtive when foraging. SONG: Mixture of churring and grating notes, e.g. *kerr-kerr-kerr - kek-kek - churuc-churuc-churuc - tuk-tuk….* CALL: *churr* and a harsher *tcharr*. HABITAT: Mainly reed-beds, also other rank herbage, bushes and crops. RACES: *A. s. fuscus* (Caspian Reed Warbler) (fig 7b) Caspian, Caucasus, E Asia Minor, Cyprus and the Levant.

8 CLAMOROUS REED WARBLER *Acrocephalus stentoreus* 18cm FIELD NOTES: Clambers clumsily among reed stems, etc. Short primary projection in contrast to Great Reed Warbler. SONG: Similar to Great Reed Warbler but less raucous and more melodious. CALL: A harsh *ke*, *chack* or *ptchuk*. HABITAT: Papyrus and reed-beds, willow scrub and other waterside vegetation.

9 ORIENTAL REED WARBLER *Acrocephalus orientalis* 18cm FIELD NOTES: Actions similar to Great Reed Warbler. Note short primary projection compared to the latter. SONG: Similar to though softer and richer than Great Reed Warbler. CALL: Very similar to Great Reed Warbler. HABITAT: Waterside vegetation, especially reeds.

10 GREAT REED WARBLER *Acrocephalus arundinaceus* 19.5cm FIELD NOTES: Sometimes difficult to see, even though often clumsy as it creeps among reed stems. SONG: Typical of genus, but deep and guttural: *karra-karra - keek-keek-keek - gurr-gurr - tchu-tchu - karra-kee - kar-kar-kar….* CALL: Harsh *tchack* and a croaking *churr*. HABITAT: Waterside vegetation, mainly reeds.

11 BASRA REED WARBLER *Acrocephalus griseldis* 17cm FIELD NOTES: Elusive, less clumsy than other large *Acrocephalus*. SONG: Like Great Reed Warbler but quieter, less guttural and grating. CALL: Harsh *chaarr*. HABITAT: Waterside vegetation, especially reeds.

12 THICK-BILLED WARBLER *Acrocephalus aedon* 18cm FIELD NOTES: Elusive, actions slow and clumsy. SONG: Fast, chattering warble with harsh and musical notes. CALL: *chok*, a longer *chok-chok-cheer-rrek-chokv* and a *tak*. HABITAT: Dense thickets; open woodland with thick undergrowth.

29 WARBLERS

1 MARMORA'S WARBLER *Sylvia sarda* 13cm FIELD NOTES: Tends to feed more in open and also higher up in tree branches, otherwise actions similar to Dartford Warbler. SONG: Similar to, but shorter than, Dartford Warbler's. CALL: Short, clear, rattling *trrut*, also a short *tik* or similar. HABITAT: Low scrubby cover with scattered trees, from coast to mountain slopes. Winters in semi-desert scrub.

2 DARTFORD WARBLER *Sylvia undata* 13cm FIELD NOTES: Skulking. Sings from prominent perch or during short song-flight. Juvenile lacks dark reddish underparts, therefore looks much like Marmora's Warbler. SONG: Brief, chattering warble, consisting of sweet piping notes and soft, metallic, chattering phrases. CALL: Harsh *tchir-rr* and a *tak*, often repeated; *tchirr-chirri-it* when alarmed. HABITAT: Coastal heath and scrub, inland heath, scrub-covered rocky hillsides, and pinewoods with under-scrub.

3 TRISTRAM'S WARBLER *Sylvia deserticola* 12.5cm FIELD NOTES: Skulking. Sings from prominent perch or short song-flight. SONG: Subdued chattering interspersed with harsh grating notes. CALL: Sharp *chit*, *chit-it*, *cheerup* and a rapid *chit-it-it-it-it-it*.... HABITAT: Open scrubby hillside, mountains and valleys; open forests of cistus, evergreen oak or juniper. Winters in semi-deserts with scrubby areas.

4 SUBALPINE WARBLER *Sylvia cantillans* 12.5cm FIELD NOTES: Skulking. Constantly flicks wings and cocks tail. Sings from exposed perch or in 'up and down' song-flight. SONG: Prolonged, scratchy, chattering warble. CALL: Soft *tek* or *chat*, also a rattling *trrrrrt*. HABITAT: Bushy hills and mountainsides with scattered trees. Migrants found in many types of bush and scrub.

5 SPECTACLED WARBLER *Sylvia conspicillata* 12.5cm FIELD NOTES: Shy. Sings from exposed perch or song-flight, in which bird rises to about 9m then descends on outstretched, fluttering wings and spread tail. SONG: Like Whitethroat, but higher, with sweeter notes at start. CALL: Nasal chattering *tchrrrrrr-tchrrrrrr*..., sometimes interspersed with a high *swee*, also a high-pitched *tseet*. HABITAT: Wide variety of bush or scrub.

6 WHITETHROAT (COMMON WHITETHROAT) *Sylvia communis* 14cm FIELD NOTES: Inquisitive, often showing on bush top before diving into cover. Sings from prominent perch or short, ascending song-flight. SONG: Lively scratchy warble, consisting of 12 or so notes, based on an opening phrase of *che-che - worra - che-wi*. CALL: Soft, scolding *tcharr*, a low *churr* and a sharp *tac-tack*. HABITAT: Wide variety, including heathland, hedgerows, woodland edge and open woodland with scrubby undergrowth.

7 LESSER WHITETHROAT *Sylvia curruca* 12.5cm FIELD NOTES: Very skulking. Often sings from thick cover, less often from bush top or in flight. SONG: Variable, dependent on race; nominate consists of quiet warble followed by a disyllabic, repeated rattle, *chika-chika-chika*.... CALL: Hard, repeated *tac-tac*..., a scolding *charr* or *churr*. HABITAT: Various bushy areas, e.g. heathland, woodland edge, hedgerows, parks and gardens. RACES: *S. c. althaea* (Hume's Lesser Whitethroat) (fig 7b) Iran eastward, sometimes treated as a full species; *S. c. minula* (Desert Lesser Whitethroat) (fig 7c) W China, sometimes treated as a full species.

8 DESERT WARBLER *Sylvia nana* 11.5cm FIELD NOTES: Skulking, usually in thick scrub, although often seen on ground, scuttling between patches of vegetation. SONG: Series of rich trilled and whistling phrases preceded by a purring trill. CALL: Feeble purr, *drrrrrrrr*, also a *chrr-rrr* and a rapid *chee-chee-chee-chee*. HABITAT: Sandy desert with scattered bushy vegetation. RACES: *S. n. deserti* (fig 8b) NW Africa. Sometimes treated as a full species.

9 GARDEN WARBLER *Sylvia borin* 13.5cm FIELD NOTES: Very skulking, usually allows only brief glimpses. SONG: Rich jumbled warble, very like Blackcap but less varied, said to sound like a rippling brook. CALL: Abrupt *chack-chack* and a rasping *tchurr-r-r-r*. HABITAT: Broadleaved and mixed woodland with understorey of thick shrubs; hedgerows, thickets and large gardens.

30 WARBLERS

1 MÉNÉTRIES' WARBLER *Sylvia mystacea* 13cm FIELD NOTES: Shy. Cocks and waves tail from side to side, as though loosely hinged. Sings from exposed perch, or during short display-flight. SONG: Quiet, dry chatter. CALL: *tak* and a rattled *tzerr-r-r*, also a chattering *chip-chip-chip*. HABITAT: Bush and scrub on hill-, mountain- and riversides. RACES: *S. m. rubescens* (fig 1b) Levant, SE Turkey, Iraq, SW Iran.

2 SARDINIAN WARBLER *Sylvia melanocephala* 13.5cm FIELD NOTES: Skulking, although can be inquisitive. Often sings from a prominent perch or during display-flight. SONG: Sustained chatter interspersed with rattling call notes. CALL: Fast, rattling chatter *chret-tret-tret-tret-tret*, a soft *scherr-err-err-err*, a short *tchur* and a double-noted *cherk-cherk*. HABITAT: Various scrubby areas, with or without scattered trees; orchards, parks and gardens.

3 RÜPPELL'S WARBLER *Sylvia rueppelli* 14cm FIELD NOTES: Mostly very skulking. Often sings and 'keeps guard' from a prominent (bush-top) perch. Also performs a short butterfly-like display-flight. SONG: Much like Sardinian Warbler but softer, more pulsating. CALL: Short *churr*, which, when alarmed, may develop into a rattle; also an abrupt *pip-pit*. HABITAT: Mountain and hillside scrub, undergrowth in open woodland.

4 CYPRUS WARBLER *Sylvia melanothorax* 13cm FIELD NOTES: Usually shy and skulking, although often 'keeps guard' from a prominent perch. Sings from exposed perch or during display-flight. SONG: Similar to Sardinian Warbler, but weaker. CALL: Harsh *tcharr-tcharr-tcharr-tcharr…*, a short *tchek* and a loud *pwit*. HABITAT: Hillside and coastal scrub, undergrowth in open pine and oak woodland.

5 ARABIAN WARBLER *Sylvia leucomelaena* 14.5cm FIELD NOTES: Constantly down-flicks tail. Usually shy, although sings from exposed perch. SONG: Slow, rich, Blackcap-like warble. CALL: Quiet *tchak* and a churring rattle, *tchrrrrrrrrrrr*. HABITAT: Thorn bushes in arid, semi-desert areas.

6 ORPHEAN WARBLER *Sylvia hortensis* 15cm FIELD NOTES: Shy and skulking, keeps to thick cover. Often sings from within tall shrubs rather than exposed perch, or, less so, during short display-flight. SONG: Loud, variable, thrush-like warble *pju-ply - we-duu - we-du - we-du - pitchee-pitchee-pitchee - chiwiroo-chiwiroo*; eastern races have more complex phrases, including warbles and rattles. CALL: Sharp *tak* and a scolding *trrrrrr*. HABITAT: Variable, including open woodland with shrubby undergrowth, orchards, parkland, large gardens and olive, fig and orange groves.

7 BLACKCAP *Sylvia atricapilla* 13cm FIELD NOTES: Presence usually revealed by song, otherwise shy and skulking. SONG: Rich, often loud, warble; softer versions can be very similar to Garden Warbler. CALL: *tac-tac*, *churr*, and a quick *teck-teck-teck-teckcherr*. HABITAT: Thick undergrowth in open deciduous or mixed woodland; thickets, parkland and large gardens.

8 BARRED WARBLER *Sylvia nisoria* 15cm FIELD NOTES: Usually shy and skulking with lumbering, clumsy, food-searching actions. Sings from atop, or inside, a bush and during butterfly-like display-flight. Juvenile usually has dark eye, and can superficially resemble a Garden Warbler. SONG: Similar to Garden Warbler, but with shorter, deeper-toned phrases and often interspersed with rattling call note. CALL: *chak-chak*, which may be extended into a rapid rattle, also a *charr* or *tch-tchurr-tchurr*. HABITAT: Shrubby thickets of forest edge, riverine areas, commons, meadows and orchards, hedgerows and shelterbelts.

9 YEMEN WARBLER *Parisoma buryi* 15cm FIELD NOTES: More often heard than seen. Tail often cocked and fanned. Frequently hangs upside-down, tit-like, to feed. SONG: A melodic warble, *bi - woo - woo - woo - woo-eee-too-chit - too-chit*, also *did - id - chee - eeyou-eeyou-eeyou*. CALL: Various harsh or mewing whistles, e.g. *piiuu-ptyii-ptii*, *tchak't-sak-tiv-huit*, a scolding *skee* and a rolling *tschee-tchee*. HABITAT: Mainly mountain- and hillside juniper forests, also cultivated valleys and waterside scrub.

31 WARBLERS AND LEAF WARBLERS

1 OLIVACEOUS WARBLER *Hippolais pallida opaca* 13cm FIELD NOTES: Typical feeding actions of the genus, e.g. clambering, often clumsily, through foliage, stretching neck to gather insects. Pumps tail up and down. SONG: Reed Warbler-like chattering, faster and more monotonous, with musical notes along with rattles and trills. Eastern race, *H. p. elaeica*, more rasping and includes mimicry. CALL: Sharp *tec* and a *tick-tick-tick*; also sparrow-like chatter. HABITAT: Open bushy areas in dry country; olive groves, orchards, parks and gardens. RACES: *H. p. elaeica* (fig 1b) SE Europe eastwards. Regarded by some authors as a separate species.

2 BOOTED WARBLER *Hippolais caligata* 11.5cm FIELD NOTES: Slight upward tail-flicking. SONG: Several fast, bubbling phrases with neat transition from one to another, starting softly and moving to a crescendo. CALL: Sharp *tsek* and a dry *churr-r*. HABITAT: Tall herbaceous plants and shrubs, often near water. Southern race *H. c. rama* usually in arid areas. RACES: *H. c. rama* (Sykes's Warbler) (fig 2b) NE Arabia, Iran. Often considered to be a full species.

3 UPCHER'S WARBLER *Hippolais languida* 14cm FIELD NOTES: Tail often appears 'unhinged' when moved up, down and sideways. Other actions typical of genus. SONG: Resembles Whitethroat, although less grating and more musical. CALL: *chuk-chuk*, said to sound like 2 stones being struck together, also *churr*. HABITAT: Arid scrubby areas, on hill- and mountainsides, in vineyards and orchards, also thickets near watercourses.

4 OLIVE-TREE WARBLER *Hippolais olivetorum* 15cm FIELD NOTES: Slight downward tail-flicks. SONG: Likened to a melodious Great Reed Warbler, transcribed as *chak - chü - chi-chak - chira - chuk - chi-chi - chak-era - chak - chü - chi-chak….* CALL: Deep *tuk-tuk*, also *tr-trik*. HABITAT: Open broadleaf forest, orchards, olive groves, almond plantations, vineyards and hillside scrub.

5 ICTERINE WARBLER *Hippolais icterina* 13cm FIELD NOTES: Shallow tail-flick. Active feeder; strong, dashing flight between cover. SONG: Marsh Warbler-like, but slower and higher pitched with typical call note *chi-chi-vooi* and repeated, nasal *geea-geea*, or similar, added. CALL: Resonant *tack-tack*. On breeding grounds a *chi-chi-vooi*. HABITAT: Many types of broadleaved woodland, forest edge, parkland, orchards, hedgerows and gardens.

6 MELODIOUS WARBLER *Hippolais polyglotta* 13cm FIELD NOTES: Skulking, lethargic, methodical feeder, fluttering flight between cover. Shallow tail-flick. SONG: Faster, more rattling than Icterine Warbler, lacking repeated nasal notes. CALL: Soft *tuk*, a harsh rattled *trrrrr* and a chattering *chret-chet*. HABITAT: Much as Icterine Warbler, but also in more bushy areas.

7 PLAIN LEAF WARBLER *Phylloscopus neglectus* 9cm FIELD NOTES: Often hovers to glean insects from leaves. Active, flitting feeding movements, typical of genus. SONG: Short, rising warble, *pt-toodla-toodla*. CALL: Harsh, low *churr*, also nasal *chit* or *chi-ip*. HABITAT: Juniper, pistachio or oak stands in mountains, also low scrub in gorges. Winters in acacia woodland and scrub on foothills and plains.

8 WOOD WARBLER *Phylloscopus sibilatrix* 12.5cm FIELD NOTES: Feeds in upper layers of woodland canopy, often fly-catching or hovering to capture insects. SONG: Distinctive, starting slowly, accelerating into a shivering trill, *zip - zip - zip - zip - zip-zip-zip-zipzipzipzipzvürrrrürrrr…*; second type is sometimes added or used independently, *pew-pew-pew-pew-pew….* CALL: Plaintive *pew* and a soft *wit-wit-wit*. HABITAT: Mature deciduous and mixed woodland.

9 EASTERN BONELLI'S WARBLER *Phylloscopus orientalis* 11.5cm FIELD NOTES: Recently split from Western Bonelli's Warbler. Actions similar. SONG: Much as Western Bonelli's Warbler, but shorter and less vigorous. CALL: Short, hard *tsiup* or *chip*. HABITAT: As Western Bonelli's Warbler.

10 WESTERN BONELLI'S WARBLER *Phylloscopus bonelli* 11.5cm FIELD NOTES: Actions much as others of genus, including fly-catching. SONG: Dry trill, *twee-wee-wee-wee-wee-wee….* CALL: *hoo-eet* or *doo-eeo*. HABITAT: Open deciduous, mixed and coniferous forests. On migration, also found in more bushy areas.

32 LEAF WARBLERS

1 RADDE'S WARBLER *Phylloscopus schwarzi* 12cm FIELD NOTES: Many actions recall a small *Hippolais* warbler. Feeds low down or on ground, usually in thick cover. SONG: Clear trill, often preceded by 1 or 2 quiet notes. CALL: Soft *chek - chek* and a nervous *pwit*. HABITAT: Open woodland with dense undergrowth, bushy forest edge and clearings, hill- or waterside thickets.

2 YELLOW-STREAKED WARBLER *Phylloscopus armandii* 12cm FIELD NOTES: Skulking, slow, deliberate feeder, in bushes and lower tree branches. SONG: Weak version of Radde's Warbler's trill. CALL: Sharp *click*, *zit*, *dzik* or *tick*, and a metallic *tack* or *tschak*. HABITAT: Mainly poplar and willow groves on mountain slopes or in valleys.

3 DUSKY WARBLER *Phylloscopus fuscatus* 11.5cm FIELD NOTES: Skulking but active feeder, usually low in thick vegetation or on ground, occasionally in tree canopy. SONG: *chewee-chewee-chewee-chewee* or similar, with a concluding trill. CALL: Sharp, often repeated, *chett*. HABITAT: Birch and willow thickets, often near water, scrub in open forest, dwarf willows, birch scrub and low conifers in subalpine zone.

4 SMOKY WARBLER *Phylloscopus fuligiventer* 11cm FIELD NOTES: Skulking, difficult to flush, prefers to scurry along ground into thick cover. When feeding, nervously flicks wings and tail, the latter often cocked. SONG: Repetition of single note, *tsli-tsli-tsli* or similar. CALL: *tzik* or *tsrr*, also a soft *stup* and a sharp *chek*. HABITAT: Rocky alpine pasture, dwarf juniper, rhododendrons and other low scrub above the tree line.

5 SULPHUR-BELLIED WARBLER *Phylloscopus griseolus* 11cm FIELD NOTES: Usually a ground feeder, Dunnock-like, becoming more arboreal in winter. SONG: Short, rapid repetition of 1 note, *tsi-tsi-tsi-tsi-tsi-tsi*, sometimes preceded by a call similar to 'smacking of lips'. CALL: *quip* or *pick*. HABITAT: Low mountain scrub on dry stony slopes, usually above tree line.

6 TYTLER'S LEAF WARBLER *Phylloscopus tytleri* 10.5cm FIELD NOTES: Difficult to see, usually located by song. Active, acrobatic feeder. SONG: Variously transcribed, e.g. *whittle-di-wee-you*, *jitsu-chissyu - jitsu-chissyup* and *kitchu-qwishu - kitchu-qwishu*. CALL: Plaintive *sooeet*. HABITAT: Mainly coniferous forest, also dwarf willow and birch near tree line.

7 BUFF-THROATED WARBLER *Phylloscopus subaffinis* 10.5cm FIELD NOTES: Skulking forager low down in thick vegetation; also feeds on ground. SONG: *tuee-tuee-tuee-tuee*. CALL: Soft, weak *trrup* or *trrip*. HABITAT: Alpine scrub, and high-elevation forest edge.

8 CHIFFCHAFF *Phylloscopus collybita* 11cm FIELD NOTES: Forages, actively, from ground level to tree canopy, with nervous flicking of wings and tail. SONG: *chiff-chaff-chiff-chaff-chiff-chaff…*, often continuing for 20sec or more. Variations occur, *P. c. brehmii* has a distinctive *tit-tit-tit-tit-tswee-tswee-chit-it-it-it…*, *P. c. tristris* an equally distinct, hurried *ch-ch-chewy-chewy-chewy-chewy-ch*. CALL: Monosyllabic *hweet*. HABITAT: Open deciduous, mixed and coniferous forests, scrubby thickets, hedgerows, parks, gardens, etc. RACES: *P. c. tristris* (Siberian Chiffchaff) (fig 8b) Urals eastward; *P. c. brehmii* (Iberian Chiffchaff) (fig 8c) Iberia, NW Africa; *P. c. canariensis* (Canary Islands Chiffchaff) (fig 8d) W Canary Islands. These races often considered as full species.

9 WILLOW WARBLER *Phylloscopus trochilus* 11.5cm FIELD NOTES: Actions very similar to Chiffchaff. SONG: Distinctive series of sweet notes, faint at first, then increasing in volume before drifting to a quieter, descending flourish. CALL: Disyllabic *hoo-eet*. HABITAT: Avoids pure conifer stands, otherwise much as Chiffchaff.

10 MOUNTAIN CHIFFCHAFF *Phylloscopus sindianus* 11cm FIELD NOTES: Often considered conspecific with Chiffchaff, hence actions similar. SONG: Very similar to Chiffchaff. CALL: Slightly disyllabic *huit*, and a loud *tiss-yip*. HABITAT: Willow, poplar, birch, alder and pine in mountain areas, 2500–4400m; often winters in coastal scrub. RACES: *P. s. lorenzii* (Caucasian Chiffchaff) (fig 10b) Caucasus, NE Turkey, NW Iran.

33 LEAF WARBLERS

1 WHITE-TAILED LEAF WARBLER *Phylloscopus davisoni* 10.5cm FIELD NOTES: Generally a canopy feeder with typical actions of the genus. When agitated, flicks both wings simultaneously. SONG: Variously transcribed, Coal Tit-like *pitsu-titsui-titsui-titsui* or *itsi-itsi-chee-wi-itsi-itsi-chee-wi....* CALL: *pitsiu* or *wit-chee* and *pitsitsui* or *ti'chee-wi.* HABITAT: Mountain pine or mixed deciduous and evergreen forests.

2 BLYTH'S LEAF WARBLER *Phylloscopus reguloides* 11cm FIELD NOTES: When agitated, slowly flicks 1 wing at a time. Often hangs head-down to feed. SONG: Variable, strident, undulating series of phrases, *chi-chi- pit-chew-pit-chew-swee-swee-swee-swee-swee.* CALL: *pit-chew-a-pit-chew-a-pit-chew-a* or *pit-cha - pit-cha - pit-cha.* HABITAT: Various mountain forests.

3 EASTERN CROWNED WARBLER *Phylloscopus coronatus* 12.5cm FIELD NOTES: Very active, restless feeder, from undergrowth to tree canopy. SONG: Tit-like *sweetoo-sweetoo-sweetoo-swe-swe-zueee* or similar. CALL: Variously transcribed, e.g. *phit-phit, swe-zueee* or *zweet.* HABITAT: Open deciduous or mixed, middle- or lower-altitude forests.

4 WESTERN CROWNED WARBLER *Phylloscopus occipitalis* 13cm FIELD NOTES: Active, restless feeder. Alternate wing-flicks leave 1 wing half-open at any one time. SONG: Rapid, piercing *stic-swee-swee-swee-swee-swee..., chwi-chwi-chwi-chwi-chwi...* or *tityu-tiu-tiu-tiu-tiu-tiu....* CALL: *stic* or *stic-swick.* HABITAT: All types of well-wooded country from lowlands to the tree line.

5 IJIMA'S LEAF WARBLER *Phylloscopus ijimae* 12cm FIELD NOTES: Often acts like a flycatcher to take insects, otherwise most actions typical of genus. SONG: Mechanical *swee-seww-swee-swee-swee*, usually ending in *chew.* CALL: Loud *twee* and a thin *phi-phi-phi.* HABITAT: Forest undergrowth, alder thickets, and bushes around habitations.

6 ASHY-THROATED WARBLER *Phylloscopus maculipennis* 10cm FIELD NOTES: Active, restless feeder, usually in the tree canopy. SONG: Thin, sweet *wee-ty-wee-ty-wee-ty* or *du-ze-zuu-ze-za.* CALL: Repeated *zip* or *zit.* HABITAT: Open, mixed forests.

7 PALLAS'S WARBLER *Phylloscopus proregulus* 10cm FIELD NOTES: Frequent wing- and tail-flicking. Often hovers around foliage in search of insects. SONG: Loud, vibrant whistles and trills. Has been called 'the canary of the taiga'. CALL: Soft, nasal *duee*, also a soft *wseep* or *deeht.* HABITAT: Mainly mixed and coniferous forest, with thick undergrowth.

8 LEMON-RUMPED WARBLER *Phylloscopus chloronotus* 10cm FIELD NOTES: Actions as Pallas's Warbler. SONG: *tsirrrrrrrrrrrrrr-tsi-tsi-tsi-tsi-tsi-tsi...* or stuttering, endless *tsi-ts-tsi-tsi-tsu-tsu-tsi-tsi-tsu-tsi-tsi-tsididididididididi-tsi-tsi-tsu-tsu....* CALL: A high *uist.* HABITAT: As Pallas's Leaf Warbler. RACES: *P. c. kansuensis* (Gansu Leaf Warbler) (fig 8b) China (Gansu, Qinghai). Due to vocal studies, will probably be confirmed, by all authorities, as a full species.

9 CHINESE LEAF WARBLER *Phylloscopus sichuanensis* 10cm FIELD NOTES: Feeds mainly in tree canopy. Sings from treetops. Little studied. SONG: Monotonous, can last for more than 1min, *tsiridi-tsirdi-tsiridi-tsiridi....* CALL: Variable, *tueet-tueet-tueet-tueet...* or *tueet-tuee-tee-tee-tee....* HABITAT: Low, secondary deciduous growth in mountain regions.

10 BROOKS'S LEAF WARBLER *Phylloscopus subviridis* 10cm FIELD NOTES: Active, restless feeder in tree canopy. Often hovers around foliage to catch insects. SONG: Series of single notes followed by a reeling *wet-wet-wet-wet-weet-whir-r-r-r-r-r-r* or similar. CALL: *cwit-chwit-chwit, tissuwee-tisuwee* and a shrill, tinkling, *tiss-yip.* HABITAT: Montane conifer forests.

11 YELLOW-BROWED WARBLER *Phylloscopus inornatus* 10cm FIELD NOTES: Shy. Actions much as others of genus. SONG: Short, thin *tsee-oo-tsee-oo-eep-tsee-eep.* CALL: High, Coal Tit-like *tswe-eeet* or *tsuee-eep.* HABITAT: Open deciduous, mixed and coniferous forests, often near water.

12 HUME'S LEAF WARBLER *Phylloscopus humei* 10cm FIELD NOTES: Very shy. Actions much as other leaf warblers. SONG: Excited repeated *wesoo*, often ending in a nasal, falling *zweeeeeeeee* or *eeeeeeeezzzzzzzz.* CALL: *wesoo* or *dsweet.* HABITAT: Hillside and mountain forests.

34 LEAF WARBLERS

1 TICKELL'S LEAF WARBLER *Phylloscopus affinis* 10cm FIELD NOTES: Skulking, feeds low down in thick vegetation, or on ground. Appears not to flick wings or tail. SONG: Rapid *tchip-chi-chi-chi-chi-chi*. CALL: Sharp *chep*, and rapidly repeated *tak-tak* when alarmed. HABITAT: Open, bushy, alpine scrub, low vegetation in rocky valleys, and dwarf bamboo and bushes in upland cultivation. Lower-elevation scrub and thick bush in winter.

2 GREENISH WARBLER *Phylloscopus trochiloides viridanus* 10cm FIELD NOTES: Mainly arboreal. Highly mobile, dashing among foliage, or hovering to capture insects. Flicks wings, but tail-flicking less pronounced. Eastern, nominate race is darker above and tends to show a wing bar on median coverts more often than *viridanus*. SONG: Variable, high-pitched, accelerating phrases that culminate in an abruptly ending trill, e.g. *si-ti-twee-si-ti-twe-si-ti-twe-si-twe-sitwesitsititi*. CALL: *ch-wee* or *tseelee*. HABITAT: Deciduous, mixed and coniferous woodlands with rich undergrowth. RACES: *P. t. nitidus* (Green Warbler) (fig 2b) Caucasus, Iran, Turkmenistan, SE Uzbekistan; *P. t. plumbeitarsus* (Two-barred Greenish Warbler) (fig 2c) C Siberia, Mongolia, NE China. Both races are often considered full species.

3 LARGE-BILLED LEAF WARBLER *Phylloscopus magnirostris* 12cm FIELD NOTES: Shy. Arboreal; feeds along boughs rather than among leaves. SONG: Far-carrying, descending *tee-ti-tii-tu-tu*. CALL: *dir-tee* or *pe-pi*, also a trisyllabic, ascending whistle, *yaw-wee-wee*. HABITAT: Open spaces and glades in mountain coniferous or mixed forests, usually near water.

4 ARCTIC WARBLER *Phylloscopus borealis* 12cm FIELD NOTES: Mainly arboreal, urgent feeder, dashing in and around cover, flicking wings and tail; also hovers to catch insects. SONG: Shivering trill *dyryryryryryry…*, often interspersed with call notes. CALL: Sharp, metallic *dzik* or *dzrt*. HABITAT: Open birch or coniferous woodland, northern taiga willow scrub, and tundra edge, often near water. RACES: *P. b. xanthodryas* (fig 4b) Japan, Kuril Islands, Kamchatka.

5 PALE-LEGGED LEAF WARBLER *Phylloscopus tenellipes* 11.5cm FIELD NOTES: Movements rather sluggish, flicks tail in a downward movement. Keeps to middle and lower storeys of forests. SONG: High-pitched, cricket-like *sresresresresre….* CALL: Metallic *til-tic* or *pit-pit*; also a loud *peet*. HABITAT: Moist broadleaf and coniferous forest on hills and mountains.

6 BUFF-BARRED WARBLER *Phylloscopus pulcher* 10cm FIELD NOTES: Typical nervous leaf-warbler actions. Feeds mainly in tree canopy. SONG: 2 types (sometimes combined): musical *dioo-dioo-dioo-dioo…* and *tick-tick-tick*, followed by a loud call, much like Wood Warbler. CALL: *tsip* or *twick*, occasionally repeated to form a vibrating trill. HABITAT: Coniferous forests, oak and birch woods, rhododendron and other scrub above the tree line.

7 SAKHALIN LEAF WARBLER *Phylloscopus borealoides* 11.5cm FIELD NOTES: Little studied. Suspect actions as Pale-legged Leaf Warbler? SONG: Repeated series of high-pitched whistles, *hee-tsoo-kee*. CALL: As Pale-legged Leaf Warbler? HABITAT: Dark coniferous or mixed mountain forests.

8 BROWN WOODLAND WARBLER *Phylloscopus umbrovirens* 11cm FIELD NOTES: Active, energetic. In worn plumage upperparts become paler grey/brown. SONG: Loud, fast and slow phrases often ending with a fast trill, transcribed as *tititititititi-wit-vuit-vuit-vuit-wit-wit-wit-wit-tu-vi-tu-vi-tuvi-twit-diu-diu-diu-diu*. CALL: Descending *dziieep*; also a low *psew* and *swee-vik* when alarmed. HABITAT: Hillside and highland trees and bushes, wadis and gorges with lush growth.

35 GOLDCRESTS, TIT-WARBLERS, FLYCATCHER-WARBLERS AND TESIA

1 RUBY-CROWNED KINGLET *Regulus calendula* 10cm (Vagrant) FIELD NOTES: Restless, acrobatic feeder. SONG: Several high notes followed by descending notes, ending in a warble. CALL: Thin *ze-zeet*. HABITAT: In native N America, mainly coniferous forests.

2 GOLDCREST *Regulus regulus* 9cm FIELD NOTES: Agile forager, always on the move, flicks wings and tail, hovers to catch insects. Often a member of winter mixed feeding parties. SONG: Jingling, high-pitched *ze-zezeezee-ze-zezeezee-ze-zezeezee....* CALL: High-pitched *zee-zee-zee* or *zit-zit-zit*, given while on the move. HABITAT: Coniferous and various types of mixed woodland, including parks and gardens. RACES: *R. r. tristris* (fig 2b) C Asia.

3 CANARY ISLANDS KINGLET (CANARY ISLANDS GOLDCREST) *Regulus teneriffae* 9cm FIELD NOTES: Actions as Goldcrest. Often regarded as subspecies of Goldcrest or Firecrest. SONG: Very like Goldcrest, perhaps more variable? CALL: *see-see-see-see-charr*. HABITAT: Pine or laurel forest with understorey of tree-heath, or in stands of pure tree-heath.

4 FIRECREST *Regulus ignicapilla* 9cm FIELD NOTES: Often feeds at low levels in bushes and shrubs. SONG: High-pitched, accelerating *zi-zi-zi-zi-zi-zi-zi-zi-zi-zi-zi-zizizit*. CALL: *ze-ze-zeep*, also a single, or repeated, *zeep*. HABITAT: Deciduous, coniferous and mixed woodland, all with rich undergrowth; scrubby Evergreen Oak, Cork Oak, bushes in parks and large gardens. RACES: *R. i. madeirensis* (Madeira Firecrest) (fig 4b) Madeira. Often treated as full species.

5 SEVERTZOV'S TIT WARBLER *Leptopoecile sophiae* 10cm FIELD NOTES: Acrobatic feeder, in thick undergrowth. Often a member of mixed species feeding flocks. SONG: Little information. Said to be a sweet, loud, chirping cry. CALL: High-pitched, metallic *tzret*. HABITAT: Dwarf scrub above the tree line. Descends in winter, often to streamside vegetation.

6 CRESTED TIT WARBLER *Leptopoecile elegans* 10cm FIELD NOTES: Very active, behaves much like Goldcrest. Usually feeds high in tree canopy. Often joins feeding parties of mixed species. SONG: Little recorded. CALL: Said to be a soft peeping and a shrill chatter, similar to wren. HABITAT: Coniferous forest, also dwarf alpine juniper and birch scrub above the tree line.

7 GREY-HOODED WARBLER *Seicercus xanthoschistos* 10cm FIELD NOTES: Actions very leaf warbler-like, including much fly-catching, hence group name of 'flycatcher-warblers'. Fans and cocks tail, also shivers wings. Arboreal. SONG: Frequently uttered, bright, cheerful *tsiri-siri-trip-ottzee-pseet-tzerra*, one of the dominant calls of Himalayan forests. CALL: High-pitched *psit-psit* or *pritt-pritt*, also a plaintive *tyee-tyee*. HABITAT: Open hill forest.

8 GOLDEN-SPECTACLED WARBLER *Seicercus burkii* 10.5cm FIELD NOTES: Skulking. Arboreal, feeds from middle and lower storeys down to undergrowth. Fans and cocks tail, flicks wings. SONG: Series of mellow notes, *dee-de-deep - dee-de-deep*. CALL: Loud *chut-chut* or *chup-chup*. HABITAT: Mixed coniferous and deciduous or evergreen forests on hills and mountains. (Recent work by ornithologists may lead to the species being split into at least 5 full species.)

9 GREY-CHEEKED WARBLER *Seicercus poliogenys* 10cm FIELD NOTES: Frequently flicks wings, also fans and cocks tail. SONG: No information. CALL: Loud *chee-chee* or *chi-chi*, also wren-like *tsik*. HABITAT: Bamboo jungle and dense undergrowth in evergreen hill forests.

10 CHESTNUT-CROWNED WARBLER *Seicercus castaniceps* 10cm FIELD NOTES: Behaves much like a leaf warbler. Continuously flicks wings. SONG: No information. CALL: Loud *chi-chi*, wren-like *tsik* and a buzzing *z-z-z-z-z-z* when alarmed. HABITAT: Dense wet oak, pine and evergreen forests in hills and mountains. Altitudinal wanderer to the region.

11 CHESTNUT-HEADED TESIA *Tesia castaneocoronata* 9cm FIELD NOTES: Feeds wren-like in and around dense undergrowth. SONG: Loud and shrill *sip - sit-it-up*. CALL: Piercing *tzeet*, a chattering *chiruk-chiruk* and a frequent delivered *wee*. HABITAT: Undergrowth in high-elevation open forests.

36 FLYCATCHERS

1 FERRUGINOUS FLYCATCHER *Muscicapa ferruginea* 12.5cm FIELD NOTES: Retiring, typical fly-catching actions, e.g. making sallies after flying insects, returning to same or nearby perch. SONG: Probably a high-pitched *tsit-tittu-tittu*. CALL: Soft trill, *si-si-si*. HABITAT: Fir or oak forests, 1800–3300m.

2 DARK-SIDED FLYCATCHER (SIBERIAN OR SOOTY FLYCATCHER) *Muscicapa sibirica* 13cm FIELD NOTES: Actions and habits much as other flycatchers. SONG: Series of repetitive thin notes combined with trills and whistles. CALL: Tinkling *chi-up-chi-up-chi-up*. HABITAT: Open broadleaved evergreen, rhododendron, coniferous and mixed deciduous forest up to 4000m. Lower on migration and in winter.

3 GREY-STREAKED FLYCATCHER (GREY-SPOTTED FLYCATCHER) *Muscicapa griseisticta* 14cm FIELD NOTES: Shy. SONG/CALL: Loud, melodious *chipee - tee-tee*. HABITAT: Dense or open forests, mainly larch, forest edge and urban parks, often near streams.

4 RUSTY-TAILED FLYCATCHER (RUFOUS-TAILED FLYCATCHER) *Muscicapa ruficauda* 14cm FIELD NOTES: Unobtrusive, forages in tree canopy, snapping up insect prey while flitting from branch to branch. SONG: 3 or 4 loud, clear notes repeated at short intervals. CALL: When alarmed a plaintive *peup*, ceaselessly repeated, followed by a soft *churr*; a *te-peup* when excited. HABITAT: Mixed conifer and deciduous forest or fir, Deodar, pine and birch forest

5 BROWN FLYCATCHER (ASIAN BROWN FLYCATCHER) *Muscicapa daurica* 13cm FIELD NOTES: Crepuscular. Feeding actions similar to Ferruginous Flycatcher. SONG: Faint, squeaky, melodious warble. CALL: Short, thin *tzi* and a soft *churr*, and a soft, rattling *tze-te-te-te* when alarmed. HABITAT: Deciduous and mixed woodland, preferring glades or open areas, sometimes coniferous woodland, parks and gardens.

6 SPOTTED FLYCATCHER *Muscicapa striata* 14cm FIELD NOTES: Fly-catching sallies take the bird out in a sweeping circle returning to its favoured perch, or one nearby. SONG: Weak series of squeaky notes, often with lengthy intervals between phrases, *tsee - chup - chup - tsee - tsee - chup-tsee-chup - tsee*. CALL: Squeaky *zeee* or *chick*; *zee-zucc* when agitated. HABITAT: Open deciduous or coniferous woodland, woodland edge, glades, parks, orchards and large gardens.

7 GAMBAGA FLYCATCHER *Muscicapa gambagae* 12cm FIELD NOTES: Habits similar to Spotted Flycatcher. SONG: Quiet, high-pitched squeaking, combined with trills and creaking notes. CALL: *chick, zick-zick-zick*. HABITAT: Wooded highlands and bushy, mainly acacia, scrub.

8 RUFOUS-GORGETED FLYCATCHER (ORANGE-GORGETED FLYCATCHER) *Ficedula strophiata* 13cm FIELD NOTES: Feeds by flitting from bush to bush, picking insects from foliage or, occasionally, from ground; also makes short aerial sallies. Constantly jerks cocked tail. SONG: Spirited 3-note *tin-ti-ti*. CALL: Low *tik-tik* or *pink*; a croaking *churr* when alarmed. HABITAT: Oak, rhododendron, conifer, birch and mixed forests. From 2400 to 3950m.

9 KASHMIR FLYCATCHER *Ficedula subrubra* 13cm FIELD NOTES: Actions and habits similar to Rufous-gorgeted Flycatcher. SONG: Said to be sweet, loud and Robin-like? CALL: Sharp *chack* and a subdued, harsh *purr*. HABITAT: Mixed forests of hazel, walnut, cherry, willow, etc.

10 RED-BREASTED FLYCATCHER *Ficedula parva* 13cm FIELD NOTES: Actions much as Rufous-gorgeted Flycatcher. SONG: Series of sweet, descending notes. CALL: *chick* or *chick-chick*, or slurred to form a wren-like rattle, *serrrt*. HABITAT: Mainly mixed and deciduous woodlands, especially where there are glades, clearings or watersides.

11 TAIGA FLYCATCHER (RED-THROATED FLYCATCHER) *Ficedula albicilla* 13cm FIELD NOTES: Only recently split from Red-breasted Flycatcher. Actions and habits as well as female colouring very similar to Red-breasted Flycatcher. SONG: Sweet *swee-de-de* followed by rising and falling notes, not descending like Red-breasted Flycatcher. CALL: Creaking *trrrrr*, otherwise as Red-breasted Flycatcher. HABITAT: Deciduous and mixed taiga forests.

37 FLYCATCHERS

1 ULTRAMARINE FLYCATCHER *Ficedula superciliaris* 11.5cm FIELD NOTES: Forages in foliage of low trees and bushes. Occasionally descends to feed on ground. Constantly jerks tail. SONG: Repeated *chi-chi-purr*. CALL: Soft *tick*; a low, rattling *trrrt* when alarmed. HABITAT: Open mixed forests of oak, rhododendron, pine, fir, etc. RACES: *F. s. aestigma* (fig 1b) E Himalayas.

2 SEMI-COLLARED FLYCATCHER *Ficedula semitorquata* 13cm FIELD NOTES: Actions and habits similar to Pied Flycatcher. SONG: Similar to Collared Flycatcher with repeated Pied Flycatcher-style phrases. CALL: Whistling *eep* or *tseep* or *tüüp* when alarmed. HABITAT: Deciduous and mixed woodlands, favouring oak and hornbeams, in lowlands and mountains, also orchards and riverside copses.

3 COLLARED FLYCATCHER *Ficedula albicollis* 13cm FIELD NOTES: Actions and habits similar to Pied Flycatcher. SONG: Like Pied Flycatcher but slower and interspersed with thin, high notes. CALL: Far-carrying, drawn-out *eep* and a soft *tsrr*. HABITAT: Deciduous woodland, especially oak, with glades and clearings, orchards, parks and gardens.

4 PIED FLYCATCHER (EUROPEAN PIED FLYCATCHER) *Ficedula hypoleuca* 13cm FIELD NOTES: Rarely returns to same perch after fly-catching sallies; usually darts out from fairly hidden perch in the middle or top of tree, returning to a similar position nearby or to cover some distance away. SONG: Sweet warble, individually variable and variously transcribed, e.g. *chee-chee-chee-tsri-tsri-chee* or *zi-vreezi-vreezi-vreezi-tsu-tsu-chu-vee-chu-vee-zi-zi-zi*. CALL: Various, e.g. *hweet* and *tic*, often combined as *whit-tic* or *whee-tic*. HABITAT: Deciduous and mixed woodland, favouring oak and beech, with glades, often near water, also parks and large gardens. RACES: *F. h. speculigera* (Atlas Flycatcher) (fig 4b) N Africa. Considered by some authors to be a full species.

5 LITTLE PIED FLYCATCHER *Ficedula westermanni* 11.5cm FIELD NOTES: Forages in treetops, constantly on the move, making short flights to catch insects. SONG: Thin, high *pi-pi-pi-pi* followed by low, rattling *churr-r-r-r-r* or *pi-churr-r-r-r-pi-pi-pi-pi*. CALL: Mellow *tweet*. HABITAT: Dense evergreen forest, 900–2600m.

6 MUGIMAKI FLYCATCHER *Ficedula mugimaki* 13cm FIELD NOTES: Usually forages in middle storey or canopy. Flicks and spreads tail. SONG: Fast twittering warble. CALL: Soft, rattled *trrrrr*. HABITAT: Mature mixed forest, often in hill country.

7 YELLOW-RUMPED FLYCATCHER (TRICOLOURED FLYCATCHER) *Ficedula zanthopygia* 13cm FIELD NOTES: Actions much as Narcissus Flycatcher. SONG/CALL: Dry, rattling *tr-r-r-rt*. HABITAT: Mountain woodland forest, often near water, forest edge and lowland scrub.

8 NARCISSUS FLYCATCHER *Ficedula narcissina* 13cm FIELD NOTES: Makes sallies from middle storey and canopy. SONG/CALL: Repeated warbles and whistles, transcribed as *o-shin-tsuk-tsuk*, often including some mimicry of other bird calls. HABITAT: Deciduous, mixed or coniferous forests with dense undergrowth, on hills and mountains. RACES: *F. n. elisae* (Chinese or Chinese Narcissus Flycatcher) (fig 8b) E China. This race may prove to be a full species.

9 WHITE-GORGETED FLYCATCHER *Ficedula monileger* 11.5cm FIELD NOTES: Retiring. Forages low down in dense undergrowth and thickets; often makes short sallies to take flying insects, occasionally takes insects from ground. Jerks and spreads tail when perched. SONG: High-pitched whistling, said to be weak but pleasant. CALL: Scolding, rattling, short whistle and a metallic *dik*. HABITAT: Dense bush, scrubby ravines in broken country and thick undergrowth in forests.

38 FLYCATCHERS AND NILTAVAS

1 SAPPHIRE FLYCATCHER *Ficedula sapphira* 11cm FIELD NOTES: Tame and confiding. Forages in trees from middle to upper storeys. Feeds in the foliage with occasional sallies to catch flying insects, also picks insects off ground. SONG: High-pitched, insect-like *chiki-riki-chicki*. CALL: Low, rattled *tit-tit-tit*. HABITAT: Evergreen forests, 900–2565m.

2 SLATY-BLUE FLYCATCHER *Ficedula tricolor cerviniventris* 11cm FIELD NOTES: Secretive. Frequents undergrowth and lower branches of trees. Takes much of its insect food from ground. Actions Robin-like. SONG: 3-note whistle, written as *zieth-ti-zietz*. CALL: When agitated, an *ee-tick*; also a rapid *ee-tick-tick-tick-tick*. HABITAT: Evergreen mountain forests. RACES: *F. t. tricolor* (not shown) has white throat and underparts. SW China.

3 SLATY-BACKED FLYCATCHER (RUSTY-BREASTED BLUE FLYCATCHER) *Ficedula hodgsonii* 13cm FIELD NOTES: Circles out after flying insects from tree-canopy perch. Very occasionally takes insects from ground. SONG: Constant ripple of descending, whistling notes, *per-ip-it-u-or-per-ip-it-tu…*. CALL: Hard *tchat* and a rattled *terrht*. HABITAT: Damp evergreen forests with thick undergrowth, also oak, pine and rhododendron forests, 2440–4270m.

4 SNOWY-BROWED FLYCATCHER (RUFOUS-BREASTED BLUE FLYCATCHER) *Ficedula hyperythra* 11cm FIELD NOTES: Forages low down in scrub and thickets, flits among branches or runs about on, or near, ground; actions chat-like. SONG: Quiet, wheezy, shrill phrases, e.g. *tsit-sit-si-sii*, *tsi-sii-swrri* or *tsi-sit-i*. CALL: Repeated, thin *sip* notes. HABITAT: Dense montane forest with thick undergrowth.

5 HILL BLUE FLYCATCHER (LARGE-BILLED BLUE FLYCATCHER) *Cyornis banyumas* 15cm FIELD NOTES: Sits quietly, hawks from low perch. SONG: Short, metallic trill of 6–10 notes, the first half descending, the second ascending. CALL: Hard *tac* and a scolding *trrt-trrt-trrt…*. HABITAT: Dense humid forest with abundant undergrowth.

6 PYGMY BLUE FLYCATCHER *Muscicapella hodgsoni* 9cm FIELD NOTES: Forages, leaf warbler-like, in dense foliage of bushes or trees. Occasionally picks insects from ground. SONG: High-pitched *tzit-che-che-che-cheeee*. CALL: Feeble *tsip* and a low *churr*. HABITAT: Tall, dense forest and secondary scrub up to 3000m.

7 BLUE-AND-WHITE FLYCATCHER *Cyanoptila cyanomelana* 17cm FIELD NOTES: Feeds high in tree canopy; little recorded of other actions. SONG: Erratic, fluty *hi-hwi-pipipi - tsi-tsi-tsi*. CALL: Harsh *tchk-tchk*. HABITAT: Deciduous and mixed mature forests, with tall trees and streams, in foothills and on mountain slopes.

8 VERDITER FLYCATCHER *Eumyias thalassina* 15cm FIELD NOTES: Flits from exposed branch to branch, rather than returning to original perch, to make sallies after flying insects, usually in the top of tall trees or bushes. SONG: Pleasant trill, *pe-tititi-wu-pititi-weu*. CALL: *tze-ju-jui*. HABITAT: Light forest and bushes along streams, also evergreen and coniferous forest.

9 RUFOUS-BELLIED NILTAVA *Niltava sundara* 16.5cm FIELD NOTES: Often drops to ground from low perch to capture insect prey. Constantly flicks tail. SONG: Rasping *zi-i-i-f-cha-chuk*. CALL: Hard *tic*, a thin *see* and a soft *chacha*. HABITAT: Open woodland and hill forests, 1500–3000m.

10 FUJIAN NILTAVA *Niltava davidi* 18cm FIELD NOTES: Actions typical of the genus. SONG/CALL: Repeated, high-pitched *sssssew* or *siiiii*; also a sharp metallic *tit-tit-tit…* or *trrt-trrt-trrt…trrt-trrt-tit-tit…*, given in alarm. HABITAT: Dense forest undergrowth in mountains.

11 VIVID NILTAVA *Niltava vivida* 17.5cm FIELD NOTES: Feeds by making sallies after flying insects in the middle and upper storey. SONG: Slow mellow whistles interspersed with scratchy notes, transcribed as *beu-wii-riu-chrt-trrt-heu-wii-tiu-wii-u…*. CALL: Whistled *yiyou-yiyou*. HABITAT: Evergreen or mixed mountain forests, 2000–2700m.

39 NILTAVA, FLYCATCHER, FANTAILS AND PARADISE FLYCATCHERS

1 LARGE NILTAVA *Niltava grandis* 20.5cm FIELD NOTES: Skulks and flits about in low bushes, occasionally feeds on ground. Less agile than most flycatchers. SONG: Ascending, whistled *whee-whee-wip*, *tee-ti-tree* or *tee-ti-tiree*. CALL: Scolding, nasal *djuee*. HABITAT: Sub-montane and montane forests.

2 GREY-HEADED FLYCATCHER *Culicicapa ceylonensis* 10.5cm FIELD NOTES: Returns to same perch after making acrobatic sallies after flying insects. Often joins mixed feeding parties in winter. SONG: Clear, sweet whistle, *chic...chiree-chilee*, *tee-tata-tei* or *tyissi-a-tyi*. CALL: Soft *pit - pit - pit*, a clear *kitwik...kitwik*; also a *kui-whi-whi* and a quiet *chichictrr* or similar. HABITAT: Evergreen forests, wooded ravines, bamboo, 1000–2000m.

3 YELLOW-BELLIED FANTAIL *Rhipidura hypoxantha* 14cm FIELD NOTES: Lively and restless, often encountered in mixed feeding parties. Many actions similar to a *Phylloscopus* warbler. Tail often held erect and fanned. SONG: A feeble trill. CALL: Thin, high *sip - sip*. HABITAT: Mixed coniferous and birch or rhododendron forests.

4 WHITE-THROATED FANTAIL *Rhipidura albicollis* 17cm FIELD NOTES: Restless forager, often working up or down main trunk or nearby branches; also makes sallies after flying insects. Tail often fanned and held partly erect. SONG: Mostly descending, clear *tut-tut-tut-sit-sit-sit-sit*, or similar. CALL: Sharp *cheep* or *chuck*. HABITAT: Moist montane forests, up to 3000m. Altitudinal wanderer to the region.

5 AFRICAN PARADISE FLYCATCHER *Terpsiphone viridis* 20cm (male with tail 36cm) FIELD NOTES: Rufous males sometimes have white tail-streamers; white wing-patch variable in size or occasionally absent. Quite secretive. Feeds on insects, by foraging among foliage or in aerial sallies. SONG: Pleasant *twee-twoo-twoo-twoo-twoo*, which has thrush-like quality. CALL: Harsh *tsveit* or *scheep* and a harsh *tscaeae-tseaeaet*. HABITAT: Semitropical wadis with trees, 1000–2400m.

6 ASIAN PARADISE FLYCATCHER *Terpsiphone paradisi* 20cm (male with tail 45cm) FIELD NOTES: Usually hunts from a perch in lower part of canopy. Mainly in pairs or with mixed-species feeding parties. SONG: Clear, rolling *chu-wu-wu-wu-wu-wu....* CALL: Loud *chee-tew*, a harsh *tst*; *weep-poor-willie - weep - poor-willie* when mobbing. HABITAT: Open forests, bushes, gardens and groves.

7 JAPANESE PARADISE FLYCATCHER *Terpsiphone atrocaudata* 18cm (male with tail 38cm) FIELD NOTES: Actions much as Asian Paradise Flycatcher. SONG: Whistled *tsuki-hi-hoshi-hoi-hoi-hoi*. CALL: Querulous *jouey*. HABITAT: Shady, mature deciduous or mixed forest, plantations, wooded valleys with streams, also broadleaved evergreen forest.

40 SCIMITAR BABBLERS AND WREN-BABBLERS

1 RUSTY-CHEEKED SCIMITAR BABBLER *Pomatorhinus erythrogenys* 25cm
FIELD NOTES: Skulks in long grass or dense scrub. Usually in pairs with small parties in winter. Sometimes calls from treetops. SONG: Loud duet, *callow-cree - callow-cree* or variant, the high *cree* given in answer to male's lower *callow*. CALL: Rattling *whih-whihihihihi* when alarmed. HABITAT: Dense bramble and scrub at the edge of forests, also bush-clad grassy hillsides.

2 SPOT-BREASTED SCIMITAR BABBLER *Pomatorhinus erythrocnemis* 23cm
FIELD NOTES: Actions and habits much as Rusty-cheeked Scimitar Babbler. SONG: Loud duet, male with *queue-pee*, female answering with *quip*. CALL: *wi-wi-chitit* or *whoip-tutututututututut* when agitated. HABITAT: Scrub, thickets and forest edge.

3 STREAK-BREASTED SCIMITAR BABBLER *Pomatorhinus ruficollis* 19cm
FIELD NOTES: Wary. Mainly forages on ground, in pairs in breeding season or small parties at other times. When disturbed, flies into thick cover. SONG: Mellow 2- or 3-note hoot, *u-hu-hu* or *wu-wu-wu*; female sometimes answers with a squeaky note. CALL: When alarmed gives a harsh scolding rattle, transcribed as *whi-whi-whi-whi-whi-whi-wichita - chrrururur - whi-wi-chututut - chutititititit*. HABITAT: Mixed, evergreen or scrubby secondary forests with bamboo.

4 CORAL-BILLED SCIMITAR BABBLER *Pomatorhinus ferruginosus* 23cm FIELD NOTES: Elusive. Forages on ground, usually in pairs or small parties. SONG: Number of fluty notes, *oo-pü-pü* or *oo-pü-pü-pü*. CALL: When alarmed, a harsh, grating *churr*; also recorded, *weeitch-oo*, a shrill *wheep-wheep* and a typical harsh scolding *whit-whit-tchrrrt - tchrrrt-tchrrrt*. HABITAT: Evergreen hill forests.

5 SLENDER-BILLED SCIMITAR BABBLER *Xiphirhynchus superciliaris* 20cm FIELD NOTES: Shy, noisy and restless. Forages on or near ground, in pairs or small parties. SONG: Rapid hollow, piping *wuwuwuwuwuwu* and a slower *put-put-put-put-put*; both may be followed by a high-pitched *u-wi*. CALL: Harsh chattering when alarmed. HABITAT: Thick bamboo, bushes and brambles on steep grassy hillsides.

6 PYGMY WREN-BABBLER (LESSER SCALY OR BROWN WREN-BABBLER) *Pnoepyga pusilla* 9cm FIELD NOTES: Shy and secretive; scuttles, mouse-like, about the forest floor, flicking wings as though nervous. Often adopts upright posture. Usually in pairs, but often singly in winter. SONG: Very high-pitched *ti - ti - tu*, or *ti - tu*, repeated every 3–5sec. CALL: Repeated, sharp *tchit* or *chit*. HABITAT: Broadleaved evergreen forest.

7 SCALY-BREASTED WREN-BABBLER *Pnoepyga albiventer* 10.5cm FIELD NOTES: Actions and habits very similar to Pygmy Wren-babbler. SONG: High-pitched, jumbled and warbler-like, written as *wisisititititiwi* or *wiswisiwitwisititui*. CALL: Repeated, loud *tschik* or *tchik*. HABITAT: Broadleaved evergreen forest, in winter along mossy, fern-lined stream banks.

8 NEPAL WREN-BABBLER *Pnoepyga immaculata* 10cm FIELD NOTES: Actions and habits typical of genus. SONG/CALL: 8 high-pitched piercing notes, fairly quickly delivered, *si-su-si-si-swi-si-si-si*. HABITAT: Tall herbage in dense forest.

9 BAR-WINGED WREN-BABBLER (SPOTTED LONG-TAILED WREN-BABBLER) *Spelaeornis troglodytoides* 13cm FIELD NOTES: Forages, restlessly, on ground or by clambering on bamboo stems and mossy trunks, but not to any great height. SONG: Repeated, husky, rolling *chi'whi-whi'whi-whi'whi-whi'whi*. CALL: Subdued *cheep* and, in alarm, a faint *churr*. HABITAT: Undergrowth and bamboo in montane forests.

10 RUFOUS-THROATED WREN-BABBLER (TAILED WREN-BABBLER) *Spelaeornis caudatus* 9cm FIELD NOTES: Actions typical of genus, terrestrial, solitary, restless and very elusive. SONG/CALL: High-pitched *tzit* and a quiet *birrh-birrh-birrh* when alarmed. HABITAT: Undergrowth in montane evergreen forest.

rufous phase

pale
phase

7

pale
phase

1

2

3

4

5

rufous phase

6

fous
hase

pale phase

8

9

10

41 BABBLERS

1 IRAQ BABBLER *Turdoides altirostris* 22cm FIELD NOTES: Gregarious, usually in groups of up to 10, sometimes furtive, sometimes inquisitive; feeds on or near ground, often stands with tail raised. Groups often first catch the eye as they fly 'follow-my-leader' from cover to cover. SONG: Said to be similar to the *phist* and *phic* calls. CALL: Commonest contact note is a drawn-out, whistled *pherrrreree*, also a chattering *pherr-pherr-pherr*.... When alarmed, produces a squeaking *phsioe* and during aggression gives series of *phist* or *phic* notes: *phist - phist - phist - phic phic-phic - phist - phist*. HABITAT: River, canal and marsh margins, frequenting various trees, scru and reeds, spreading into nearby thickets, palm groves and the edges of cultivation.

2 COMMON BABBLER *Turdoides caudatus* 23cm FIELD NOTES: Actions and habits typical of genus, *see* Iraq Babbler. SONG: Undescribed. CALL: Loud, slow, descending, whistling *pi-pee-pee-pee-pee-peerrrrr* and a mournful *piooooo-pioo-poor*; Nuthatch-like *qui-qui-qui-qui*... given when alarmed. HABITAT: Thickets and scrub in lowlands and hills; edges of cultivation, palm groves, citrus orchards and gardens.

3 ARABIAN BABBLER *Turdoides squamiceps* 27cm FIELD NOTES: Action and habits typic of genus, *see* Iraq Babbler. SONG: Quiet, high-pitched warble. CALL: Series of loud, piercing whistles, *peee - peee - peee - peee*... or *piu - piu - piu - piu*..., a hoarse trill and a loud *pew*; a soft whinnying when groups are at roost. HABITAT: Open acacia woodland, scrub thickets, palm-grove undergrowth, edges of reed-beds and gardens.

4 FULVOUS BABBLER (FULVOUS CHATTERER) *Turdoides fulvus* 24cm FIELD NOTE: Actions and habitats typical of genus, *see* Iraq Babbler. Said to be more secretive than other babblers. SONG: Subdued squeaking and chirruping. CALL: Series of piping notes, *peeoo-peeoo-peeoo-peeoo-peeoo-peeoo*, also a hollow rattle and a sharp *pwit*; a clear *peep* in flight. HABITAT: Open acacia woodland, scrub, thickets and palm groves with undergrowth.

5 CHINESE BABAX *Babax lanceolatus* 28cm FIELD NOTES: Skulking. Feeds on ground or in low scrub, although does ascend trees to forage in topmost branches, especially mornings and evenings. Usually in small, noisy, groups. SONG/CALL: Wailing *ou-phee-ou-phee* repeated severa times. Groups keep up a continual flow of soft musical notes interspersed with some harsher outbursts. Also recorded is a note that sounds like a creaky gate hinge. HABITAT: Scrub thicket: and undergrowth of montane and hill forests.

6 KOZLOV'S BABAX (TIBETAN BABAX) *Babax koslowi* 28cm FIELD NOTES: Actions and habits said to be much as others of genus. SONG/CALL: Undescribed. HABITAT: Scrubland, rocky areas and abandoned agricultural fields.

7 GIANT BABAX *Babax waddelli* 31cm FIELD NOTES: Skulks in dense bushes. Forages on ground, turning over dead leaves in search of food. Usually occurs in small parties. SONG: Serie of quavering, whistled, thrush-like notes. CALL: Harsh grating. HABITAT: High-altitude arid scrub and thickets.

8 RUFOUS-TAILED BABBLER *Moupinia poecilotis* 15cm FIELD NOTES: Usually skulks in scrub and tall grass, often feeds on ground. Occurs in small flocks outside breeding season. SONG/CALL: Unrecorded. HABITAT: In grass and scrub, 1500–3810m.

9 RUFOUS-CAPPED BABBLER *Stachyris ruficeps davidi* 12cm FIELD NOTES: Actions rather tit-like. Forages in pairs during breeding season, otherwise in small parties, often in company with other small babblers. SONG: A low *pi-pi-pi-pi-pi-pi*. CALL: Low 4-note whistle, *whi-whi-whi-whi*, and a harsh *trrrrt-trrrrt-trrrrt* or *ttrrutut-trrrrt-trrrrt*. HABITAT: Broadleaved evergreen forest, scrub and bamboo.

42 PARROTBILLS

1 GREAT PARROTBILL (GIANT PARROTBILL) *Conostoma oemodium* 28cm FIELD NOTES: Feeds on or near the ground. SONG: Repeated, loud *wheou-wheou*…. CALL: Nasal wheezes, cackling, churring and squeals. HABITAT: Bamboo and rhododendron thickets in subalpine forest

2 BROWN PARROTBILL *Paradoxornis unicolor* 20cm FIELD NOTES: Acrobatic, often hanging upside-down to feed. SONG: Repeated, loud *it'ik'ik - ii-wuu-iiew*, also repeats a high *hee-hew*. CALL: Shrill *whi-whi-whi*, a low *brrh* and a cackling *churrh*. HABITAT: Dense bamboo thicket

3 SPECTACLED PARROTBILL *Paradoxornis conspicillatus* 14cm FIELD NOTES: Forages lo down in bamboo, in small, active flocks. SONG/CALL: Twangy, high-pitched *triiih-triiih-triiih*…, also shorter *triit* notes. HABITAT: Bamboo layer in montane forests.

4 SPOT-BREASTED PARROTBILL *Paradoxornis guttaticollis* 20cm FIELD NOTES: Noisy, usually in small parties. SONG: Series of 3–7 staccato notes. CALL: *chut-chut-chut*; some group chittering. HABITAT: Secondary growth, scrub and tall grass, 1050–2135m.

5 THREE-TOED PARROTBILL *Paradoxornis paradoxus* 23cm FIELD NOTES: Actions and habits as other large parrotbills. SONG: High-pitched, plaintive *tuwi-tui* or *tuii-tew*, also a weaker *tidu-tui-tui* and a low chuntering, interspersed with high *tuwii, tuwii* or *tuuu* notes. CAL Harsh *chah* and *chao*. HABITAT: Bamboo thickets in broadleaf and conifer forests, 1500–3660m

6 BROWN-WINGED PARROTBILL *Paradoxornis brunneus* 12cm FIELD NOTES: Forages active flocks, sometimes consisting of 30+ birds. SONG/CALL: Continuous twittering. Nothing more documented. HABITAT: Bamboo thickets, scrub and tall grass, 1830–2800m.

7 VINOUS-THROATED PARROTBILL *Paradoxornis webbianus* 12cm FIELD NOTES: Forages in small, fast-moving, active flocks. SONG: Repeated, high-pitched *tw'i-tu - tititi* or *tw' tu - tiutiutiutiu*, interspersed with short *twit* notes. Occasionally only *tiutiutiutiu*…. CALL: Continuous chirpy rattle. HABITAT: Scrub, thickets and forest edge up to 1500m.

8 GREY-HOODED PARROTBILL *Paradoxornis zappeyi* 13cm FIELD NOTES: Found in small flocks in bamboo understorey. SONG/CALL: Only recorded as *shh…shh…shh*. HABITAT: Mountain bamboo understorey, 2350–3200m.

9 PRZEVALSKI'S PARROTBILL (RUSTY-THROATED PARROTBILL) *Paradoxorn przewalskii* 13cm FIELD NOTES: Actions and habits much as other small parrotbills. SONG/CALL Contact call consists of short rattles, interspersed with thin, high notes. HABITAT: Montane scrub, also bamboos and grasses in open larch forests, 2440–3050m.

10 FULVOUS PARROTBILL *Paradoxornis fulvifrons* 14cm FIELD NOTES: Clambers, feverishl up and down bamboo stems. Forms flocks of 20+. SONG/CALL: Continual twittering and a faint mouse-like *cheep*. HABITAT: Bamboo thickets in mixed woodland, also spruce or juniper forests

11 REED PARROTBILL (CHINESE PARROTBILL) *Paradoxornis heudei* 18cm FIELD NOTES: Occurs in small, active flocks. SONG/CALL: Undescribed. HABITAT: Reed-beds.

12 BLACK-THROATED PARROTBILL *Paradoxornis nipalensis* 11cm FIELD NOTES: Acrobatic, active feeder in small to large groups, often accompanied by tits and other babblers. SONG/CALL: Constant high-pitched twittering with various cheeps and chirrs, also a loud purring chatter and a plaintive bleat. HABITAT: Broadleaf montane forest, undergrowth and bamboo. RACES: *P. n. poliotis* (fig 12b) SE Tibet; *P. n. humii* (fig 12c) E Himalayas.

13 GOLDEN PARROTBILL *Paradoxornis verreauxi* 11cm FIELD NOTES: Actions much as Black-throated Parrotbill. SONG/CALL: Similar to Black-throated Parrotbill and possibly a thin high-pitched *ssii-ssii-ssu-ssii*. HABITAT: Bamboo thickets in evergreen montane forests.

14 BEARDED REEDLING (BEARDED TIT OR PARROTBILL) *Panurus biarmicus* 14cm FIELD NOTES: Usually detected by pinging call. SONG: Soft *tchin-tchik-tchraay*. CALL: Far-carrying *ping* or *pching*, also a harsh, buzzing *tjipp* and a soft *pitt*. HABITAT: Extensive reed-beds.

43 LAUGHINGTHRUSHES

1 MASKED LAUGHINGTHRUSH *Garrulax perspicillatus* 30cm FIELD NOTES: Mainly a ground feeder, turning over leaf litter. Usually in small parties. SONG/CALL: Contact and alarm call loud and piercing, has been transcribed as *jhew* or *jhow*, also a harsh chattering. HABITAT: Bamboo thickets, thick scrub, reeds, cultivation and parks.

2 WHITE-THROATED LAUGHINGTHRUSH *Garrulax albogularis* 28cm FIELD NOTES: Feeds both on ground and in trees, in small, noisy flocks. Winter flocks may contain 100+ individuals. SONG/CALL: Buzzing *tzzzzzzzzzzz* when alarmed, and a gentle *ter-ter* contact note; also squeals and laughing sounds when excited. Flocks have a wheezy *tsu'ueeeee-hiuuuu-huiiii* call or similar. HABITAT: Broadleaved evergreen forest, secondary growth and bamboo, 1200–4600m.

3 STRIATED LAUGHINGTHRUSH *Garrulax striatus* 30cm FIELD NOTES: Feeds mainly in trees, from canopy to lower branches and undergrowth. Forms small, noisy winter parties. SONG/CALL: Shrill contact cries and discordant cackles, and a repeated, loud, musical *o-will-you-will-you-wit* or variants, also a whistled *teo-wo*. HABITAT: Dense thickets near streams, in broadleaved and mixed forests.

4 VARIEGATED LAUGHINGTHRUSH *Garrulax variegatus* 26cm FIELD NOTES: Skulking. Forages in pairs, forms small parties during winter. SONG/CALL: Loud musical whistles *weet-a-weer* or *weet-a-woo-weer*, which is usually taken up by other group members; also a *pte-weer* given by winter flocks. When alarmed, utters muttering and squealing notes. HABITAT: Undergrowth of rhododendron and other bushes in open oak and mixed forests.

5 PÈRE DAVID'S LAUGHINGTHRUSH (PLAIN LAUGHINGTHRUSH) *Garrulax davidi* 23cm FIELD NOTES: Actions as other laughingthrushes. SONG/CALL: Repeated series of short notes, starting with weak whining notes and followed by lower, weaker notes, transcribe as *wia - wa- WIKWIKWIK-woitwoitwoitwoit*; also utters a series of single *wiau* notes. HABITAT: Mountain thickets and scrub.

6 SUKATSCHEV'S LAUGHINGTHRUSH (SNOWY-CHEEKED LAUGHINGTHRUSH) *Garrulax sukatschewi* 28cm FIELD NOTES: Usually in small parties that feed mainly on ground. Birds shake head, flick tail and quiver feathers when calling. SONG/CALL: Various melodious notes, nothing more recorded. HABITAT: Coniferous hill forest and scrub, 2000–3500m.

7 RUFOUS-CHINNED LAUGHINGTHRUSH *Garrulax rufogularis* 22cm FIELD NOTES: Very skulking. Feeds mainly on ground, or in low bushes. Less gregarious than most laughingthrushes. SONG/CALL: Chuckles and chattering; loud squealing when agitated. HABITAT: Broadleaved evergreen forests. Altitudinal wanderer to the region.

8 MOUSTACHED LAUGHINGTHRUSH *Garrulax cineraceus* 23cm FIELD NOTES: Feeds on ground in pairs or small parties. SONG: Loud *diu-diuuid*. CALL: Not well documented, only mentioned as low and musical. HABITAT: Thick bushes in damp forests, thick scrub and secondary growth near villages or cultivation.

9 BIET'S LAUGHINGTHRUSH (WHITE-SPECKLED LAUGHINGTHRUSH) *Garrulax bieti* 26cm FIELD NOTES: Little known, actions probably as Barred Laughingthrush, which has been treated by some authors as conspecific. SONG/CALL: Undescribed. HABITAT: Bamboo thickets in conifer and secondary forests, 3050–3650m.

10 HWAMEI (MELODIOUS LAUGHINGTHRUSH) *Garrulax canorus* 22cm FIELD NOTES: Rather skulking. Mainly a ground feeder, in leaf litter. Occurs in pairs or small parties. SONG/CALL: Variable, rich and high-pitched with regular repetition. Starts slowly then increases in volume and pitch. HABITAT: Scrub and secondary forest.

44 LAUGHINGTHRUSHES

1 GIANT LAUGHINGTHRUSH *Garrulax maximus* 34cm FIELD NOTES: Secretive. Mainly a ground feeder. Gregarious, often in association with other laughingthrushes. SONG/CALL: Jerky rattling chorus and shrill calls that are said to sound like those of a Large Hawk Cuckoo, e.g. *pi-peea* or *pwi-pwee-wru*. HABITAT: Dense, dry subalpine forest with undergrowth and glades.

2 SPOTTED LAUGHINGTHRUSH (WHITE-SPOTTED LAUGHINGTHRUSH)
Garrulax ocellatus 31cm FIELD NOTES: Actions very similar to Giant Laughingthrush. SONG: Repeated, rich and fluty *wu-it - wu-u - wu-u - wi-u - wi-u - w'you - w'you - uu-i - w'you - uu-i*. CALL: *cacree-cree-cree-cree-rrr-cacree-cree*, also said to utter a squawking alarm. HABITAT: Light mountain forest with undergrowth, rhododendron scrub and bushes. RACES: G. o. artemesiae (fig 2b) China (S Gansu, C Sichuan mountains).

3 BARRED LAUGHINGTHRUSH (BAR-BACKED LAUGHINGTHRUSH)
Garrulax lunulatus 23cm FIELD NOTES: Forages in groups. Little more recorded. SONG/CALL: *wu-chi - wi-wuoou*, repeated at short intervals. Nothing more recorded. HABITAT: Bamboo understorey in broadleaf and coniferous forest, 1200–3660m.

4 STREAKED LAUGHINGTHRUSH *Garrulax lineatus* 21cm FIELD NOTES: Feeds mostly on ground; forms small parties during winter. SONG/CALL: Constant murmuring and crying with a clear *pity-pity-we-are*; a plaintive *sweet-pea-pea-pea* when alarmed. HABITAT: Scrub and bush-covered open hillsides, 1700–3300m. RACES: G. l. imbricatus (fig 4b) China (SE Tibet).

5 BLUE-WINGED LAUGHINGTHRUSH *Garrulax squamatus* 26cm FIELD NOTES: Skulking. Forages mostly on ground. SONG: Written as *cur-white-to-go* and *free-for-you*. CALL: Buzzy *jrrrrr-rrr-rrr…* and a harsh, buzzy, liquid *cher-cherrrru*. HABITAT: Dense bushes, bamboo and rhododendron, often near streams and rivers. Altitudinal wanderer to the region.

6 ELLIOT'S LAUGHINGTHRUSH *Garrulax elliotii* 26cm FIELD NOTES: Actions similar to others of genus. SONG/CALL: Far-carrying double note and group chattering. HABITAT: Undergrowth and bamboo of open and secondary forests and thickets, 1200–4800m.

7 SCALY LAUGHINGTHRUSH (PLAIN-COLOURED LAUGHINGTHRUSH)
Garrulax subunicolor 24cm FIELD NOTES: Occurs in pairs, or small parties in non-breeding season. SONG: Clear 4-note whistle. CALL: Squeaky chatters and a sharp alarm note. HABITAT: Mixed deciduous forest undergrowth, secondary growth, dwarf rhododendron, bamboo and scrub.

8 PRINCE HENRI'S LAUGHINGTHRUSH (BROWN-CHEEKED LAUGHINGTHRUSH) *Garrulax henrici* 26cm FIELD NOTES: Secretive. Moves around in pairs during breeding season and small parties at other times. SONG/CALL: Fluty *whoh-hee* and noisy chattering. HABITAT: Forest and scrubby valleys in wet and dry zones, 2800–4600m.

9 BLACK-FACED LAUGHINGTHRUSH *Garrulax affinis* 26cm FIELD NOTES: Runs rat-like over moss-covered boulders and fallen trees, seldom takes to the wing. Usually in pairs or small parties. SONG: Repetitive, mournful, *to-wee-you, tsi-tsitu-wiu* or *you-weary-wheeooo-ee-rr-kay-luck*. CALL: Rolling *whirr-whirrer*, also some harsh scolding notes. HABITAT: Rhododendron and juniper thickets, scrub oak and bamboo in mixed forests, 1500–4500m.

10 CHESTNUT-CROWNED LAUGHINGTHRUSH *Garrulax erythrocephalus* 28cm FIELD NOTES: Skulking. SONG: Several repeated, short phrases, *pearl-lee - to-reaper - to-real-year - you - reap* or variants. Also a whistled *too-rit-a-reill* answered by *wroo-wroo*. CALL: Constant twittering and chuckling, also a churring *grrrrt-grrrt*. HABITAT: Dense undergrowth of dwarf rhododendron, scrub, forest edge and bamboo thickets. RACES: G. e. nigrimentum (fig 10b) China (S Tibet).

11 RED-WINGED LAUGHINGTHRUSH *Garrulax formosus* 28cm FIELD NOTES: Shy. Actions typical of genus. SONG: Repeated loud, whistled *chu-weewu* or rising *chi-wee*, also a loud *wu-eeoo*. Duets include *chi-wee - u-weeoo* or a quicker *u-weeoo - wueeoo*. CALL: A soft *wiii*. HABITAT: Dense evergreen forest, secondary growth and bamboo.

45 LIOCICHLA, MYZORNIS, LEIOTHRIX, SHRIKE-BABBLERS, MINLAS, BARWINGS AND SIBIAS

1 EMEI SHAN LIOCICHLA *Liocichla omeiensis* 21cm FIELD NOTES: Secretive. Actions similar to other babblers? SONG/CALL: Loud whistling consisting of 6 or more notes, falling in pitch at the end. HABITAT: Undergrowth in primary and secondary forest, 1000–2400m.

2 FIRE-TAILED MYZORNIS *Myzornis pyrrhoura* 13cm FIELD NOTES: Found singly or in small parties. Probes rhododendron flowers for nectar. Also captures prey by running up tree-trunks in treecreeper-like fashion, or occasionally by fly-catching. SONG/CALL: Usually silent but sometimes utters a high *tsi-tsit* contact note. Also recorded is *trrrr-trrrr-trrr*, preceded by a high squeak, also *tzip* when alarmed. HABITAT: Rhododendron and juniper bushes, montane forests and bamboo thickets, 3000–3660m.

3 RED-BILLED LEIOTHRIX (PEKING ROBIN) *Leiothrix lutea* 15cm FIELD NOTES: Forages in noisy parties, often on ground. SONG: Loud, thrush-like warble, consisting of 15 or so notes. CALL: When alarmed utters harsh, scolding, buzzy rattles. HABITAT: Undergrowth of secondary forest and scrub.

4 WHITE-BROWED SHRIKE-BABBLER *Pteruthius flaviscapis validirostris* 17cm FIELD NOTES: Arboreal. Regularly hops sideways along branches in search of insects, etc. SONG: Loud *cha-chew-cha-cha-chip* or *chu-wip-chip-chip*. CALL: Harsh grating, often repeated 10 or more times in quick succession. HABITAT: Montane forest of oak, rhododendron, etc.

5 BLACK-HEADED SHRIKE-BABBLER *Pteruthius rufiventer* 21cm FIELD NOTES: Arboreal. Lethargic. Often part of mixed-species foraging parties. SONG: Mellow *wip-wiyu* repeated every few seconds, or a descending *you-wu-uu*. CALL: Scolding *rrrrt-rrrrt-rrrrt…* and a quick *ukuk-wrrrrrii-yiwu*. HABITAT: Montane evergreen forest. Altitudinal wanderer to region.

6 GREEN SHRIKE-BABBLER *Pteruthius xanthochlorus* 13cm FIELD NOTES: Acts like a sluggish leaf warbler. Often in mixed-species feeding parties. SONG: Rapid monotonous repetition of a single note. CALL: Repeated *whit*. HABITAT: Subalpine, mixed and conifer forests, 760–5600m.

7 RED-TAILED MINLA *Minla ignotincta* 14cm FIELD NOTES: Agile, acrobatic feeder. SONG: Loud, ringing *twiyi-twiyuyi…*. CALL: High-pitched *wi-wi-wi* and a repeated *chik*, along with various high-pitched titters. HABITAT: Montane broadleaf forest.

8 CHESTNUT-TAILED MINLA *Minla strigula* 16cm FIELD NOTES: Agile, arboreal feeder. Often part of mixed-species foraging parties. SONG: Hoarse *tsi-tsu-ti-si* or slurred *chu-u-wee - chu-u-wee*. CALL: Metallic *chew* or *pe-eo*, also a mellow *peera-tzip*. HABITAT: Lower trees and bushes of montane broadleaf and conifer forests.

9 HOARY-THROATED BARWING *Actinodura nipalensis* 21cm FIELD NOTES: Arboreal. Usually in small parties, foraging for insects concealed in mossy branches and tree trunks. SONG/CALL: Whistled *tui-whee-er*; when alarmed, a rapid *je-je…*, repeated several times. HABITAT: Oak, oak with conifer and also rhododendron forests.

10 STREAK-THROATED BARWING *Actinodura waldeni daflaensis* 21cm FIELD NOTES: Actions as Hoary-throated Barwing. SONG/CALL: Soft *chup-chup*, also a mewing and *churr*. HABITAT: Evergreen and mixed forests.

11 BLACK-CAPPED SIBIA (RUFOUS SIBIA) *Heterophasia capistrata* 24cm FIELD NOTES: Arboreal, lively feeder, foraging amongst mossy branches. Often forms part of mixed-species feeding flocks. SONG: Fluty *tee-dee-dee-dee-dee-o-lu*. CALL: Rapid *chi-chi*; a harsh *chrai-chrai-chrai…* when alarmed. HABITAT: Mixed forests, 2200–2600m.

12 BEAUTIFUL SIBIA *Heterophasia pulchella* 24cm FIELD NOTES: Actions much as Black-capped Sibia. SONG: Shrill *ti-ti-titi-tu-ti*, descending slightly towards end. CALL: Generally silent but often breaks into a great variety of notes, including a series that is said to sound like the jingling of a bunch of keys. HABITAT: Mossy forests, 1650–2745m.

46 FULVETTAS AND YUHINAS

1 GOLDEN-BREASTED FULVETTA (GOLDEN-BREASTED TIT BABBLER)
Alcippe chrysotis 11cm FIELD NOTES: Actions very tit-like. Forages low down in thickets, often in large winter flocks. SONG/CALL: Continuous low twitter, also a descending, high-pitched, 5-note series. HABITAT: Dense growth on steep hillsides.

2 RUFOUS-WINGED FULVETTA (CHESTNUT-HEADED TIT BABBLER) *Alcippe castaneceps* 10cm FIELD NOTES: Occurs in highly active, large winter flocks; actions much as other fulvettas. SONG: Rich, undulating and slightly descending *ti-du-di-du-di-du-di*. CALL: 3-note crescendo *tu-twee-twe*; a high, wheezy *tsi-tsi-tsi-tsirr* and a quiet *chip* or *chup*. HABITAT: Thick evergreen undergrowth at forest edge.

3 WHITE-BROWED FULVETTA (WHITE-BROWED TIT BABBLER) *Alcippe vinipectus* 11cm FIELD NOTES: Actions as others of genus, occurs in small parties or flocks of 20 or so. SONG: Faint *chit-it-it-or-key*, given while tail flicked and head held forward. CALL: Incessant, high-pitched *chip-chip*; a *churr* when alarmed. HABITAT: Scrub and undergrowth in subalpine forest.

4 CHINESE FULVETTA *Alcippe striaticollis* 12cm FIELD NOTES: Actions and habits similar to other fulvettas. SONG/CALL: Clear, ventriloqual *tsway - ahh-tsway - ahh*. HABITAT: Prickly oak scrub and thickets, 2200–4300m.

5 SPECTACLED FULVETTA *Alcippe ruficapilla* 12cm FIELD NOTES: Actions and habits similar to other fulvettas? SONG/CALL: Undescribed. HABITAT: Evergreen oak forests, 1250–2500m.

6 STREAK-THROATED FULVETTA (BROWN-HEADED TIT BABBLER) *Alcippe cinereiceps* 12cm FIELD NOTES: Actions and habits typical of genus. SONG: Rattling 3 or 4 notes. CALL: Tit-like *cheep*. HABITAT: Bamboo brakes plus undergrowth and thickets of mixed and coniferous forests.

7 LUDLOW'S FULVETTA (HIMALAYAN BROWN-HEADED TIT BABBLER) *Alcippe ludlowi* 12cm FIELD NOTES: Forages in small flocks. Actions as other fulvettas. SONG/CALL: A rattling alarm. HABITAT: Rhododendron forests and bamboo thickets.

8 WHISKERED YUHINA (YELLOW-NAPED YUHINA) *Yuhina flavicollis* 14cm FIELD NOTES: Actions tit-like, also fly-catches from bush tops. Forages in small, noisy parties, often in company with tits, warblers, nuthatches, sibias and small babblers. SONG: Transcribed as *twe-tyurwi-tyawi-tyawa*. CALL: Thin, squeaky *swii-swii-swii* and a metallic ringing note. Flocks utter a constant twittering. HABITAT: Evergreen forests, forest edge and secondary growth, 1500–2285m.

9 STRIPE-THROATED YUHINA *Yuhina gularis* 15cm FIELD NOTES: Actions much as Whiskered Yuhina. Flocks work through tops of flowering trees. SONG/CALL: Descending, nasal mewing, *mherr* or *wher*, which is sometimes followed by a hurried *whu-whu-whu-whi-whi-whi*, also a short *wiht*. HABITAT: Mainly montane broadleaf forest.

10 WHITE-COLLARED YUHINA *Yuhina diademata* 17.5cm FIELD NOTES: Actions and habits as other yuhinas. SONG/CALL: A weak white-eye-like cheeping; also recorded is a subdued *wi-wrrr-i-wrrr-wrrr-i*. HABITAT: Montane scrub and secondary growth, 1100–3600m.

11 RUFOUS-VENTED YUHINA (SLATY-HEADED YUHINA) *Yuhina occipitales* 13cm FIELD NOTES: Often associates with Stripe-throated Yuhina, in tree canopy and on moss-covered trunks. SONG: High-pitched *zee-zu-drrrr - tsip-che-e-e-e*. CALL: Short buzzing and *z-e-e* when alarmed. HABITAT: Evergreen forest, especially rhododendron and oak, 1800–3700m, lower in winter.

47 PENDULINE TITS AND LONG-TAILED TIT

1 FIRE-CAPPED TIT *Cephalopyrus flammiceps* 10cm FIELD NOTES: Active, agile; many actions similar to leaf warblers. Often in large mixed- or single-species flocks. Juvenile like adult, whiter below. SONG: Variable, with many phrases; some individuals can have up to 9 song types, including a high-pitched *tink-tink-tink-tink*, a slow *pitsu-pitsu*, a quicker *pissu-pissu-pissu* and a vibrant *psing-psing-psing*. CALL: Abrupt, high-pitched *tsit*, repeated for long periods. HABITAT: Deciduous mixed forests, orchards, poplars and maples.

2 PENDULINE TIT *Remiz pendulinus* 11.5cm FIELD NOTES: Agile feeder. Unobtrusive, but can be quite confiding. Juvenile like dull female but lacking black facial mask. SONG: Made up from a combination of the various calls. CALL: Thin *tssssseeoo* with variations, e.g. *ssss-lu-lu-lu* and a buzzing *tizzz*. HABITAT: Reeds, rank vegetation with patches of bushes and small trees. RACES: *R. p. caspius* (fig 2b) N and W Caspian; *R. p. macronyx* (Black-headed Penduline Tit) (fig 2c) WC Asia, N Iran, sometimes considered to be a full species; *R. p. nigricans* (fig 2d) E Iran (this would become a race of *R. p. macronyx* if the latter was made a full species); *R. p. coronatus* (White-crowned Penduline Tit) (fig 2e) C Asia, sometimes considered a full species; *R. p. consobrinus* (Chinese Penduline Tit) (fig 2f) Manchuria, N China, Korea, sometimes considered a full species.

3 SOOTY TIT *Aegithalos fuliginosus* 11.5cm FIELD NOTES: Typical agile feeder. Forms family flocks post-breeding. Juvenile like a dull adult but with broad white central crown-stripe. SONG: Rolling *sir-rrup*, a thin *si-si-si - si-si-si - si-si-si* and a low *trrr*. CALL: Thin *chit* repeated at irregular intervals. HABITAT: Mixed forests, with scrub of willow, birch, rhododendron or bamboo, 1000–2600m.

4 BLACK-BROWED TIT *Aegithalos iouschistos* 11cm FIELD NOTES: Typically agile. Forms family flocks post-breeding. Juvenile like dull adult with uniform dull buff underparts. SONG/CALL: Similar to Long-tailed Tit. HABITAT: Forest undergrowth, 2200–4000m. RACES: *A. i. bonvaloti* (Black-headed Tit) (fig 4b) SE Tibet.

5 WHITE-THROATED TIT *Aegithalos niveogularis* 11.5cm FIELD NOTES: Typical of genus, agile, often tame. Forms flocks post-breeding. SONG: Long, complex phrases, including rapid, chattering *teet-teet*, combined with rapid *tsi-tsi-tsi* and short warbling. CALL: *tze-tze-tze*, similar to Black-throated Tit. Also a *wi* contact note. HABITAT: Conifer and birch forests, willows and rhododendrons, 2440–3965m.

6 WHITE-CHEEKED TIT *Aegithalos leucogenys* 11cm FIELD NOTES: Active. Feeds in small parties of 6 or so. Also joins mixed winter flocks. Juvenile as adult, but lacks dark bib and crown is paler. SONG: Weak jumble of squeaky and piping notes. CALL: *si-si-si-si*, sometimes more slurred at end, also a fuller *see-see-see* and a buzzing *trrrp*. HABITAT: Oak, holly and juniper scrub, 1220–2600m.

7 BLACK-THROATED TIT *Aegithalos concinnus iredalei* 10.5cm FIELD NOTES: Gregarious, often forms large flocks. Typically restless and agile when feeding. Juvenile as adult, but crown paler and lacks dark bib. Upper breast has collar made up of small dark streaks. SONG: Repeated twittering combined with the odd single chirp. CALL: *si-si-si-si*, also a rattling *churr-trrrt-trrrt*. Song and call very similar to Long-tailed Tit. HABITAT: Mainly deciduous forest edge, but also bush, secondary growth, bamboo and gardens, 1000–3000m.

8 LONG-TAILED TIT *Aegithalos caudatus* 14cm FIELD NOTES: Always on the move, often in large flocks or mixed species flocks. Juvenile has distinctively different head pattern, a white crown-stripe and a dark facial mask, also greyish, not pink, scapulars. SONG: *tsee* and *tsirrup* notes repeated as a jumbled twittering. CALL: Very vocal with various *tup* and *ssrit* notes used to keep contact. Also a thin *tsee-tsee-tsee* given as flocks move through trees. HABITAT: Mixed woodland with undergrowth, scrub, hedges and heathland with scattered bush. RACES: *A. c. europaeus* (fig 8b) C Europe (British race, *A. e. rosaceus* very similar); *A. c. siculus* (fig 8c) Sicily; *A. c. tephronotus* (fig 8d) Asia Minor; *A. c. passekii* (fig 8e) SW Iran; *A. c. glaucogularis* (fig 8f) C China.

1 MARSH TIT *Parus palustris* 11.5cm FIELD NOTES: Generally seen in pairs. Agile feeder. SONG: Liquid, monotonous *tchip-tchip-tchip…*, *tew-tew-tew…* or a faster *chipchipchipchip…*, also other variations. CALL: Explosive *pichay* and a scolding *chicka-dee-dee-dee-dee*. HABITAT: Mainly mature deciduous woodland, mixed woodland and riverine woodland. RACES: *P. p. hypermelaena* (Black-bibbed Tit) (fig 1b) W China. Considered by some authors to be a full species.

2 SOMBRE TIT *Parus lugubris* 14cm FIELD NOTES: Usually in pairs. Less acrobatic than many of genus. SONG: Piping, buzzy *be-zoo-be-zoo-be-zoo…* and a *doodle-lu-doodle-lu-doodle-lu….* CALL: Harsh, churring *zi-zi-zi-z-chrrr*. HABITAT: Open mixed or deciduous woodland or tall scrub, mostly in hilly, rocky areas. RACES: *P. l. hyrcanus* (Caspian Tit) (fig 2b) N Iran, Azerbaijan, considered by some authors to be a full species; *P. l. dubius* (fig 2c) W and NE Iran.

3 WILLOW TIT *Parus montanus* 11cm FIELD NOTES: Generally more skulking than Marsh Tit? SONG: Variable, *tsiu-tsiu-tsiu-tsiu…*, *du-duu-duu-duu…*, etc. CALL: Harsh, nasal *tchar-tchar-tchar* or *tsi-tsi-chay-chay*, also a buzzing *zi-zi-zeerr-zeerr*. HABITAT: Thickets, deciduous and mixed woodland, preferably willow, alder or birch, with undergrowth. Frequents coniferous forests in northern and montane regions. RACES: *P. m. kamtschatkensis* (fig 3b) Kamchatka peninsula; *P. m. songarus* (Songar Tit) (fig 3c) C Asia, China, often considered a full species.

4 SIBERIAN TIT *Parus cinctus* 13.5cm FIELD NOTES: Can be very confiding, usually in pairs or small groups. SONG: Loud, hoarse *cheeoop-cheeoop-cheeoop…* or similar. CALL: Harsh, ringing *cheer-cheer-cheer*, a scolding *chierr*, and a soft, high-pitched *tsi*, *tsitsi* or *tsit*. HABITAT: Mainly mature coniferous or mixed coniferous and birch forest.

5 PÈRE DAVID'S TIT (RED OR RUSTY-BELLIED TIT) *Parus davidi* 12cm FIELD NOTES: Acrobatic feeder, mainly in the canopy of tall trees. Usually in small flocks. SONG/CALL: *sip* or *tsip*, a sibilant *psit*, a hard *chit* and a *t'sip-zee-zee*. HABITAT: Mature mixed forest, 2135–3350m.

6 COAL TIT *Parus ater* 11cm FIELD NOTES: Active, restless feeder. Gregarious in winter, in single-species or mixed-species parties. SONG: *teechu-teechu-teechu…* or *chickwee-chickwee-chichwee…*, sometimes ends in abrupt *dit*. CALL: *tsuu* or *hseeoo*, a high *psit* or *psitisit*, and a buzzing *tsee-tsee-tsee-tsee….* HABITAT: Coniferous and mixed woodland, parks and gardens. RACES: *P. a. cypriotes* (fig 6b) Cyprus; *P. a. chorassanicus* (fig 6c) NE Iran, SW Turkmenistan; *P. a. ledouci* (fig 6d) Tunisia, Algeria; *P. a. aemodius* (fig 6e) E Himalayas, W China.

7 SPOT-WINGED TIT *Parus melanolophus* 11cm FIELD NOTES: Active, forages in mixed-species flocks. SONG: Very similar to Coal Tit. CALL: Similar to Coal Tit. HABITAT: Mainly coniferous forest, often mixed with birch or rhododendron.

8 GREY-CRESTED TIT *Parus dichrous* 12cm FIELD NOTES: Shy. In pairs or small parties. SONG: *whee-whee-tz-tz-tz*. CALL: Various, e.g. a high *zai* and a rapid *ti-ti-ti-ti-ti*. HABITAT: Various forests, including oak, fir and birch. RACES: *P. d. dichroides* (fig 8b) SW China, NE Tibet.

9 RUFOUS-VENTED TIT *Parus rubidiventris* 12cm FIELD NOTES: Habits much as others of genus. SONG: Rattled *chi-chi-chi-chi-chi-chi…*, also some slurred whistles and trills. CALL: A high *see*, a sharp *chit* and a scolding *chit-it-it-it*. HABITAT: High-altitude forests, including oak, birch, pine and rhododendron. RACES: *P. r. beavani* (Sikkim Black Tit) (fig 9b) C Nepal, Tibet, SW China.

10 RUFOUS-NAPED TIT *Parus rufonuchalis* 13cm FIELD NOTES: Actions as Rufous-vented Tit. SONG: Trilling *tip'tip-pee-trrrrrrrr* and a whistled *tsi-tsi-peeduw*. CALL: Plaintive *cheep*, a deep *chut-chut* and a squeaky *trip-ip-ip*. HABITAT: Coniferous forests at high elevations.

11 CRESTED TIT *Parus cristatus* 11.5cm FIELD NOTES: Restless, flicks wings and tail. Usually found singly or in pairs, forms small parties in the winter. SONG: Rapid *seeh-i-i-burrurlt-seeh-i-i-burrurlt….* CALL: Low *brrrrrr-t'brrrrrr*, often preceded by thin *zizizi…*; also *sith-sith-silililili*, a nasal *sniu-zhih* and a *see-see-see*. HABITAT: Conifer forests in north; in south frequents a wider variety of woodland, from mixed forest to Cork Oak. RACES: *P. c. abadiei* (fig 11b) NW France.

49 TITS

1 BLUE TIT *Parus caeruleus* 12cm FIELD NOTES: Very acrobatic. Often tame. SONG: Variable may have up to 8 different types, e.g. *tee-tee - see-see - tee-tee - see-se - psi-dada - psi-dada - psi-dada* or *pee-pee-ti - sihihihihihi - pee-pee-ti - sihihihihi*. CALL: Many, e.g. a scolding *churrrrit* and a thin *sissississississ*. HABITAT: Deciduous woodlands, although utilises evergreen forests in N Africa and Middle East, also orchards, parks, hedgerows and gardens. RACES: *P. c. teneriffae* (fig 1b) Gomera, Tenerife, Gran Canaria; *P. c. persicus* (fig 1c) S and SW Iran.

2 AZURE TIT *Parus cyanus* 13.5cm FIELD NOTES: Active, noisy; feeds in cover of low trees, bushes and reeds. Hybridises with Blue Tit: the progeny can look very like *flavipectus* race. SONG: Variable, includes a descending trill, *tii-tsi-dji-daa-daa-daa*, a Blue Tit-like *tee-tee-tee-chup-chup* and a repeated *tea-cher*. CALL: Various, e.g. a slurred *tstirrup*, a nasal *tsee-tsee-dze-dze* and a scolding *chr-r-r-rit*. HABITAT: Willow, birch and poplar thickets, preferably near water, also light deciduous and mixed woodland and reed-beds in winter. RACES: *P. c. flavipectus* (Yellow-breasted Tit) (fig 2b) C Asia. Sometimes considered to be a full species.

3 GREAT TIT *Parus major* 14cm FIELD NOTES: Bold. Less acrobatic than smaller tits. SONG: Very variable, e.g. simple *ti-ta-ti-ta-ti-ta…* or *tea-cher - tea-cher - tea-cher*. CALL: Various, e.g. a harsh *tcha-tcha-tcha* or *chich-ich-ich-ich* and a ringing *pink-pink-pink*. HABITAT: Open deciduous and mixed woodlands, thickets, orchards, olive groves, hedgerows, parks and gardens. RACES: *P. m. cinereus* (Cinereous Tit) (fig 3b) NE Iran; *P. m. corsus* (fig 3c) Portugal, S Spain, Corsica *P. m. minor* (Japanese Tit) (fig 3d) SE Russia, Japan; *P. m. nigriloris* (fig 3e) Japan.

4 TURKESTAN TIT *Parus bokharensis* 15cm FIELD NOTES: Actions very similar to Great Tit. SONG: Similar to Great Tit. CALL: As Great Tit, although sometimes contains trilling note HABITAT: Riverine thickets in desert, semi-desert and plains, also gardens, orchards and parks.

5 YELLOW-CHEEKED TIT *Parus spilonotus* 14cm FIELD NOTES: Actions much as Great Tit. SONG: Rapidly repeated *chee-chee-piu - chee-chee-piu - chee-chee-piu*. CALL: Great Tit-like. HABITAT: Mainly light oak or pine forest, up to 2400m.

6 BLACK-LORED TIT *Parus xanthogenys* 13cm FIELD NOTES: Actions typical of genus. SONG: *pui-pui-tee - pui-pui-tee* or similar. CALL: *si-si-tzee-tzee-wheep-wheep-wheep - tsi-tsi-pit-tui* and a rattling *ch-chi-chi-chi-chi*. HABITAT: Light, open oak or pine forest.

7 GREEN-BACKED TIT *Parus monticolus* 12.5cm FIELD NOTES: Actions very similar to Great Tit. SONG: Variable, including *seta-seta-seta*, *tu-weeh-tu-weeh…* and, less often, *pli-pli-pli-plipli-pli*. CALL: Like Great Tit, but louder and shriller. HABITAT: Evergreen, deciduous and mixed forests.

8 YELLOW-BELLIED TIT *Parus venustulus* 10cm FIELD NOTES: Usually in pairs or small parties. SONG: Coal Tit-like *swi-swi-swi - suwi-suwi-suwi - sipu-sipu-sipu…*. CALL: Variable, includes *dzee-dzee-dzee…*, a high *si-si-si-si-si* and a quiet *sit-oo*. HABITAT: Open broadleaved deciduous and evergreen forests, also bamboo, willow and larch plantations.

9 VARIED TIT *Parus varius* 12cm FIELD NOTES: Secretive. Feeds in canopy. SONG: Variable *peee-spit'tit - peee-spit'tit…*, *tsre-tsre-peee-triri-peee-triri-peee-triri*; all variants appear to include the *peee* whistle. CALL: Thin *pit*, a high-pitched *spit-spit-see-see* and a scolding *ch-chi-chi*. HABITAT: Coniferous forests in Russia, and deciduous, mixed and evergreen forests with thick undergrowth in Japan. RACES: *P.v. owstoni* (fig 9b) Izu Islands.

10 WHITE-BROWED TIT *Parus superciliosus* 13.5cm FIELD NOTES: Actions typical of genus. Feeds low down in scrub. SONG: Very variable and complex, *tsee-tsee-tsee-pwi-pee*, *tsir'r'r'r'r'r-pee-pee-pee*, *peta-peta-peta-peta-pata*, etc. CALL: Thin *si-si*, insect-like *trrrrrp* or *tsirrrrr*, and a repeated *sip*. HABITAT: Dwarf shrubs, 3000–4250m. Winters in taller shrubs.

11 YELLOW-BROWED TIT *Sylviparus modestus* 10cm FIELD NOTES: Flits among foliage recalling a leaf-warbler, but also acrobatic like a typical tit. SONG: Not well documented, possibly a shrill *zee-zi-zee-zi-zee-zi….* CALL: Variable, e.g. *tsip*, *tchup*, a rapid, trilling *tsziziziziziz-tsziziziz…* and a metallic *pli-pli-pli-pli*. HABITAT: Mainly oak forests.

110

50 NUTHATCHES

1 YUNNAN NUTHATCH *Sitta yunnanensis* 12cm FIELD NOTES: Little known, said to forage tit-like among tree foliage. SONG: Unknown. CALL: Various, e.g. a nasal *nit*, often repeated, and a harsh *schri-schri-schri*. HABITAT: Pine forests, 2440–3960m, lower in winter.

2 CHINESE NUTHATCH *Sitta villosa* 11.5cm FIELD NOTES: Little known, actions said to be typical of genus. SONG: Series of upward-inflected whistles, *tsi-pui-pui-pui-pui*. CALL: Harsh *schraa-schraa*, a *wip-wip-wip* and a repeated *quir-quir*. HABITAT: Coniferous forests, 780–2600m.

3 KRÜPER'S NUTHATCH *Sitta kruepri* 12.5cm FIELD NOTES: Black forehead less pronounced on female. When agitated, sits upright flicking wings. SONG: Various trills, *pip-pip-pip-pip…*, *veet-veet-veet…* or *yu-di - yu-di - yu-di - yu-di…*. CALL: Low *cha*, often repeated, also a *pwit* and *dui*. HABITAT: Coniferous forests, from sea-level to 2500m.

4 CORSICAN NUTHATCH *Sitta whiteheadi* 12cm FIELD NOTES: Feeds tit-like among branches, or feeds by hovering or fly-catching. SONG: Rapid, quavering *hididididid…* and an ascending *dew-dew-dew…*, sometimes combined. CALL: *pu* often repeated, a thin *tsi-tsi-tsi* and nasal *pink*; *chay-chay-chay* when agitated. HABITAT: Corsican Pine, mainly 1000–1500m.

5 ALGERIAN NUTHATCH *Sitta ledanti* 13.5cm FIELD NOTES: Actions as Corsican Nuthatch, though not thought to fly-catch. SONG: Fluty *quair-di - quair-di - quair-di…*, a fast *du-wid-du-wid-du-wid…* or faster *vid-vid-vid-vid…*. CALL: Various; a soft *kna*, *quuwee*, a rasping *schrr-shrr-schrr* and a loud *chwa-chwa-chwa*. HABITAT: Mainly Atlas Oak and cedar, above 1450m.

6 RED-BREASTED NUTHATCH *Sitta canadensis* 11.5cm (Vagrant) FIELD NOTES: Active; usually feeds high in trees. SONG: Quavering *tee-you-you-you*. CALL: Nasal *kng-kng-kng* or *yaaa-yaaa-yaaa*. HABITAT: In native N America: coniferous and mixed woodland.

7 WHITE-CHEEKED NUTHATCH *Sitta leucopsis* 13cm FIELD NOTES: Shy, feeds in treetops. SONG: Prolonged, rapid, wailing squeaks. CALL: *kner-kner* or *nit-nit*. HABITAT: Coniferous forest, 2100–4575m, slightly lower in winter. RACES: *S. l. przewalskii* (fig 7b) W China.

8 WHITE-TAILED NUTHATCH *Sitta himalayensis* 12cm FIELD NOTES: Usually in upper branches. SONG: Fast, rising *dwi-dwi-dwi…* or similar, also a slow *tui-tui-tui-tui*. CALL: Includes *nit*, *chak*, *shree* and a *chak-kak*, which may be repeated as *chic-kak-ka-ka-ka-ka*. HABITAT: Mainly oak and rhododendron forests, 1800–3500m. Lower in winter.

9 NUTHATCH (EURASIAN NUTHATCH) *Sitta europaea* 14cm FIELD NOTES: Agile feeder on main tree trunks or larger branches; in winter, often visits bird-tables or nut feeders. SONG: Variable, from a slowish *pee-pee-pee…* to a rapid *wiwiwiwiwiwiwi….* CALL: Liquid *dwip* or *dwip-dwip*, a shrill *sirrrr*, a harsh *trah* and a thin *tsee-tsee-tsee*. HABITAT: Mainly deciduous or mixed forest, also parks and large gardens. RACES: *S. e. caesia* (fig 9b) W and C Europe, N Mediterranean; *S. e. asiatica* (fig 9c) Russia, N Asia, N Japan; *S. e. sinensis* (fig 9d) W and S China.

10 KASHMIR NUTHATCH *Sitta cashmirensis* 14cm FIELD NOTES: Actions much as Nuthatch. SONG/CALL: *tsi-tsi*, a rapid *pee-pee-pee-pee*; also a harsh *kraaa*. HABITAT: Mainly mixed forests of oak, spruce and pine, 1800–3500m.

11 CHESTNUT-VENTED NUTHATCH *Sitta nagaensis* 13cm FIELD NOTES: Often feeds on ground. SONG: Rapid *chichichichichi…* or a slower *chi-chi-chi-chi-chi-chi….* CALL: *sit* or *sit-sit*, a *quir* and *tsit*, which is often repeated. HABITAT: Evergreen, pine and mixed forests.

12 EASTERN ROCK NUTHATCH *Sitta tephronota* 15cm FIELD NOTES: More arboreal than Rock Nuthatch. SONG: Very similar to Rock Nuthatch. CALL: Like Rock Nuthatch but generally louder, lower and slower. HABITAT: Rocky mountain slopes, cliffs and gorges.

13 ROCK NUTHATCH (WESTERN ROCK NUTHATCH) *Sitta neumayer* 13cm FIELD NOTES: Restless, feeds on ground as well as rocks. Often perches upright. SONG: Loud trill, *iti-tit tuit-tuit-tuit-tuit….* CALL: *chik*, a harsh *charr*, a screeching *creea*, and a trill resembling main song. HABITAT: Rocky slopes, gorges, etc., in dry or arid areas. RACES: *S. n. tschitscherini* (fig 13b) W Iran

51 WALLCREEPER, TREECREEPERS AND WHITE-EYES

1 WALLCREEPER *Tichodroma muraria* 16.5cm FIELD NOTES: Wary. Flicks wings open to reveal red and white markings. SONG: Slow, drawn-out piping, *tu-tuee-zreeeeeeu* or *chewee-cheweeoo*. CALL: Rapid twitter, a buzzing *zree*, a short *tui* and *chup*. HABITAT: Cliff and rock faces up to 3000m. In bad weather often forced lower to streamsides, sea cliffs and large buildings.

2 BAR-TAILED TREECREEPER (HIMALAYAN TREECREEPER) *Certhia himalayana* 14cm FIELD NOTES: Forages by climbing up tree trunks and along branches; occasionally feeds on ground or by fly-catching. SONG: Lilting *tsee-tsu-tsu-tsut-tut-ti-lee* or *ti-ti-tu-du-du-du-du*; also a longer *tsee-tsui-tsui-tsui-tsui-tsui-tsui-tsui-tsui-tsuip*. CALL: Thin *tsui*, sometimes given as a descending series, also *tsee* and a rising *tseet*. HABITAT: Mainly coniferous forest, 2000–3700m.

3 RUSTY-FLANKED TREECREEPER (NEPAL OR STOLICZKA'S TREECREEPER) *Certhia nipalensis* 14cm FIELD NOTES: Forages among mosses and plants on trunks and branches. SONG: High-pitched accelerating trill. CALL: Thin *sit*. HABITAT: Forests of oak or mixed oak and rhododendron, fir and hemlock with understorey of dwarf bamboo, 1980–3600m.

4 BROWN-THROATED TREECREEPER (SIKKIM TREECREEPER) *Certhia discolor* 14cm FIELD NOTES: Actions typical of genus. SONG: Monotonous *chit-it-it-it-it-it-it-it-it-it…* or similar. CALL: Explosive *tchip*, a high *tsit* and a rattling *chi-r-r-it*. HABITAT: Mature broadleaved evergreen and deciduous forests.

5 SICHUAN TREECREEPER *Certhia tianquanensis* 14cm FIELD NOTES: Actions typical of genus. Forages on trunks and branches in the upper storey. SONG/CALL: Said to be very different from others of genus? HABITAT: Stands of mature, open conifer, 2500–2830m.

6 TREECREEPER (EURASIAN TREECREEPER) *Certhia familiaris* 12.5cm FIELD NOTES: Typically feeds by climbing tree trunks and large branches. Some of the western and central races have underparts very similar to those of Short-toed Treecreeper. SONG: *tsee-tsee-tsi-tsi-si-si-si-sisisisi* or similar. CALL: High-pitched, often repeated *tsrree*; also a sharp *tsee*. HABITAT: Deciduous and mixed woodland, occasionally in pure conifer forests.

7 SHORT-TOED TREECREEPER *Certhia brachydactyla* 12.5cm FIELD NOTES: Actions as Treecreeper. SONG: Series of loud, plaintive whistles, *seet-seet-seet-e-roi-deitt* or similar. CALL: Explosive, shrill *zeet*, often given as a rapid series, also a tremulous *tsrree* like Treecreeper, but lower. HABITAT: Deciduous, mixed and coniferous woodland, parks, orchards and large gardens.

8 BONIN HONEYEATER (BONIN WHITE-EYE) *Apalopteron familiare* 13.5cm FIELD NOTES: Feeds on fruits of papaya, acacia, etc., and various flowers. SONG: A melodious warble. CALL: Soft *pee-you*, *weet* and *pit*, an explosive *tit-tit*, a harsh *weet-weet* and a *zhree-zhree*. HABITAT: Secondary forest, forest edge, bushes, plantations and gardens.

9 JAPANESE WHITE-EYE *Zosterops japonicus* 11cm FIELD NOTES: Forages restlessly through treetop foliage. SONG: Sweet, melodious and varied. CALL: Thin, twittering *tsee-tsee*. HABITAT: Thickets and undergrowth in deciduous and mixed woodland and forest edge.

10 ABYSSINIAN WHITE-EYE (WHITE-BREASTED WHITE-EYE) *Zosterops abyssinicus* 12cm FIELD NOTES: Actions as Japanese White-eye. SONG: Squeaky and descending slurs in a random series. CALL: Soft, fine *tilu* or *teuu*, and a low *waouw*. HABITAT: Trees (mainly acacia), wooded mountain slopes and gardens.

11 ORIENTAL WHITE-EYE (INDIAN OR SMALL WHITE-EYE) *Zosterops palpebrosus* 10cm FIELD NOTES: Actions as others of genus. SONG: Wispy, made up of slurred call notes. CALL: Twittering *dzi-da-da* or metallic *dza-dza*. HABITAT: Primary and secondary vegetation.

12 CHESTNUT-FLANKED WHITE-EYE (RED-FLANKED WHITE-EYE) *Zosterops erythropleurus* 12cm FIELD NOTES: Actions typical of genus. SONG/CALL: Twittering *dze-dze*. HABITAT: Primary and secondary forests, usually above 1000m.

52 SUNBIRDS AND FLOWERPECKERS

1 PYGMY SUNBIRD *Anthreptes platurus* 10cm (male with tail 16cm) FIELD NOTES: Active agile forager after insects, spiders and nectar. SONG: Soft, silvery trilling, like a weak Skylark song. CALL: *cheek* or *cheek-cheek*. HABITAT: Acacia scrub, open woodlands and gardens.

2 NILE VALLEY SUNBIRD *Anthreptes metallicus* 10cm (male with tail 16cm) FIELD NOTES: Actions as Pygmy Sunbird. Often in small parties in non-breeding season. SONG: High-pitched warble, *pruüit-prruüit-pruüit-tiririri-tiririri*. CALL: Grating *pee* or *pee-ee*. HABITAT: Scrub, usually acacia, also gardens.

3 PURPLE SUNBIRD *Nectarinia asiatica* 10cm FIELD NOTES: Actions as other sunbirds. Feeds mainly on flower nectar. Erects yellow/orange pectoral tufts during display. SONG: Repeated *cheewit-cheewit*. CALL: *dzit-dzit* and *tsweet*. HABITAT: Dry forests, riverside vegetation, thorn scrub, cultivation and gardens with large trees.

4 SHINING SUNBIRD *Nectarinia habessinica* 13cm FIELD NOTES: Typical sunbird, active and agile. SONG: Fast, fluty, trilling and whirring *tuu-tuu-tuu-tuu-vita-vita-vita-vita-du-du-du-du* often ends in Wren-like trill. CALL: Hard *tshak*, *dzit* or *chewit-chewit*, also a fast, dry *tje-tje-tje-tje* HABITAT: Flowering trees and plants on hills, slopes and coastal cultivation.

5 PALESTINE SUNBIRD *Nectarinia osea* 11cm FIELD NOTES: Typical sunbird actions and habits. Erects orange pectoral tufts during display. SONG: Fast, rambling, high-pitched trill, *dy-vy-vy-vy-vy-vy*, or rising *tveeit-tveeit-tveeit* or similar, often ending in Serin-like trill. CALL: Variable, includes a thin *ftift* and a hard *tsak*, also a loud *te-weeit-teweeit* and a Siskin-like *tiu*. HABITAT: Well-vegetated wadis, river banks, acacia savannah and gardens.

6 MRS GOULD'S SUNBIRD *Aethopyga gouldiae* 10cm (male with tail 15cm) FIELD NOTES: Actions and habits similar to other sunbirds. Often feeds on rhododendron and rubus. SONG/CALL: Lisping *squeeee* that rises in middle, also a quickly repeated *tzip* and a rattling alarm HABITAT: Montane evergreen forest, up to 4300m.

7 GREEN-TAILED SUNBIRD *Aethopyga nipalensis* 10cm (male with tail 15cm) FIELD NOTES: Actions and habits similar to other sunbirds. SONG: Described as *tchiss...tchiss-iss-iss* CALL: Loud *chit-chit*. HABITAT: Mossy forests of oak, rhododendron, etc., in moist valleys, 1800–3600m.

8 FIRE-TAILED SUNBIRD *Aethopyga ignicauda* 10cm (male with tail 18cm) FIELD NOTES: Actions and habits similar to other sunbirds. Aggressive to other sunbirds when feeding at flowering bushes. SONG: Monotonous *dzidzi-dzidzidzidzi*. CALL: Quiet *shweet*. HABITAT: Open coniferous forest with thick undergrowth of rhododendron or other flowering bushes, on or above tree line.

9 YELLOW-BELLIED FLOWERPECKER *Dicaeum melanoxanthum* 12cm FIELD NOTES: Elusive. Agile feeder with liking for mistletoes; also makes fly-catching sallies. SONG/CALL: Harsh, agitated *zit-zit-zit*. HABITAT: Evergreen forest edge and clearings, 1400–4000m.

10 FIRE-BREASTED FLOWERPECKER (BUFF-BELLIED FLOWERPECKER) *Dicaeum ignipectus* 9cm FIELD NOTES: Lively forager among parasitic *Loranthus*. SONG: High-pitched chittering, *titty-titty-titty*. CALL: Clicking *chip*. HABITAT: Hill forests, 800–2200m.

11 THICK-BILLED FLOWERPECKER *Dicaeum agile* 9cm FIELD NOTES: Twitches tail from side to side. Actively forages among foliage, especially attracted to parasitic *Loranthus*. SONG/CALL: Sharp, metallic *chik-chik-chik*. HABITAT: Deciduous or semi-evergreen forests. Altitudinal wanderer to region.

53 SHRIKES

1 ROSY-PATCHED SHRIKE *Rhodophoneus cruentus* 23cm FIELD NOTES: Mainly terrestrial although often perches on bush tops. Usually located by song. SONG/CALL: Monotonous, duetted *twee-u-twee-u-twee-u…* or *tswee-ur - tswee-ur - tswee-ru…*. HABITAT: Acacia and thorn scrub in arid regions.

2 BLACK-CROWNED TCHAGRA (BLACK-HEADED BUSH SHRIKE) *Tchagra senegala* 22cm FIELD NOTES: Usually secretive as it clambers through bushes. Hops on ground with tail raised. SONG: Given from perch or during display-flight, a series of descending whistles, *wheee-wooo-wuuu…*. CALL: Harsh *grrr*; a rapid *ter-rac-rac* when alarmed. Also recorded is a trilled *truit-truit-drirriririvivir*. HABITAT: Riverside scrub, thickets and groves, also large gardens with dense bushes.

3 ISABELLINE SHRIKE *Lanius isabellinus* 17cm FIELD NOTES: Usually perches prominently on bush tops or other vantage points from where it can pounce on large insects or small vertebrates. In flight, shows white flashes at base of primaries. Most prey taken on ground but will take some flying insects in the air. Impales prey items. SONG: Babbling and warbling that contains mixture of melodious whistles and harsh notes. Very similar to Red-backed Shrike. CALL: Similar to Red-backed Shrike. HABITAT: Arid areas with scattered bushes, cultivation edge and bushy areas in lowlands and hills. RACES: *L. i. phoenicuroides* (Red-tailed Shrike) (figs 3b & 3c) West part of range.

4 BROWN SHRIKE *Lanius cristatus* 17cm FIELD NOTES: Actions and habits similar to Isabelline Shrike. SONG: Like Red-backed Shrike, but less rich and varied. CALL: Harsh *chr-r-ri* or *cheh-cheh-cheh*. HABITAT: Open cultivation, open mixed forest of birch and spruce or larch, forest edge and forest stands along steppe rivers. RACES: *L. c. lucionensis* (fig 4b) Parts of N and E China, Korea and Japan.

5 TIGER SHRIKE (THICK-BILLED SHRIKE) *Lanius tigrinus* 17cm FIELD NOTES: Usually perches more in cover of tree foliage than other *Lanius* species. Catches most prey from tree leaves and branches. SONG: Resonant and musical. CALL: *tcha-tcha-tcha-tcha* and *tchik*. HABITAT: Open forest, forest edge, forest clearings, cultivated country with trees and suburban parks.

6 RED-BACKED SHRIKE *Lanius collurio* 17cm FIELD NOTES: Actions and habits similar to Isabelline Shrike. In flight, shows grey rump. SONG: Subdued, jerky warbling, which includes mimicry of other birds. CALL: Hard *shack* or *shak-shak* and a harsh *churruck-churruck*. HABITAT: Woodland edge and clearings, open country with scattered trees and bushes, hedgerows, heathland, orchards, parks and gardens. RACES: *L. c. kobylini* (fig 6b) Crimea to Iran.

7 BAY-BACKED SHRIKE *Lanius vittatus* 18cm FIELD NOTES: Actions and habits typical of genus. Often aggressive towards other shrikes. In flight, shows pale grey rump and white flashes at base of primaries. SONG: Pleasant loud warble interspersed with mimicry of other birds. CALL: Scolding *chur-r* or *chee-urr*. HABITAT: Open rocky country with scattered trees and scrub.

8 BULL-HEADED SHRIKE *Lanius bucephalus* 19cm FIELD NOTES: Actions and habits much as others of genus. In flight, shows white flashes at base of primaries. SONG: Loud and Marsh Warbler-like, consisting of clear whistles and mimicry of other birds and insects, e.g. cicadas. CALL: Chattering *ju-ju-ju* or *gi-gi-gi*, a trilling *kürrrririri* and a short *kew* repeated 3 or 4 times when a male first notices a female. HABITAT: Light hill forest, tree-lined meadows, light riverine forests. In the Kuril Islands and Japan, frequents clearings in taiga forest and bamboo as well as cultivated areas with scattered trees, roadside trees and shrubs, parks and gardens.

54 SHRIKES AND WOODSWALLOW

1 LONG-TAILED SHRIKE *Lanius schach* 24cm FIELD NOTES: Conspicuous and noisy, other actions and habits typical of genus. In flight, shows rusty rump and white flashes at base of primaries. SONG: Metallic warble interspersed with mimicry of other bird calls. CALL: Sharp, harsh *chakerek*, *rrrre*, a *tchick* and a buzzing *grennh*. HABITAT: Open woodland, thickets, tall scrub, hedgerows, cultivation edge, orchards and gardens. RACES: *L. s. tricolor* (Black-headed Shrike) (fig 1b) Nepal, part of WC China.

2 GREY-BACKED SHRIKE (TIBETAN SHRIKE) *Lanius tephronotus* 22cm FIELD NOTES: Actions and habits typical of genus. SONG: Similar to Long-tailed Shrike, sustained for several minutes. CALL: Harsh grating notes, typical of genus. HABITAT: Forest clearings, mountain meadows with small trees or bushes, open high-altitude scrub, 2700–4500m.

3 GREY-BACKED FISCAL SHRIKE *Lanius excubitoroides* 25cm FIELD NOTES: Gregarious, usually in parties of up to 20. Confiding. In flight, shows white patches at base of primaries and large black tip to white-sided tail. Feeding actions and habits much as others of genus. SONG/CALL: Very varied: *kyoir-l - kyoi - kyo-ooh*, also screaming and chattering notes when moving from tree to tree. HABITAT: Wooded savannah, woodland, open bush with scattered thorn trees.

4 LESSER GREY SHRIKE *Lanius minor* 20cm FIELD NOTES: Actions and habits typical, although tends to use hovering more than others of genus. In flight, shows white patches at base of primaries. SONG: Long babbling chatter that includes mimicry of birds and mammals, e.g. dogs. CALL: *kerrib-kerrib*, a warning *tscheck-tscheck* sometimes accompanied by a *tr-tr-tr-trrr*. HABITAT: Open country with scattered trees and bushes, woodland edge, orchards, vineyards and parks.

5 GREAT GREY SHRIKE (NORTHERN SHRIKE) *Lanius excubitor* 24cm FIELD NOTES: Perches prominently, often using same vantage point for long periods. Feeds mainly on small vertebrates, especially voles. In flight, shows large white patches at base of primaries. SONG: *trrr-turit-trrr-turit*…. CALL: Ringing *shreee*; also an often repeated nasal *shack*. HABITAT: Various types of open country with scattered trees, bushes or scrub. RACES: *L. e. meridionalis* (Southern Grey Shrike) (fig 5b) S France, Iberia, often considered a full species; *L. e. pallidirostris* (Steppe Grey Shrike) (fig 5c) C Asia, winters in Middle East.

6 CHINESE GREY SHRIKE (LONG-TAILED GREY SHRIKE) *Lanius sphenocercus* 29cm FIELD NOTES: Actions and habits similar to Great Grey Shrike. In flight, shows large white wing-bar. SONG: Repetition of 2 melodious notes, *tschriii*, the first lower in pitch. CALL: Harsh, nasal *tscheee*. HABITAT: Open country with scattered trees and bushes, open steppe and semi-deserts. In Japan, frequents cultivated plains, open woodland and reclaimed land.

7 MASKED SHRIKE (NUBIAN SHRIKE) *Lanius nubicus* 17cm FIELD NOTES: Often perches partly hidden. Usually feeds in typical shrike fashion, although will often take flying insects by making aerial sallies. In flight, shows large white patches at base of primaries. SONG: Long, chattering warble. CALL: Various harsh notes, including *keer-keer-keer*. HABITAT: Open woodland, woodland edge, bushy hillsides, orchards and olive groves.

8 WOODCHAT SHRIKE *Lanius senator* 18cm FIELD NOTES: Actions and habits typical of family. In flight, shows a pale rump and large white patch at base of primaries. SONG: Warble, containing harsh and musical notes with some mimicry. CALL: Rattling *trr-trr-trr*, a *gek-gek-gek*; also a short *crex* and a *kwikwik*. HABITAT: Open woodland, woodland edge, scrubby hillsides, farmland with hedges, orchards and groves.

9 WHITE-BREASTED WOODSWALLOW *Artamus leucorynchus* 18cm (Vagrant) FIELD NOTES: Gregarious, many perch together on same bare branch. Makes sallies after flying insects. SONG: Chattering that includes some mimicry of other bird calls. CALL: Rasping *wek-wek-wek* and a sharp *pirt-pirt*…. HABITAT: In native SE Asia: open areas with scattered trees.

55 JAYS AND GROUND JAYS

1 JAY (EURASIAN JAY) *Garrulus glandarius* 34cm FIELD NOTES: Wary, harsh alarm calls and white rump, as bird flies from tree to tree, is often the first sign of bird's presence. SONG: Quiet, often unnoticed warble. CALL: Harsh *skaaaak-skaaaak*; also a weak *piyeh*. HABITAT: Deciduous, mixed and coniferous forests, parks and large gardens. RACES: *G. g. atricapillus* (fig 1b) Iraq, W Iran; *G. g. cervicalis* (fig 1c) E Algeria, Tunisia; *G. g. bispecularis* (fig 1d) W Himalayas; *G. g. japonicus* (fig 1e) N Japan; *G. g. hyrcanus* (fig 1f) N Iran; *G. g. brandtii* (fig 1g) NE Russia, C and NE Asia.

2 LIDTH'S JAY *Garrulus lidthi* 38cm FIELD NOTES: Sociable bird, often forms large parties in winter. Juvenile much duller than adult, especially chestnut areas, lacks white tips to wing and tail feathers. SONG/CALL: Harsh, variously pitched *kraah*. HABITAT: Coniferous, deciduous and mixed forest.

3 LANCEOLATED JAY (BLACK-THROATED JAY) *Garrulus lanceolatus* 33cm FIELD NOTES: Actions much like Jay when feeding in forest, also recorded feeding on scraps around isolated houses and villages. SONG: Quiet mewing, whistling and bubbling notes interspersed with some mimicry. CALL: Very like Jay. HABITAT: Montane forests, 1500–3000m.

4 SIBERIAN JAY *Perisoreus infaustus* 30cm FIELD NOTES: Usually wary, though will visit forest picnic sites. Recorded hanging upside-down, feeding in tit-like manner. SONG: Various quiet whistles, trills and creaky notes, with some mimicry. CALL: Harsh *hearrr-hearrr*, a hoarse *skaaaak* and a Buzzard-like mewing note. HABITAT: Mainly dense coniferous forest; in the far north may frequent birch forest.

5 SICHUAN JAY *Perisoreus internigrans* 30cm FIELD NOTES: Can be inquisitive, but usually unobtrusive. SONG/CALL: High *kyip-kyip*, sometimes repeated to make longer series; also a Buzzard-like mewing note. HABITAT: Steep mountainside spruce and pine forests, 3350–4300m.

6 HENDERSON'S GROUND JAY (MONGOLIAN GROUND JAY) *Podoces hendersoni* 28cm FIELD NOTES: Shy. Ground feeder, digging for seeds and insects. Usually runs; when put to flight, shows conspicuous white primary wing-patch. SONG/CALL: Poorly recorded. Harsh whistles and *clack-clack-clack*, said to sound like a wooden rattle. HABITAT: Flat stony or gravel desert with scattered trees.

7 BIDDULPH'S GROUND JAY (WHITE-TAILED GROUND JAY) *Podoces biddulphi* 28cm FIELD NOTES: Shy, actions typical of genus. In flight, shows white wing-patch, white trailing edge to secondaries and a mainly white tail. SONG/CALL: *chui-chui-chui*, last syllable higher than rest; also a succession of low whistles in a rapidly descending scale. HABITAT: Sandy wastes and semi-deserts with scattered trees.

8 PANDER'S GROUND JAY (GREY GROUND JAY) *Podoces panderi* 25cm FIELD NOTES: Feeding actions typical of genus. In flight, wings appear mainly white. SONG/CALL: Ringing *chweek-chweek-chweek*. HABITAT: Sandy deserts with scattered Saxaul shrubs.

9 PLESKE'S GROUND JAY (PERSIAN GROUND JAY) *Podoces pleskei* 24cm FIELD NOTES: Little studied, actions suspected to be much as Pander's Ground Jay. In flight, shows large white wing-patch and white trailing edge to secondaries. SONG/CALL: Clear, rapid, high-pitched *pee-pee-pee-pee-pee*…. HABITAT: Sandy desert with scattered shrubs.

10 HUME'S GROUND-PECKER (LITTLE, TIBETAN OR HUME'S GROUND JAY) *Pseudopodoces humilis* 19cm FIELD NOTES: Can be very confiding but usually shy and wary. Looks and acts very like a wheatear. SONG/CALL: Short *chip* followed by rapid, whistled *cheep-cheep-cheep-cheep*, also a feeble *cheep*. HABITAT: Open grassy steppe and plains with scattered boulders and bushes, above tree line.

56 MAGPIES, NUTCRACKER AND CHOUGHS

1 AZURE-WINGED MAGPIE *Cyanopica cyanus* 34cm FIELD NOTES: Sociable, small family parties in breeding season, larger parties in winter. SONG/CALL: Shivering *screep*, often uttered by roving parties, also a harsh chatter, a sharp *wee-wee-wee-u*; a harsh *karrah* when alarmed, often followed by a series of *kwink* notes. HABITAT: Mixed and deciduous woodland, forest edge, parks and large gardens. RACES: *C. c. cooki* (fig 1b) Spain, Portugal.

2 GOLD-BILLED MAGPIE (YELLOW-BILLED BLUE MAGPIE) *Urocissa flavirostris* 63cm FIELD NOTES: Usually in pairs or small parties. Feeds both on trees and on the ground. Juveniles of eastern race *U. f. cucullata* (not shown) have the white nape patch extended as a streak onto the crown, recalling Blue Magpie. SONG/CALL: Varied, including mimicry, transcribed as *bu-zeep-peck-peck-peck*, *pop-unclear*, *pu-pu-weer* and a high *clear-clear*. HABITAT: Deciduous and mixed mountain forests, 1600–2700m, descending slightly in winter.

3 BLUE MAGPIE (RED-BILLED BLUE MAGPIE) *Urocissa erythrorhyncha brevivexilla* 66cm FIELD NOTES: Social, mainly arboreal bird. Often feeds in canopy of fruiting fig trees. SONG/CALL: Various: metallic, repeated *penk* given in flight, others being transcribed as a piercing *quiv-pig-pig*, a softer, repeated *beeee-trik*, a low *kluk* and a sharp *chwenk-chwenk*. HABITAT: Foothills with temperate and subtropical evergreen forests.

4 MAGPIE (BLACK-BILLED MAGPIE) *Pica pica* 45cm FIELD NOTES: Usually in pairs or small parties. Mainly a ground feeder; will raid bird nests for eggs and young, also recorded riding on domestic cattle to feed on ectoparasites. SONG/CALL: Chattering *chack-chack-chack-chack*; also *ch-chack*. HABITAT: Very varied, including open woodland, lightly wooded open country, farmland, parks, gardens, villages and towns. RACES: *P. p. mauretanica* (fig 4b) NW Africa; *P. p. asirensis* (fig 4c) W Saudi Arabia.

5 NUTCRACKER (SPOTTED NUTCRACKER) *Nucifraga caryocatactes* 32cm FIELD NOTES: Usually shy and wary, although irruptive wanderers can be quite confiding. Feeds both in trees and on ground. SONG: Quiet, musical, piping, whistling, clicking, squeaking and whining notes, interspersed with some mimicry. CALL: Dry *kraaaak*, often repeated to form a discordant rattle, also a weak *zhree*. HABITAT: Conifer or conifer-dominated mixed forest. Vagrants often in any location where there are trees, not necessarily conifers. RACES: *N. c. multipunctata* (Larger-spotted Nutcracker) (fig 5b) NW Himalayas. Regarded by some authors as a full species.

6 ALPINE CHOUGH *Pyrrhocorax graculus* 38cm FIELD NOTES: Very sociable, often in large flocks. Scavenges around mountain resorts. SONG/CALL: Rolling *churr*, rippling *preeep* and a descending, thin, whistled *sweeeeoo*. HABITAT: High mountain pastures, with rocky ravines and cliffs, above the tree line. A little lower in winter, often around ski resorts and villages.

7 CHOUGH (RED-BILLED CHOUGH) *Pyrrhocorax pyrrhocorax* 38cm FIELD NOTES: Sociable, forms large winter flocks. Ground feeder. Mountain breeder, often consorting with Alpine Choughs. Juveniles have yellowish bill so can resemble Alpine Chough. SONG/CALL: *chee-aw* and slight variants, e.g. *ker-ker-ker*. HABITAT: Mountains and mountain pastures, rocky coasts and coastal pastures in British Isles and Brittany.

57 JACKDAWS, CROWS, ROOK AND RAVENS

1 JACKDAW (WESTERN JACKDAW) *Corvus monedula* 34cm FIELD NOTES: Sociable, often forming large flocks, regularly associates with other crows and starlings. SONG/CALL: Abrupt *chjak* often repeated 7 or so times, also a low, drawn-out *chaairurr* accompanied by *chak*. HABITAT: Open country with scattered trees, including farmland and parkland, also towns and villages, and coastal and inland cliffs. RACES: *C. m. soemmerringii* (fig 1b) E Europe and Asia.

2 DAURIAN JACKDAW *Corvus dauuricus* 32cm FIELD NOTES: Actions very similar to Jackdaw. Some juveniles very like adult Jackdaw, but always has dark eye. SONG/CALL: Similar to Jackdaw. HABITAT: Mainly meadows with stands of trees, often near habitation.

3 COLLARED CROW *Corvus torquatus* 54cm FIELD NOTES: Little recorded, said to be less of a scavenger than Carrion Crow. Sometimes forms mixed flocks with Large-billed Crow. SONG/CALL: More hoarse, less rolling, than Carrion Crow; a loud *kaaarr*, also a *kaar-kaar*. HABITAT: Open lowland cultivation with scattered trees, farmland, parks and large gardens, also edges of towns and villages.

4 PIED CROW *Corvus albus* 48cm FIELD NOTES: Often scavenges around human habitation and rubbish dumps. SONG/CALL: Harsh *karrh-karrh-karrh*; also a knocking *kla-kla-kla*. HABITAT: Open country with scattered trees, cultivation, also around towns and villages.

5 HOUSE CROW (INDIAN HOUSE CROW) *Corvus splendens* 40cm FIELD NOTES: Bold very sociable, usually found around human habitations. SONG/CALL: Flat, dry *kaaa-kaaa*. HABITAT: Villages, towns and cities, often in and around ports.

6 CARRION CROW *Corvus corone* 49cm FIELD NOTES: Usually in pairs or small groups. Scavenger. SONG/CALL: Vibrant *kraaa*, often repeated, sometimes a hollow *konk-konk*. HABITAT: Farmland, open woodland, parks, large gardens, coastal cliffs and moorland. RACES: *C. c. cornix* (Hooded Crow) (fig 6b) N and E Europe; *C. c. capellanus* (Mesopotamian Crow) (fig 6c) S Iraq, SW Iran. Both these subspecies are considered by some as full species.

7 ROOK *Corvus frugilegus* 47cm FIELD NOTES: Sociable, both in nesting and feeding. Eastern race, *C. f. pastinator* (not shown), has pale bill base but lacks bare white face. Juvenile lacks bare face and pale bill base. SONG/CALL: Dry *kraah* and higher pitched *kraa-a*. Also cawing, chuckling, gurgling and clicking noises. HABITAT: Mainly agricultural land with stands of trees.

8 LARGE-BILLED CROW *Corvus macrorhynchos* 49cm FIELD NOTES: Scavenger, usually in pairs or small groups but will form larger flocks at good food sources and roosts. SONG/CALL: Loud, dry *kaaa-kaaa* and various single, hoarse, musical notes. HABITAT: Woodland and forest edge, in riverine valleys in the north and forests up to the tree line in the Himalayas, also town and city parks.

9 FAN-TAILED RAVEN *Corvus rhipidurus* 47cm FIELD NOTES: In flight, distinctly short-tailed. Often in quite large gatherings. Regularly associates with Brown-necked Ravens. SONG/CALL: High-pitched *craah-craah*, also guttural croaks, quiet high-pitched croaks, squeals, trills and clucks. HABITAT: Desert cliffs and ravines with nearby oases.

10 RAVEN (COMMON OR NORTHERN RAVEN) *Corvus corax* 62cm FIELD NOTES: In flight, shows distinctive wedge-shaped tail. Generally wary but will scavenge around human settlements. Often forms large flocks, especially at communal roosts. SONG/CALL: Deep, hollow croaking *pruk-pruk-pruk*, plus various other notes, e.g. *kraa*, *toc-toc-toc* and a guttural rattle. HABITAT: Very varied: mountains, coastal cliffs, open woodland, forests, etc.

11 BROWN-NECKED RAVEN *Corvus ruficollis* 53cm FIELD NOTES: Desert counterpart of the Raven. Small gatherings form at feeding locations, which often include rubbish dumps, larger ones often occur at communal roosts. SONG/CALL: Dry, rising *aarg-aarg-aarg* and an abrupt croak. All calls appear to be less harsh than those of Raven. HABITAT: Arid desert and semi-desert plains and foothills, also around oases and human settlements.

126

58 STARLINGS

1 TRISTRAM'S STARLING *Onychognathus tristramii* 25cm FIELD NOTES: Gregarious, noisy and fairly tame, often seen at picnic areas. In flight, shows bright orange/red primaries. SONG/CALL: Parties keep up a constant flow of wolf-whistle-like notes, *dee-oo-ee-o* or *o-eeou*; also a mewing *vu-ee-oo*. HABITAT: Rocky hills and ravines, semi-desert and various urban areas.

2 VIOLET-BACKED STARLING (AMETHYST STARLING) *Cinnyricinclus leucogaste* 18cm FIELD NOTES: Often in small parties. Fairly shy, feeds mainly in trees. SONG: Loud, gurglin warble. CALL: Long, ringing, grating, musical squeal with a rising inflection, ending in a quiet chuckle. Chuckle also used when flushed. HABITAT: Plains, hills and wadis with trees.

3 WHITE-SHOULDERED STARLING (CHINESE OR GREY-BACKED STARLING) *Sturnus sinensis* 18cm (Vagrant) FIELD NOTES: Gregarious, noisy, often congregates to feed in fruiting trees. SONG: Not described. CALL: Harsh squawks and squeals. HABITAT: In native S China, open country, scrub and urban areas.

4 DAURIAN STARLING (PURPLE-BACKED STARLING) *Sturnus sturninus* 17cm FIELD NOTES: Mainly arboreal, very gregarious, winter flocks can reach up to 100. SONG: Rich and varied, more melodious than Starling. CALL: Soft *squerhh*; also harsh whistling and whickering notes. HABITAT: Open deciduous woodland, willow thickets, groves and villages.

5 CHESTNUT-CHEEKED STARLING (RED-CHEEKED STARLING) *Sturnus philippensis* 17cm FIELD NOTES: Mainly arboreal. Forms flocks of up to 50 birds during winter. SONG: Babbling, made up of call notes. CALL: *airr* or *tschairr*; a piercing *tshick* and a soft *chrueruch* in flight. HABITAT: Open, mixed deciduous woodland, agricultural areas and urban parks.

6 BRAHMINY STARLING (PAGODA MYNA) *Sturnus pagodarum* 19cm FIELD NOTES: Usually in pairs or small family groups; forms larger flocks in winter. Mainly a ground feeder. SONG: Musical, rambling warble, transcribed as *gu-u-weerh-kwurti-kwee-ah*. CALL: Various croaking and chattering notes; short grating 'churrs' when alarmed. HABITAT: Open deciduous forest, cultivated areas and around human habitations.

7 ROSE-COLOURED STARLING (ROSY STARLING) *Sturnus roseus* 21cm FIELD NOTES: Gregarious at all times. Juvenile pale grey/brown above, dirty buff below, wings dark. Bil pale. SONG: Mix of harsh chattering and melodious warbling. CALL: Various, e.g. harsh, rattling *chik-ik-ik-ik* or *qwik-ik-ik-ik*, a throaty *chrrt-chrrt* and *tchirr*. HABITAT: Open grassland, farmland, grassy slopes with scattered rocks; disperses to wooded areas, including orchards and vineyards.

8 RED-BILLED STARLING (SILKY STARLING) *Sturnus sericeus* 22cm (Vagrant) FIELD NOTES: Gregarious in winter with flocks of 100+ recorded. Feeds on ground and in trees. SONG: Sweet and melodious. CALL: Flocks chatter, much like Starling. HABITAT: In native S China, hill country and cultivated areas with scattered trees; also scrub, groves and gardens.

9 STARLING (COMMON OR EUROPEAN STARLING) *Sturnus vulgaris* 22cm FIELD NOTES: Gregarious at all times, forms very large winter flocks. Mainly a ground feeder. Juvenile grey/brown above, slightly paler below, especially on throat. Bill dark. SONG: Medley of clicks, creaks, chirrups, warbles, etc., interspersed with drawn-out whistles and mimicry. CALL: Various, e.g. a harsh *tcheerrr*, a hard *kyik* and a grating *schaarh*. HABITAT: Varied, including farmland, woodland edge, parkland, coastal cliffs, orchards, gardens, villages, towns and cities

10 SPOTLESS STARLING *Sturnus unicolor* 22cm FIELD NOTES: Actions and habits similar to Starling. Usually in smaller flocks. Juvenile blackish above and below. SONG: Starling-like, perhaps more melodious. CALL: As Starling. HABITAT: Similar to Starling.

11 WHITE-CHEEKED STARLING (GREY STARLING) *Sturnus cineraceus* 22cm FIELD NOTES: Gregarious at all times, forms large winter flocks. Mainly a ground feeder. SONG/CALL: Monotonous, creaking *chir-chir-chay-cheet-cheet….* HABITAT: Cultivated fields, pastures, open woodland, parks, towns and cities.

59 MYNAS, WATTLED STARLING, OXPECKER, DRONGOS AND ORIOLES

1 ASIAN PIED STARLING (ASIAN PIED MYNA) *Sturnus contra* 24cm (Vagrant) FIELD NOTES: Gregarious in winter. SONG: Similar to Common Myna but more melodious. CALL: *cheek-cheurk* and a descending *treek-treek-treek*. HABITAT: In native India and SE Asia: open, usually moist areas with scattered trees, often near cultivation and human settlements.

2 BANK MYNA *Acridotheres ginginianus* 22cm FIELD NOTES: Gregarious, often tame. Juvenile browner. SONG: Tuneless gurgles and whistles. CALL: *wheek* used as contact or flight note; a raucous note when agitated. HABITAT: Towns, villages, grassy areas, rubbish dumps, etc.

3 COMMON MYNA (INDIAN MYNA) *Acridotheres tristis* 23cm FIELD NOTES: Tame, often a pest. SONG: Tuneless mixture of gurgling and whistled phrases. CALL: A querulous *kwerrh* and many gurgling and chattering notes; a drawn-out *traaahh* when alarmed. HABITAT: Around human habitations; also open, lightly wooded country.

4 CRESTED MYNA (CHINESE JUNGLE MYNA) *Acridotheres cristatellus* 24cm FIELD NOTES: Usually in flocks, feeding on ground. Sometimes forms large winter flocks that roost colonially. In flight, shows white flashes at bases of primaries. SONG/CALL: Similar to Common Myna, but more whistled, less fluty. HABITAT: Open country, cultivated areas, suburban parks and gardens.

5 WATTLED STARLING *Creatophora cinerea* 21cm (Vagrant) FIELD NOTES: Gregarious. Ground feeder. In flight, shows pale rump. SONG/CALL: High, squeaky *tsirrit-tsirrit-tseep - seeet-seeereeet*, a harsh *graaaah* when alarmed, and a harsh 3-syllable flight note. HABITAT: In native Africa, open bush and savannah.

6 RED-BILLED OXPECKER *Buphagus erythrorhynchus* 20cm (Vagrant) FIELD NOTES: Clambers about on mammals to feed. Juvenile has dark bill and dark skin around eye. SONG/CALL: Hissing *krissss-krissss* or buzzing *zzhaaaaa*, also *tsee-tsee-tsee-tsee-tsee* and a harsh *tzik-tzik-tzik*. HABITAT: In native Africa: broad-leaved and acacia savannah woodland.

7 BLACK DRONGO *Dicrurus macrocercus* 30cm FIELD NOTES: Sits upright in prominent position from which it makes fly-catching sallies. In flight, shows translucent primaries. SONG/CALL: *cheece-ti* or *cheece-titi* given in noisy duets, also a harsh *ti-tiu* and *cheece-cheece-chichuk*. HABITAT: Open deciduous forest, cultivations and around human habitations.

8 HAIR-CRESTED DRONGO (SPANGLED DRONGO) *Dicrurus hottentottus* 31cm FIELD NOTES: Feeds mainly on nectar. Aggressive to other feeders. Often among mixed feeding parties. SONG/CALL: Loud *chit-wiii*, the rising *wiii* often given singly. HABITAT: Deciduous and evergreen forests.

9 ASHY DRONGO *Dicrurus leucophaeus leucogenis* 30cm FIELD NOTES: Perches on bare branches, makes sallies after flying insects. SONG: Loud, clear *huur-uur-cheluu* or *wee-peet - wee-peet*. CALL: Variable, e.g. wheezy notes, chattering, shrill whistles and mimicry. HABITAT: Open woodland and forest edge, 600–2500m.

10 BLACK-NAPED ORIOLE *Oriolus chinensis* 26cm FIELD NOTES: Arboreal, usually stays hidden in foliage. SONG: Liquid, fluty *luwee - wee - wee-leeow* or similar. CALL: Harsh, scolding note and a plaintive whistle. HABITAT: Open woodland, plantations, parkland, etc.

11 SLENDER-BILLED ORIOLE *Oriolus tenuirostris* 25cm FIELD NOTES: Has been treated as a race of Black-naped Oriole, hence habits similar. SONG/CALL: Typical fluty notes, but also a diagnostic, high-pitched *kich*. HABITAT: Pine forests, open woods, plantations and open country with scattered trees.

12 GOLDEN ORIOLE *Oriolus oriolus* 24cm FIELD NOTES: Arboreal. Usually stays hidden in foliage. SONG: Mellow fluty whistle, *weela-weeoo*. CALL: Harsh *kweeaahk* and a fast *gigigigigi*. HABITAT: Mainly oak, poplar or ash woodland, groves, parks and large gardens.

60 SPARROWS

1 HOUSE SPARROW *Passer domesticus* 15cm FIELD NOTES: Common visitor to feeding stations. Probably one of the most well-known birds in the world. SONG: Excited series of mostly call notes, *chirrup-chirrup-cheep-chirp-chirrup…*, etc. CALL: Various, e.g. *chirrup*, *chirp*, *chissick*, a soft *swee-swee*; rolling *chur-r-r-it-it-it* when alarmed. HABITAT: Anywhere around habitations; often feeds well away from buildings. RACES: *P. d. indicus* (Indian Sparrow) (fig 1b) Saudi Arabia, S Iran eastward.

2 SPANISH SPARROW *Passer hispaniolensis* 15cm FIELD NOTES: Often wary, otherwise actions much as House Sparrow. SONG: Like House Sparrow but slightly higher and more metallic. CALL: Like House Sparrow but higher or more metallic, including *chweing-chweing*, a squeaky *cheela-cheeli* and a *chirrup* that is deeper than that of House Sparrow. HABITAT: Open hilly country, farmland, groves, thickets, urban and suburban areas, usually where House Sparrow is absent. RACES: *P. h. italiae* (Italian Sparrow) (fig 2b) Italy, Sicily, Corsica, Malta and Crete.

3 SIND JUNGLE SPARROW *Passer pyrrhonotus* 13cm FIELD NOTES: Sociable, usually in loose flocks of up to 20 or so. SONG: House Sparrow-like but softer with warbling twitters and a high White Wagtail-like note. CALL: House Sparrow-like but softer. HABITAT: Along rivers and swamps with acacia, thorn or tamarisk bushes.

4 IAGO SPARROW *Passer iagoensis* 13cm FIELD NOTES: Actions much as House Sparrow. Social, occurs in small, loose breeding colonies and larger flocks at other times. SONG: Loose series of call notes, e.g. *cheep-chirri-chip-cheep-chirri-chip-chip*. CALL: *chirrp* like House Sparrow but lower, also a nasal *cheesp* or *chew-weep*. HABITAT: Barren, arid country, stony plains, gorges, rocky cliffs, also villages and towns.

5 RUSSET SPARROW *Passer rutilans* 14cm FIELD NOTES: Actions similar to House Sparrow. SONG: Frequently repeated *cheep-chirrup-cheweep* or *chwe-cha-cha*. CALL: *cheeep* or *chilp*, also *swee - swee*; a rapid *chit-chit-chit* when alarmed. HABITAT: Open oak, rhododendron or alder woodland in mountain and upland areas, scrub near cultivation; villages and towns where House Sparrow is absent. RACES: *P. r. cinnamomeus* (Cinnamon Sparrow) (fig 5b) Himalayas, Tibet.

6 TREE SPARROW (EURASIAN TREE SPARROW) *Passer montanus* 14cm FIELD NOTES: Habits similar, although a little more retiring, to House Sparrow, with which it often mixes when feeding. SONG: Typically, rapidly alternating high and low call notes, including distinctive *tsooit*, *tsveet* and *tswee-ip*. CALL: Similar to House Sparrow, but higher pitched and more abrupt. HABITAT: Open and lightly wooded country, cultivation, hedgerows, parks and gardens; villages and towns, usually when House Sparrow is absent.

7 DEAD SEA SPARROW *Passer moabiticus* 12cm FIELD NOTES: Wary. Colonial breeder, occurs in loose flocks in breeding season and larger flocks at other times. Feeds on ground and in small trees. SONG: Rhythmic, high-pitched *tweeng-tweeng-tweeng*, *trirp-trirp-trirp* or similar. CALL: High-pitched *trrirp*, a *chet-chet-chet-chet* or similar, also the usual sparrow chirp, 'churrs' and rattles; a *chi-vit* in flight. HABITAT: Tamarisk, poplars or other thick scrub near water.

61 SPARROWS

1 SAXAUL SPARROW *Passer ammodendri* 15cm FIELD NOTES: Wary, often stays hidden in foliage of Saxaul or other shrubs. In winter, regularly forms mixed flocks with House, Spanish and Tree sparrows. SONG/CALL: Melodic chirps and a short whistle. HABITAT: Oases and river beds in deserts and foothills, usually with Saxaul, tamarisks or poplar thickets nearby, also at edge of desert settlements. RACES: *P. a. stoliczkae* (fig 1b) W China.

2 DESERT SPARROW *Passer simplex* 14cm FIELD NOTES: Shy and retiring, spends good deal of time hidden, especially in high heat of the day, usually in tops of palm trees. Ground feeder. SONG: Greenfinch-like musical trill. CALL: Soft *chup*, high-pitched *chip-chip* and usual House Sparrow-like *chirps*. HABITAT: Sandy plains with scattered trees or scrub, oases, wadis and in and around human settlements.

3 SUDAN GOLDEN SPARROW *Passer luteus* 13cm FIELD NOTES: Actions typical of genus. Highly gregarious. Breeds colonially. SONG: Repetition of call notes, *chirp-chirp-chirp*. CALL: *chirp*, *schilp* or *tchirrup* and, in flight, a rhythmic *che-che-che*. HABITAT: Arid scrub, often near cultivation.

4 ARABIAN GOLDEN SPARROW *Passer euchlorus* 13cm FIELD NOTES: Highly gregarious, breeds and roosts colonially, forms small flocks in breeding season and much larger flocks in non-breeding season. SONG/CALL: Flocks give a constant, whispering twitter, also noted is a subdued *chirp*. HABITAT: Arid thorn and acacia savannah; in non-breeding season, in cereal crops and on edges of towns.

5 PALE ROCKFINCH (PALE ROCK OR HILL SPARROW) *Carpospiza brachydactyla* 14cm FIELD NOTES: Ground feeder. In non-breeding season, often in very large flocks. May be misplaced in rock sparrow group; it would appear to have much morphology in common with the finches. SONG: Distinctive, rising buzzing, somewhat like a cicada, *tss-tss-tss-tsseeeeeeei* or *tee-zeeeze-zeeezeeei*. CALL: High, nasal *twee*, *zweee* or *twee-oo*, also a soft trill or *churr* in flight. HABITAT: Grassy plains and hillsides with rocky outcrops, arid, stony semi-deserts, wadis and sometimes in cultivation.

6 CHESTNUT-SHOULDERED PETRONIA (YELLOW-THROATED SPARROW) *Petronia xanthocollis* 14cm FIELD NOTES: On ground looks like a finch, especially female Chaffinch. In non-breeding season, often in large flocks, also forms mixed flocks with House Sparrows and Black-headed Buntings. SONG: Long series of chirping notes, *chilp-chalp…* or *chilp-chalp-cholp….* CALL: Soft, liquid *cheep*, *chilp* or *chirrup*. HABITAT: Various wooded habitats, including dry forests, jungles, scrub, date groves and gardens.

7 BUSH PETRONIA (LESSER ROCK SPARROW) *Petronia dentata* 13cm FIELD NOTES: Often sits for long periods in top of tree or bush. Usually feeds in bushes or trees, less so on ground. SONG: Fast twittering *triup-triup-triup-triup* or bunting-like *chu-chu-chu-chu*. CALL: Soft *chewee* flight note. HABITAT: Wadis and terraced slopes with scattered trees, 650–1700m.

8 ROCK SPARROW (ROCK PETRONIA) *Petronia petronia* 14cm FIELD NOTES: Sociable usually in small groups. Breeds colonially. Mainly a ground feeder. Eastern race, *brevirostris*, has less well-defined head pattern. SONG: Collection of repeated call notes, usually delivered from high vantage point. CALL: Various, vaguely similar to House Sparrow with some added metallic notes, e.g. *cheeooee* or *pee-uoo-ee*, *dliu*, *viep* or *vi-viep*; utters a *sup* or *doui* in flight. HABITAT: Various, including barren hills and mountain regions with rocky outcrops, gorges, ravines, desert edge, vineyards, villages and, in winter, farmland.

62 SNOWFINCHES AND WEAVERS

1 THERESA'S SNOWFINCH *Montifringilla theresae* 14cm FIELD NOTES: Little known. Ground feeder. In winter, joins flocks of Snowfinches, Horned Larks and Rock Sparrows. SONG/CALL: Undescribed. HABITAT: High mountains, open stony hillsides and plateaux.

2 BLANFORD'S SNOWFINCH (PLAIN-BACKED SNOWFINCH) *Montifringilla blanfordi* 15cm FIELD NOTES: Quite confiding. Runs mouse-like when foraging on ground. Has a stiff-winged, hovering display-flight. In winter, forms large flocks that include other snowfinches, sparrows and finches. Juvenile lacks black head markings. SONG/CALL: Constant, rapid twittering, given in flight and on ground, otherwise generally silent. HABITAT: Dry, stony steppes and hillsides with stunted grass. Usually associated with pika colonies.

3 RUFOUS-NECKED SNOWFINCH (RED-NECKED SNOWFINCH) *Montifringilla ruficollis* 15cm FIELD NOTES: Confiding. Elaborate display-flight that includes rushing and buzzing noises. In winter often mixes with other snowfinches. Juvenile lacks black head markings. SONG/CALL: Soft *duuid* or *doooid*; Magpie-like chattering when alarmed. HABITAT: High, barren, stony steppes, rolling grassy plateaux, rocky ravines and gullies, also rubbish tips. Has a close association with pika colonies.

4 PÈRE DAVID'S SNOWFINCH *Montifringilla davidiana* 15cm FIELD NOTES: Forms large winter flocks, which often feed around settlements, that can become quite tame. Juvenile lacks black head markings. SONG/CALL: Undescribed. HABITAT: Stony mountains and semi-desert with sparse grass, usually close to water. Closely associated with pika colonies.

5 ADAMS' SNOWFINCH (TIBETAN OR BLACK-WINGED SNOWFINCH) *Montifringilla adamsi* 17cm FIELD NOTES: Ground feeder. Very elaborate courtship-flight with somersaults, vertical drops, wing-claps and stiff-winged flight. Often in very large winter flocks. Juvenile lacks black bib and white inner secondaries. SONG: Single note repeated monotonously. CALL: Sharp *pink-pink* and a soft mewing note. Flocks keep up a constant twittering. HABITAT: Mountain tops, rocky plateaux, cliffs and rocky slopes often near water, cultivated fields close to villages.

6 WHITE-RUMPED SNOWFINCH (MANDELLI'S SNOWFINCH) *Montifringilla taczanowskii* 17cm FIELD NOTES: Generally shy. Forms large winter flocks, often mixed with Rufous-necked Snowfinches. When landing, has a distinctive bob and bow action of the tail. Lark-like display-flight and a 'drumming' courtship dance on ground. Juvenile lacks black face marks. SONG: Short *duid-ai-duid-duid*…. CALL: Sharp *duid-duid*. HABITAT: High stony plateaux, cold deserts, steppes and marsh edges. Has a close association with pika colonies.

7 SNOWFINCH (WHITE-WINGED SNOWFINCH) *Montifringilla nivalis* 17cm FIELD NOTES: Often tame and confiding. Ground feeder, in small loose flocks; forms larger flocks during winter, often containing other snow- and mountain finches. Has a circular display-flight. SONG: Monotonous *sitticher - sitticher - sitticher*…. CALL: Sharp, nasal *pschieu* or *pchie* often given in flight, also a *tsee*, a soft *pruuk*; a *pchurrt* when alarmed. HABITAT: Rocky slopes and gullies, between the tree line and snowfields of high mountains; often visits the buildings in ski resorts. RACES: M. n. henrici (fig 7b) Tibet, W China; M. n. alpicola (fig 7c) Transcaucasus, Iran, C Asia.

8 STREAKED WEAVER *Ploceus manyar* 14cm FIELD NOTES: Always gregarious. Breeds in colonies; globular nest at tip of reeds. Mainly a ground feeder. Rapid, whirring flight. SONG: Jingling phrases that end in a drawn-out wheeze. CALL: Loud *chirt-chirt*. HABITAT: Reed-beds, papyrus beds and nearby cultivation.

9 RÜPPELL'S WEAVER *Ploceus galbula* 14cm FIELD NOTES: Gregarious, frequently in large flocks, often including sparrows. Breeds colonially, nest suspended from tree branches. SONG: Wheezy chatter, ending in insect-like hiss. CALL: Dry *cheee-cheee*. HABITAT: Savannahs and wadis with acacia or other bushes, also palm groves and crops.

63 WAXBILLS, AVADAVAT, SILVERBILLS, MUNIAS, CUT-THROAT, FIREFINCH AND JAVA SPARROW

1 **COMMON WAXBILL** Estrilda astrild 11cm FIELD NOTES: Very sociable. Forms large non-breeding flocks. Feeds on ground, or acrobatically on grass stems. SONG: Harsh, rising *tcher-tcher-peeee - cher-cher-cher*. CALL: Abrupt *pit*. Flocks keep up a light twittering. HABITAT: Reed-beds, cultivation, grassy areas with trees and bushes.

2 **ARABIAN WAXBILL** Estrilda rufibarba 11cm FIELD NOTES: Social. Feeds on ground or on reed and grass seed-heads, etc. SONG/CALL: Buzzing *dzit*, or similar; a buzzing *chee-chee-chee…* in flight. HABITAT: Reed patches, weedy thickets, rocky hillsides and cultivation.

3 **ORANGE-CHEEKED WAXBILL** Estrilda melpoda 10cm FIELD NOTES: Actions and habits much as Common Waxbill. Juvenile duller, bill black. SONG: Collection of short notes, *de-de-de-sweea - sweea - sweea*, or similar. CALL: High-pitched *sieu*. HABITAT: Cultivation, grassy and weedy areas. Possibly established in France, Spain and Portugal.

4 **RED AVADAVAT (STRAWBERRY FINCH)** Amandava amandava 10cm FIELD NOTES: Sociable, roosts communally. Feeds on ground or on tall grasses. SONG: Weak, high-pitched warble combined with sweeter twittering notes. CALL: Thin *teei* or *tsi*, also various chirps and squeaks. HABITAT: Tall grass, reeds, sugarcane and scrub areas, often near water.

5 **ZEBRA WAXBILL (ORANGE-BREASTED WAXBILL)** Amandava subflava 10cm FIELD NOTES: Actions much as Common Waxbill. SONG/CALL: Short *cheep* or *chirp*; also soft clinking *zink-zink*, usually given in flight. HABITAT: Cultivation, trees and scrub.

6 **INDIAN SILVERBILL** Lonchura malabarica 10cm FIELD NOTES: Sociable. When perched, flicks, waves and spreads tail. SONG: Short, rambling trill. CALL: *cheep*, a soft *seeip*, a trilling *zip-zip* and a harsh *tchwit*. HABITAT: Dry, open grassland with thorn bush and scrub, cultivations.

7 **AFRICAN SILVERBILL** Lonchura cantans 10cm FIELD NOTES: Habits similar to Indian Silverbill. SONG: Rapid repetition of rising and falling single and then slurred double notes. CALL: Similar to Indian Silverbill. HABITAT: Similar to Indian Silverbill.

8 **WHITE-RUMPED MUNIA** Lonchura striata 11cm FIELD NOTES: Highly social. Feeds on ground or on grass seed-heads. SONG: Rising and falling series of twittering notes. CALL: Twittering *tr-tr-tr*, *prrrrit* or *brrt*. HABITAT: Lightly wooded areas, open dry scrub, cultivations and gardens.

9 **SCALY-BREASTED MUNIA (SPOTTED MUNIA OR SPICE FINCH)** Lonchura punctulata 10cm FIELD NOTES: Highly social. SONG: Hardly audible, high, flute-like whistles and low slurred notes. CALL: Harsh *chup* or *tret-tret*; also *kitty-kitty-kitty*, *kit-eeeeee*; *ki-ki-ki-ki-ki-teeee* when alarmed. HABITAT: Grasslands with scrub, forest edge, cultivation, parks and gardens.

10 **CHESTNUT MUNIA (BLACK-HEADED MUNIA)** Lonchura malacca 12cm FIELD NOTES: Social. SONG: Almost inaudible, consists of bill-snapping and 'silent' singing, ending with faint, drawn-out, whistling notes. CALL: Weak *peekt* or *pee-eet*; also a *veet-veet* and a triple *chirp* given in flight. HABITAT: Marsh and swamp edge, reed-beds, grassland and cultivated areas. RACES: *L. m. atricapilla* (fig 10b) Both this and nominate race established in Japan.

11 **CUT-THROAT** Amadina fasciata 11cm (Vagrant) FIELD NOTES: Usually in pairs or small groups. SONG: Low buzzing interspersed with toneless warbling notes. CALL: Various sparrow-like chirps, a plaintive *kee-air*; a thin *eee-eee-eee* in flight. HABITAT: In native Africa: dry bush country

12 **RED-BILLED FIREFINCH (SENEGAL FIREFINCH)** Lagonosticta senegala 10cm FIELD NOTES: Confiding. Mainly ground feeder. SONG: Short twittering phrases. CALL: Low *tweet-tweet*. HABITAT: Dry grassland with scattered bushes and trees, oases and gardens.

13 **JAVA SPARROW** Padda oryzivora 17cm FIELD NOTES: Highly social. Juvenile generally brownish. SONG: Series of bell-like, trilling and clucking notes ending with drawn-out whistle. CALL: *tup*, *t'luk* or *tack*. HABITAT: Mainly in urban and suburban areas.

64 CHAFFINCHES, BRAMBLING, CROSSBILLS AND LINNETS

1 CHAFFINCH *Fringilla coelebs* 15cm FIELD NOTES: Feeds on ground and in tree foliage, also fly-catching sorties. Gregarious in winter, flocks often include other finches and sparrows. SONG: Short accelerating and descending musical notes, *chip-chip-chip-tell-tell-cherry-erry-erry-tissi-cheweeo* or variants. CALL: *pink* or *pink-pink*, a loud *whit* and a wheezy *eeese*; a *tsup* in flight. HABITAT: All types of woodland, heath, farmland with hedges, parks and gardens, stubble fields in winter. RACES: *F. c. africana* (fig 1b) N and NW Africa; *F. c. canariensis* (fig 1c) Canary Islands.

2 BLUE CHAFFINCH *Fringilla teydea* 17cm FIELD NOTES: Habits similar to Chaffinch. SONG: Like Chaffinch, but slower, lacking end flourish. CALL: *chirp* or *chirp-chirp*; also *che-wir* or similar; sometimes a sharp *sipp* in flight. HABITAT: Pine forest, usually with rich undergrowth.

3 BRAMBLING *Fringilla montifringilla* 15cm FIELD NOTES: Actions much like Chaffinch. Sometimes in very large flocks. In flight, shows white rump. SONG: Harsh, monotonous *zweeeee* interspersed with weaker fluty notes and sometimes a rattling trill. CALL: Nasal *tsweek* or *zweee*; *chuk-chuk* in flight. HABITAT: Mixed forests, birch woods, conifer forest edge or clearings, dwarf birch and willow scrub. In winter, often on stubble fields and open weedy ground.

4 TWO-BARRED CROSSBILL *Loxia leucoptera* 16cm FIELD NOTES: Habits and many actions similar to Common Crossbill. SONG: Variable, Siskin-like, buzzing trills with harsh rattles, given from treetop or in circular display-flight. CALL: *glip-glip* or similar, also a nasal *pee*. In flight, a *chut-chut*. HABITAT: Mainly larch and cedar forests.

5 COMMON CROSSBILL *Loxia curvirostra* 16cm FIELD NOTES: Sociable. Often feeds acrobatically, even upside-down, to extract pine seeds. Frequently drinks at small pools. Juvenile generally greyish brown, streaked darker above and below. SONG: Series of call notes leading into *cheeree-cheeree-choop-chip-chip-chip-cheeree* phrase, combined with various trills, twitters and more call notes. CALL: *chip-chip* or similar, also a quieter *chuk-chuk*. HABITAT: Coniferous forests, mainly Scots Pine, larch and spruce, also alders and birch.

6 SCOTTISH CROSSBILL *Loxia scotica* 16cm FIELD NOTES: Actions, habits and juvenile as Common Crossbill. SONG/CALL: Very similar to Common Crossbill. HABITAT: Scots Pine in Scotland's Caledonian pine forest.

7 PARROT CROSSBILL *Loxia pytyopsittacus* 17cm FIELD NOTES: Tends to break off cones, extracting the seeds while holding the cone with a foot; otherwise actions and juvenile similar to Common Crossbill. SONG: Similar to Common Crossbill but deeper and slower. CALL: Much as Common Crossbill but deeper *choop-choop*, *chok-chok*; a *tsu-tsu-tsu-tsu* and a hard *cherk-cherk* when alarmed. HABITAT: Coniferous forests, especially Scots Pine.

8 LINNET *Carduelis cannabina* 13cm FIELD NOTES: White in wings shows well in flight. Often in large winter flocks. Sings from prominent perch or during display-flight. SONG: Lively musical tinkling or twittering interspersed with short trills, drawn-out whistles and twanging notes. CALL: Rapid *tett-tett-terrett* or similar, and a soft *hoooi* or *tsooeet*. HABITAT: Heaths and commons with scattered trees, farmland with hedges and thickets, parks and gardens. In winter, extends to stubble fields and various weedy areas as well as coastal marsh and shoreline.

9 YEMEN LINNET *Carduelis yemenensis* 12cm FIELD NOTES: White wing and tail patches conspicuous in flight. Winter flocks often include Yemen Serin. SONG: Rapid, melodious twittering. CALL: Musical *territ* or *wid-lee-lee* and a soft *vliet*. HABITAT: Highlands, hillsides and wadis, usually with scattered trees or scrub, also various cultivation areas.

10 TWITE *Carduelis flavirostris* 13cm FIELD NOTES: Often quite wary. Ground feeder. Forms large winter flocks. SONG: Like Linnet but harder and interspersed with call notes. CALL: Much as Linnet but with characteristic *tweee*, *chweee* or *chwaiie*. HABITAT: Grassy, rocky mountain and highland areas, moorland and open hillsides. In winter, resorts to lowland pastures, cultivation, coastal salt marshes and waste ground. RACES: *C. f. montanella* (fig 10b) W China.

65 GREENFINCHES, GOLDFINCH AND SISKINS

1 GREENFINCH (EUROPEAN GREENFINCH) *Carduelis chloris* 15cm FIELD NOTES:
Yellow wing- and tail-patches very conspicuous in flight. Often visits garden feeding stations.
Generally sociable, in winter in larger groups, often associating with other finches, sparrows
and buntings. Sings from high perch or during slow, stiff-winged display-flight. SONG: Variable
often starts with dry nasal trill then a rising *teu-teu-teu-teu* interspersed with a *tswee* note.
Sometimes just a repetition of *tswee* note. CALL: A rapid *chichichichichit* or *chill-ill-ill-ill*, single
notes, *chit* or *teu*; a *swee-it* or *tsooeet* when alarmed. HABITAT: Various, including woodland edge
copses, thickets, hedgerows, parks and gardens. In winter, often feeds on stubble fields and
various weedy areas.

2 ORIENTAL GREENFINCH (GREY-CAPPED OR CHINESE GREENFINCH)
Carduelis sinica 14cm FIELD NOTES: Habits and actions similar to Greenfinch. Juvenile pale
buff below streaked darker, and darker buff/brown above streaked darker. Wing pattern as
adult. SONG: Similar to Greenfinch with some coarser notes added, e.g. *kirr* or *korr*. CALL:
Distinct *dzi-dzi-i-dzi-i* in flight, otherwise much as Greenfinch. HABITAT: Woodland edge,
scrub, cultivations and gardens.

3 GOLDFINCH (EUROPEAN GOLDFINCH) *Carduelis carduelis* 14cm FIELD NOTES:
Feeds, often acrobatically, on plant seed-heads, e.g. teasels, sunflowers and thistles. Often in
small groups with larger flocks in winter. Juveniles uniform brown/buff on head, lacking black,
red and white markings. Wing pattern as adult. SONG: Rapid tinkling *tsswit-witt-witt*, combined
with various twittering or buzzing *zee-zee* notes. CALL: Liquid, tinkling *tickelit*, a *tsee-yu* or *pee-uu*
also a harsh *zeez*. HABITAT: Various, including woodland edge, scrub, hedgerows, waste ground,
orchards, parks and gardens. RACES: C. c. caniceps (Grey-crowned Goldfinch) (fig 3b) SC Asia

4 BLACK-HEADED GREENFINCH (TIBETAN OR YUNNAN GREENFINCH)
Carduelis ambigua 14cm FIELD NOTES: Actions very similar to Greenfinch. Occurs in pairs or
small family parties with larger winter flocks. Juvenile lacks dark head and is streaked above
and below. Wing pattern similar to adult. SONG: Similar to Greenfinch but with shrill trills and
a dry *screee* or *treeee-tertrah* added. CALL: Thin *tit-it-it-it-it* and a wheezy *twzyee* or *tzyeee*.
HABITAT: Open conifer or deciduous forests, open hillsides with scattered trees, cultivated areas

5 YELLOW-BREASTED GREENFINCH (HIMALAYAN GREENFINCH) *Carduelis*
spinoides 14cm FIELD NOTES: Most actions as Greenfinch. Often feeds in tops of pines or alders
Usually in pairs or small parties with larger winter flocks. Juvenile similar to juvenile Black-
headed Greenfinch, but paler. Wing pattern similar to adult. SONG: Similar to Greenfinch but
higher pitched. CALL: Similar to Greenfinch, twittering followed by a harsh *dzwee*, also a
sparrow-like *swee-tuu*. HABITAT: Open conifer, oak or rhododendron forests, hillsides,
cultivation, scrub and gardens.

6 SISKIN (EURASIAN SISKIN) *Carduelis spinus* 12cm FIELD NOTES: Social, usually in
small parties often mixed with redpolls or other finches. Feeds actively and acrobatically, to
extract seeds from trees, e.g. conifer, alder and birch, and from thistles and dandelions. A
frequent visitor to garden feeding stations. SONG: Given from treetop or butterfly-like display-
flight, consists of a rapid, undulating series of twittering phrases interspersed with trills and
wheezy notes, ending in a rasping *kreee*. CALL: Plaintive *dlu-ee* or *dlee-u*, also a dry *tet* or *tet-tet*.
In flight, a *tirrillilit*, *twilit* or *tittereee* or similar. HABITAT: Coniferous or mixed woods; in non-
breeding season spreads to streamside trees, hedgerows, gardens, etc.

7 TIBETAN SISKIN *Carduelis thibetana* 12cm FIELD NOTES: Usually in small flocks feeding
in treetops or occasionally on ground, under bushes or scrub. SONG: Nasal buzzing *zeezle-eezle-
eeze* interspersed with various trills. CALL: Soft, dry twittering, with the occasional wheezy
twang. In flight, flocks make a continual noisy twittering. HABITAT: Coniferous and birch forest
with rhododendron understorey, also alder, hemlock and mixed fir forests.

66 REDPOLLS AND SERINS

1 LESSER REDPOLL *Carduelis cabaret* 12cm FIELD NOTES: Actions similar to Redpoll, of which it is often regarded as a race. SONG/CALL: As Redpoll, although flight note said to be higher pitched. HABITAT: Variable, e.g. coniferous, willow, birch and alder woodlands, hawthorn thickets and large gardens.

2 REDPOLL (COMMON REDPOLL) *Carduelis flammea* 13cm FIELD NOTES: Usually in pairs or small parties; larger winter groups often include Siskins and other finches. Feeds on ground or acrobatically on catkins, etc. SONG: Given from perch or circular display-flight: a high trilling combined with rolling and call notes. CALL: Metallic twittering *chuch-uch-uch-uch* and a ringing *tsooeet* or *djueee*. HABITAT: Upland areas in dwarf birch, willow thickets, spruce and juniper.

3 ARCTIC REDPOLL (HOARY REDPOLL) *Carduelis hornemanni* 13cm FIELD NOTES: Actions similar to Redpoll, with which it often associates in winter. SONG/CALL: Very similar to Redpoll. HABITAT: Arctic tundra scrub; in winter, inhabits similar areas to Redpoll.

4 RED-FRONTED SERIN (FIRE-FRONTED SERIN) *Serinus pusillus* 12cm FIELD NOTES: Usually in small groups. Juvenile head rusty brown, lacking red forehead. SONG: Series of long twittering phrases, mixed with trills, rapid whistles and wheezy notes. CALL: Rapid, ringing trill, a soft *dueet* and twittering *bri-ihihihihi*. HABITAT: Rocky mountain slopes with grass and scrub, scattered junipers, stands of conifers and low rhododendrons. Descends in winter.

5 SERIN (EUROPEAN SERIN) *Serinus serinus* 11cm FIELD NOTES: Frequently in small flocks. SONG: Jingling mixture of notes, similar to a high-pitched Corn Bunting song, given from a prominent perch or during stiff-winged display-flight. CALL: Rapid, high-pitched trill, *tirrillilit* or *titteree*; also *tirrup* and *tsooee* or *tsswee*. HABITAT: Woodland edge, pine woods, copses, parks, orchards, cultivations and large gardens.

6 SYRIAN SERIN (TRISTRAM'S SERIN) *Serinus syriacus* 12.5cm FIELD NOTES: Most actions similar to Serin. Forms large, noisy winter flocks. SONG: Fast, Linnet-like twittering, sometimes with buzzing sounds. CALL: Dry, rolling *pe-re-ret* or *tree-der-dee*, a thin *shkeep* and a dry *tearrh* or *tsirr*. HABITAT: Open bushy slopes and light woodland on mountains. Descends in winter to cultivations, vegetated wadis, desert or semi-desert scrub.

7 CANARY (ISLAND OR ATLANTIC CANARY) *Serinus canaria* 13cm FIELD NOTES: Gregarious, often forming large flocks that frequently include other finches. Mainly ground feeder. SONG: Given from a perch or display-flight, similar to domesticated Canary: melodic fluty whistles and trills with some twitters and churrs. CALL: High-pitched *sooee*, *tsooeeet* or *sweee*, often accompanied by a light trill. HABITAT: Almost anywhere with trees or bushes.

8 CORSICAN FINCH *Serinus corsicana* 12cm FIELD NOTES: Actions similar to Citril Finch of which it is often thought to be a race. SONG: Like Citril Finch but more segmented. Also differs by having alternative song of purring, fluty, trumpeting notes. CALL: Similar to Citril Finch. HABITAT: Dry montane scrub, woodland and open vegetation.

9 CITRIL FINCH *Serinus citrinella* 12cm FIELD NOTES: Ground feeder on seeds of weeds and conifers. Perches on trees, bushes and overhead wires. SONG: Siskin or Goldfinch-like short musical phrases interspersed with harsh twittering. CALL: Metallic *tiyie* or *tsi-ew* and *check* or *chwick*. HABITAT: Montane conifer forest edge, rocky slopes with scattered conifers. Descends in winter.

10 ARABIAN SERIN *Serinus rothschildi* 12cm FIELD NOTES: Gently flicks tail. SONG: Slow, rising trill, occasionally followed by a varied musical jingle. CALL: Quiet *tsit-tsit* and a short ripple. HABITAT: Rocky hills and wadis with bushes and trees, also orchards and gardens.

11 YEMEN SERIN *Serinus menachensis* 12cm FIELD NOTES: Actions typical of genus. Tends to flock more than Arabian Serin. SONG: *chew-chee-chee-chwee*. CALL: *teee-oo*. Various flight notes e.g. *dweep*, *twi-twi-twi-twi* and *chirrip-chirrip*. HABITAT: Rocky hillsides with patches of cultivation or bushes, bare country, villages and towns.

67 MOUNTAIN FINCHES, ROSY FINCHES, CRIMSON-WINGED FINCH, DESERT FINCH AND TRUMPETER FINCHES

1 PLAIN MOUNTAIN FINCH (HODGSON'S MOUNTAIN OR ROSY FINCH)
Leucosticte nemoricola 15cm FIELD NOTES: Gregarious at all times, often flies in large, wheeling twisting flocks. Feeds, sparrow-like, on the ground. SONG: Usually given from top of a boulder, a sharp twitter, *rick-pi-vitt* or *dui-dip-dip-dip*. CALL: Soft twitter, *chi-chi-chi-chi*, and a double-noted shrill whistle. HABITAT: Mountains, hillsides and alpine meadows to 5150m. Descends in winter.

2 BRANDT'S MOUNTAIN FINCH (BLACK-HEADED MOUNTAIN FINCH)
Leucosticte brandti 17cm FIELD NOTES: Actions and habits similar to Plain Mountain Finch. SONG: Unknown. CALL: Loud *twitt-twitt*, *twee-ti-ti* or *peek-peek*, and a harsh *churr*. HABITAT: High altitude cliffs and crags, and barren, stony mountain tops, up to 6000m. Descends in winter. RACES: *L. b. haematopygia* (fig 2b) Himalayas, Tibet.

3 SILLEM'S MOUNTAIN FINCH *Leucosticte sillemi* 17cm FIELD NOTES: Almost nothing known. Actions probably much as others of genus. Pale rump probably shows in flight. SONG/CALL: Unknown. HABITAT: Known only from collected area, 5125m in W Tibet.

4 ASIAN ROSY FINCH *Leucosticte arctoa* 16cm FIELD NOTES: Tame. Ground feeder, in pairs or small parties; forms much larger winter flocks. SONG: Slow descending series of *chew* note, given from ground or in display-flight. CALL: *chew* or *cheew* repeated continuously, a dry *pert* and a high-pitched *chirp*. HABITAT: From high mountains to lower areas in winter. RACES: *L. a. giglioli* (fig 4b) Transbaikalia; *L. a. brunneonucha* (fig 4c) E Siberia, Kuril Islands.

5 GREY-CROWNED ROSY FINCH *Leucosticte tephrocotis* 16cm FIELD NOTES: Actions and habits similar to Asian Rosy Finch. SONG/CALL: As Asian Rosy Finch. HABITAT: As Asian Rosy Finch. It may prove that the birds found on Commander Island (Siberia) are not this species but only a subspecies of Asian Rosy Finch.

6 CRIMSON-WINGED FINCH *Rhodopechys sanguinea* 16cm FIELD NOTES: Sociable. Mainly ground feeder. In flight, looks long-winged, and the pink on rump and wings shows well. SONG: Grating, sparrow-like *tchili-tchwilichip*; a *turdel-edel-weep-ou* during display-flight. CALL: Musical *tlweep* or *dewleet*; also a soft, musical *wee-tll-ee* or *wee-tell-er* and a *dy-lit-dy-lit*. HABITAT: Bare mountain slopes, boulder fields, cliffs and gorges, with or without sparse scrub.

7 DESERT FINCH *Rhodopechys obsoleta* 15cm FIELD NOTES: Ground feeder, but frequently perches in trees. Forms small flocks in winter, otherwise usually in pairs. SONG: Repetitive jumble of twittering call notes, harsh trills and rolls. CALL: Soft, purring *prrryv-prrryv* or *prrrt-prrrt*, harsh *turr* and a sharp *shreep*, given in flight. HABITAT: Dry plains with scattered trees and bushes, edges of vineyards. Recorded in some city gardens in C Asia.

8 MONGOLIAN FINCH (MONGOLIAN TRUMPETER FINCH) *Bucanetes mongolica* 15cm FIELD NOTES: Confiding. Ground feeder. Social at all times, forms winter flocks of 20 or so, occasionally with Rock Sparrows and Spanish Sparrows. SONG: Slow *do-mi-sol-mi*. CALL: *djou-voud* or *djouddjou-vou*; also a continual twittering when flocks are feeding. HABITAT: Arid or semi-arid mountain country of crags, ravines and rocky slopes with herbaceous plants and the odd low bush. Descends to lower areas in winter, when often visits cultivations in valleys.

9 TRUMPETER FINCH *Bucanetes githagineus* 15cm FIELD NOTES: Ground feeder. Social at all times with larger winter flocks. Often visits small pools. SONG: Distinctive, drawn-out, nasal buzz, *cheeeeee*, interspersed with twittering, clicks and whistles. CALL: Abrupt *chee* or *chit*; a soft *weechp* in flight. HABITAT: Desert or semi-desert areas, e.g. stony plains, bare rocky hills and wadis.

68 ROSEFINCHES AND PINE GROSBEAK

1 SCARLET FINCH *Haematospiza sipahi* 18cm FIELD NOTES: Feeds in trees and bushes and on ground. Often perches prominently. Forms single-sex flocks in winter. SONG: Clear, liquid *par-ree-reeeeee*. CALL: Loud *too-eee* or *pleeau* and *kwee-i-iu* or *chew-we-ah*. HABITAT: Edges and clearings in montane coniferous forest, also in oak and bamboo forests in winter.

2 ROBOROVSKI'S ROSEFINCH (TIBETAN ROSEFINCH) *Kozlowia (Carpodacus) roborowskii* 17cm FIELD NOTES: Ground feeder, shuffling gait. Little else known. SONG/CALL: Generally silent, apart from a short, plaintive whistle, often repeated as a trill. HABITAT: Barren rocky and alpine steppes, 4500–5400m. Slightly lower in winter.

3 PINE GROSBEAK *Pinicola enucleator* 22cm FIELD NOTES: During breeding season usually unobtrusive, often staying relatively hidden as it clambers about in foliage in search of food. Forms small winter flocks, when less secretive, feeding in berry-bearing trees and shrubs, especially Rowan. SONG: Loud, musical, fluty warble, often sung from top of a conifer. CALL: Explosive, fluty *chulee-woo-chuleewoo* and a low *pew* or *puee*. HABITAT: Northern coniferous and mixed forests, mainly spruce or larch, with rich undergrowth of berry-bearing shrubs. Moves to mostly deciduous trees in winter.

4 CRIMSON-BROWED FINCH (RED-HEADED ROSEFINCH) *Pinicola subhimachalus* 19cm FIELD NOTES: Unobtrusive, feeds low down in bushes or on ground, usually in pairs or small parties. SONG: Bright, varied warble, also *ter-ter-ter*. CALL: Generally silent apart from sparrow-like chirp. HABITAT: Dense juniper or dwarf-rhododendron scrub and open forests, near or above tree line.

5 SINAI ROSEFINCH *Carpodacus synoicus* 15cm FIELD NOTES: Shy and retiring, usually in small ground-feeding parties. Often larger parties at waterholes. SONG: Not well documented, said to be a musical jumble, often containing buzzing notes. CALL: *cheeup* or *chip*, a high *touit* or similar, and a weak *stip*. HABITAT: Arid mountains, foothills, rocky desert, wadis, cliffs and gorges.

6 PALLAS'S ROSEFINCH (SIBERIAN ROSEFINCH) *Carpodacus roseus* 16cm FIELD NOTES: Feeds in trees, bushes or on ground, usually in pairs or small parties with larger winter flocks. SONG: Series of quiet, rising and falling notes. CALL: Generally silent apart from a low, short whistle. HABITAT: Conifer, cedar and birch forests, alpine meadows, shrub thickets and sparse scrub on mountains; cedar groves and scrub-covered hillsides in winter.

7 BLANFORD'S ROSEFINCH (CRIMSON ROSEFINCH) *Carpodacus rubescens* 15cm FIELD NOTES: Mainly ground feeder. Forms small winter flocks of 30 or so birds. Little else known. SONG: Unknown. CALL: Thin, high-pitched *sip* and a series of short, rising and falling notes, *pitch-ew*, *pitch-it*, *chit-it*, *chit-ew*, etc. HABITAT: Open areas in coniferous or mixed conifer and birch forests.

8 GREAT ROSEFINCH *Carpodacus rubicilla* 19cm FIELD NOTES: Wary. Feeds on the ground or in low bushes. Generally occurs singly or in pairs; forms small flocks that often mix with other rosefinches in winter. SONG: Slow, descending *fyu-fyu-fyu-fyu-fyu*, often including some shrill whistles. *C. r. severtzovi*'s song consists of a mournful *weeep* and soft chuckles. CALL: *peu* o *peeu-een*. HABITAT: Alpine meadows, valleys, boulder-strewn areas with shrubby thickets, foothills, etc., 2500–5000m. RACES: *C. r. severtzovi* (Severtzov's Rosefinch) (fig 8b) W China.

9 STREAKED ROSEFINCH (EASTERN GREAT ROSEFINCH) *Carpodacus rubicilloides* 19cm FIELD NOTES: Secretive. Ground feeder, often roosts communally in willows. Frequently mixes with other rosefinches. When alarmed, flicks wings and tail. SONG: Slow, descending *tsee-tsee-soo-soo-soo*, sometimes with first phrase repeated. CALL: Chaffinch-like *twink*, *pink* or *sink*, also a soft *sip* and melancholic *dooid-dooid*. HABITAT: High-altitude rocky slopes, screes, plateaus and hillsides with scrub; often winters in thickets near villages.

69 ROSEFINCHES

1 DARK-BREASTED ROSEFINCH (DARK OR NEPAL ROSEFINCH) *Carpodacus nipalensis* 15cm FIELD NOTES: Shy, feeds in cover or on ground in pairs or small groups, occasionally in larger, single-sex flocks mixed with other rosefinches. SONG: Monotonous chirping. CALL: Plaintive, wailed double whistle, twittering and *cha-a-rr* alarm note. HABITAT: Mixed forests of oak with conifer and rhododendron, also scrub, low bushes and weedy areas above tree line.

2 BEAUTIFUL ROSEFINCH *Carpodacus pulcherrimus* 15cm FIELD NOTES: Feeds on ground or low down in bush or scrub in pairs or small flocks. When alarmed tends to raise short crest and sit motionless in cover until danger has passed. SONG: Unrecorded. CALL: Subdued *trip, trilp* or *trillip*, also a tit-like twitter; in flight, a harsh *chaaannn*. HABITAT: Dwarf oak, juniper and rhododendron scrub and forest edge, on and above the tree line.

3 PINK-RUMPED ROSEFINCH (STRESEMANN'S ROSEFINCH) *Carpodacus eos* 13cm FIELD NOTES: Little known, actions said to be similar to Common Rosefinch. Occurs in small flocks; larger winter flocks often include Beautiful Rosefinches. SONG: Unrecorded. CALL: Forceful *pink* or *tink* and *tsip* or *tsick*, also a harsh *pitrit* and rattling *tvitt-itt-itt*. HABITAT: Open alpine meadows and dry valleys with bushes and scrub.

4 SPOT-WINGED ROSEFINCH *Carpodacus rhodopeplus* 15cm FIELD NOTES: Ground feeder. Often perches prominently on bush tops, but usually shy, otherwise very little else recorded. SONG: Unrecorded. CALL: Usually silent, but occasionally gives loud, Canary-like chirp. HABITAT: Rhododendron scrub and bushes on alpine slopes and meadows. Descends to bamboo, bushes and mixed forest in winter.

5 PINK-BROWED ROSEFINCH *Carpodacus rhodochrous* 14cm FIELD NOTES: Unobtrusive ground feeder, flying up to perch in bushes if disturbed. Usually in pairs, or small, loose flocks in winter. SONG: Sweet and lilting. CALL: Loud *per-lee* or *chew-wee*, and Canary-like *sweet*. HABITAT: Undergrowth of mixed birch and fir subalpine forest, also willows, dwarf juniper, rhododendrons and grassy slopes.

6 VINACEOUS ROSEFINCH *Carpodacus vinaceus* 15cm FIELD NOTES: Feeds low in bushes or on ground. Often sits unobtrusively in a bush or undergrowth for long periods. SONG: Simple, 2sec-long *pee-dee - be - do-do*. CALL: Whiplash-like *pwit* or *zieh*, occasionally repeated several times, also a high-pitched *tip* and a low *tink, pink* or *zick*. HABITAT: Scrubby open hillsides and bamboo forests.

7 DARK-RUMPED ROSEFINCH *Carpodacus edwardsii* 16cm FIELD NOTES: Shy and skulking, feeds on ground under bushes. Flicks wings and tail when anxious. Usually alone or in small parties. SONG: Unrecorded. CALL: Metallic *twink* and rasping *che-wee*, but usually silent. HABITAT: Stands of dwarf rhododendron, juniper and bamboo, also thorny thickets and scrub in alpine meadows or open hillsides.

8 RED-MANTLED ROSEFINCH *Carpodacus rhodochlamys* 18cm FIELD NOTES: Feeds on ground or low down in bushes, usually secretive. Generally in pairs or small groups, occasionally alone in winter. SONG: Unrecorded. CALL: Plaintive, buzzing whistle, *kwee* or *squee*, also a sharp *wir*. HABITAT: Juniper and deciduous forests, bushes or woods in alpine meadows, 2720–4900m. Winters at lower levels, in scrub, rose bushes, cultivation edge, orchards and gardens. RACES: *C. r. grandis* (Blyth's Rosefinch) (fig 8b) W Himalayas.

70 ROSEFINCHES, SPECTACLED FINCH AND GOLDEN-NAPED FINCH

1 COMMON ROSEFINCH (SCARLET ROSEFINCH OR GROSBEAK) *Carpodacus erythrinus* 15cm FIELD NOTES: Skulking, usually feeds in bushes or trees. Solitary, in pairs or small parties, occasionally joins with other finches, sparrows or buntings. SONG: Variable, repeated, fluty, rising and falling *sooee-teeew, weeeja-wu-weeeja, te-te-wee-chew, tiu-wee-tiu*, etc. CALL: Distinctive rising whistle, *ooeet, ueet* or *too-ee*; a sharp *chay-eeee* when alarmed. HABITAT: Variable, e.g. deciduous or mixed woodland, juniper, thorn bushes, thickets, waterside willow scrub, damp bushy meadows, forest edge, orchards, parks, etc. RACES: *C. e. roseatus* (Hodgson's Rosefinch) (fig 1b) Himalayas, Tibet, China.

2 WHITE-BROWED ROSEFINCH *Carpodacus thura* 17cm FIELD NOTES: Tame and confiding. Mainly ground feeder. Usually in pairs or small, loose flocks, sometimes with other rosefinches. SONG: Linnet-like twitter. CALL: Sharp, buzzing *deep-deep-deep-de-de-de-de* or *veh-ve-ve-ve-ve-ve*, also a rapid, piping *pupupipipipi*. HABITAT: High-altitude open forest or forest edge, dwarf rhododendron, juniper and bamboo scrub above tree line. Open hillsides with berberis bushes or scrub in winter.

3 THREE-BANDED ROSEFINCH *Carpodacus trifasciatus* 18cm FIELD NOTES: Lethargic, often sitting immobile for long periods hidden in bushes or trees. Mainly a ground feeder, but also in bushes and trees; especially fond of crab apples. SONG/CALL: Generally silent? No records. HABITAT: Undergrowth and thickets in light coniferous forest, 1800–3000m. Winters at lower elevations in farmland hedges, orchards, bushes, etc.

4 RED-BREASTED ROSEFINCH *Carpodacus puniceus* 20cm FIELD NOTES: Ground feeder, rarely flies far when disturbed. Usually in small parties. SONG: Short *twiddle-le-de*, also warbling CALL: Loud, cheery *are-you-quite-ready*, a cat-like *maaau* and sparrow-like chirp, given in flight. HABITAT: High-altitude rocky screes, glaciers, alpine meadows, dry valleys, etc., 3900–5700m.

5 LONG-TAILED ROSEFINCH *Uragus sibiricus* 17cm FIELD NOTES: Actions can recall Long-tailed Tit: feeds acrobatically, picking at seed-heads, usually singly or in pairs. Juveniles often form small flocks of 12 or so. In flight, wings make *frrrrp-frrrrp* sound. SONG: Various pleasant, rippling trills. CALL: Liquid 3-note warble, *pee-you-een* or *su-we-su-wee-sweeeoo-cheweeoo*, and rising *sit-it-it*. HABITAT: Dense thickets, grassland, wet meadows, woodland with rich undergrowth, riverine woods of pine, birch, alder, willow, larches and poplars. RACES: *U. s. lepidus* (fig 5b) NW China.

6 PRZEWALSKI'S ROSEFINCH (PINK-TAILED ROSEFINCH) *Urocynchramus pylzowi* 16cm FIELD NOTES: Feeds on ground and in bushes, perches on bush tops. Occurs mainly singly or in pairs in breeding season, in winter in small groups of 5–10. SONG: Hurried, chattering *chitri-chitr-tri* or *chitri-chitri-chitri-chitri*. CALL: Clear, ringing *kvuit-kvuit*, otherwise generally silent. HABITAT: Bushes, scrub and alpine thickets usually near water, 3000–5000m.

7 SPECTACLED FINCH (RED-BROWED FINCH) *Callacanthis burtoni* 17cm FIELD NOTES: An unobtrusive feeder of the forest floor or under bushes, feeding mainly on Deodar seeds. Usually in pairs during breeding season, often in flocks of 12 or more out of breeding season. SONG: Loud, trilling *il-til-til…*; also a monotonous, repeated single note, given from a high, bare branch. CALL: Loud *pweee* or *chew-we*, often followed by *pweeu, pweuweu* or *chipeweu*, also a light *chip*; a rising *uh-eh* or *twee-yeh* when alarmed. HABITAT: Subalpine Deodar, birch, rhododendron and fir forests; oak and hemlock forests in winter.

8 GOLDEN-NAPED FINCH (GOLDEN-HEADED OR GOLDEN-CROWNED BLACK FINCH) *Pyrrhoplectes epauletta* 15cm FIELD NOTES: Secretive, keeps to interior of bushes and undergrowth. Small winter flocks often associate with rosefinches. SONG: Rapid, high-pitched *pi-pi-pi-pi*, also a low piping. CALL: Thin, high-pitched, repeated whistle, *teeu, tseu* or *peeuu*, also *pur-lee* and a *plee-e-e*. HABITAT: Undergrowth in high-altitude oak and rhododendron forests.

71 BULLFINCHES

1 BROWN BULLFINCH *Pyrrhula nipalensis* 16cm FIELD NOTES: Confiding, usually in pair or small parties. Feeds mainly in tops of trees and bushes, on buds, seeds and blossoms. Fast, direct flight. Juvenile generally more buff/brown, with buffy wing-bar. SONG: Hastily repeated, mellow *her-dee-a-duuee*, usually rendered from treetop cover. CALL: Mellow *per-lee*, and a soft whistling twitter when feeding. HABITAT: Dense undergrowth or thick forest, especially oak bu also rhododendron and fir, 1350–3300m.

2 ORANGE BULLFINCH *Pyrrhula aurantiaca* 14cm FIELD NOTES: Feeds mainly in bushes and also on ground. Usually quiet and unobtrusive, often sitting motionless for long periods in bushes or trees. Generally alone, in pairs or small flocks. White rump shows well in flight. Juvenile like adult female, except brownish/grey head. SONG: Loud call followed by rapidly repeated, metallic *tyatlinka-tlinka*. CALL: Soft, clear, low-pitched *tew*. HABITAT: Open fir, birch or mixed forest, 2700–3900m.

3 GREY-HEADED BULLFINCH (BEAVAN'S BULLFINCH) *Pyrrhula erythaca* 17cm FIELD NOTES: Can be confiding and approachable, in pairs in breeding season and in small flock during winter. Feeds in bushes, usually low down or on ground. White rump shows well in flight. Juvenile similar to adult female, but head colour uniform with mantle. SONG: Unrecorded CALL: Slow *soo-ee* or *poo-ee*, frequently repeated or given as triple whistle. HABITAT: Mixed coniferous and rhododendron, birch or larch forest, also in willows, poplars, junipers and buckthorn, 2500–4100m. In winter, descends to 2000–3200m, exceptionally to 1700m.

4 RED-HEADED BULLFINCH *Pyrrhula erythrocephala* 17cm FIELD NOTES: Feeds low dow in bushes or on ground, on buds, seeds, catkins and berries. Often sits motionless in bushes for long periods. Generally in pairs or small, often single-sex, parties. Juvenile similar to female, but generally more brown above and buff below, wing-bars buff. SONG: Low, mellow *terp-terp-tee*. CALL: Very similar to Bullfinch: a soft, plaintive *pew-pew*. HABITAT: Dense cedar, pine or juniper forests, also mixed forests that include fir, birch and rhododendron; 2700–4200m.

5 BULLFINCH (COMMON OR EURASIAN BULLFINCH) *Pyrrhula pyrrhula* 16cm FIELD NOTES: Generally wary; often first sign of bird's presence is the melancholic call or flash o white rump as bird flies into cover. Acrobatic feeder in bushes, shrubs or trees and on plant seed-heads, also forages on ground. Usually in pairs or small, loose flocks. Juvenile like female but head lacks dark cap and face, and is basically uniform buff/brown. SONG: Weak, scratchy warble interspersed with soft whistles. CALL: Low, melancholic, piping *peeu, pew, teu, due* or *due-due*. HABITAT: Coniferous and deciduous woodlands with dense undergrowth, hedgerows, thickets, orchards, parks and gardens. RACES: *P. p. griseiventris* (Oriental or Grey-bellied Bullfinch) (fig 5b) NW China, Sakhalin, Korea, S Japan; *P. p. cineracea* (Grey Bullfinch) (fig 5c) W Lake Baikal to N Altai and N Mongolia; *P. p. murina* (Azores Bullfinch) (fig 5d) Azores. All 3 races are often considered full species, or *cineracea* being a race of *griseiventris*, if the latter is regarded as a full species.

72 GROSBEAKS AND HAWFINCH

1 GOLDEN-WINGED GROSBEAK *Rhynchostruthus socotranus percivali* 15cm FIELD NOTES: Feeds on seeds, buds and fruit. Usually occurs singly or in pairs, and in small parties of about 20 in winter. Often inactive, sitting unobtrusively in trees or bushes. Females lack black face and are slightly duller. Juveniles lack dark head markings and are generally browner, streaked darker above and below. SONG: Liquid, musical and jingling phrases, e.g. *whit-whee-c* or *tvit-te-vyt-te-viit*, interspersed with clear, fluty notes. CALL: Very variable, e.g. *wip* or *tzee*, a rippling *tut-tut-tut* or *did-did-ee*, and a soft, often repeated *tlyit*; also a rapid *dy-dy-dy* followed a dry trill. HABITAT: Hills and wadis with euphorbia, acacia or juniper.

2 BLACK-AND-YELLOW GROSBEAK *Mycerobas icterioides* 22cm FIELD NOTES: Feeds mainly in treetop foliage, in pairs or loose flocks. SONG: Rich, clear *prr-trweeet-a-troweeet*; also rich *tookiyu-tuukiyu*. CALL: High-pitched *pi-riu - pir-riu - pir-riu* or *tit-te-tew - tit-te-tew*; also a short *chuck* used as a contact note when feeding. HABITAT: Mainly conifer and Deodar forest, less often in forest-edge oak and scrub.

3 COLLARED GROSBEAK (ALLIED GROSBEAK) *Mycerobas affinis* 22cm FIELD NOTES: Frequents mainly treetops, but freely descends to feed on ground. Usually in pairs or small parties. SONG: Loud, clear, piping whistle, *ti-di-li-ti-di-li-um*, also a constantly repeated, loud, creaky phrase, interspersed with musical bulbul-like notes. CALL: Mellow, rapid *pip-pip-pip-pip-pip-pip-ugh*; a sharp *kurr* alarm note. HABITAT: Oak, rhododendron or mixed conifer an deciduous forests, occasionally in dwarf rhododendrons and juniper above the tree line.

4 SPOT-WINGED GROSBEAK *Mycerobas melanozanthos* 22cm FIELD NOTES: Shy; usuall sits and feeds in treetops, also feeds lower down or on ground. Generally in pairs or flocks of 3 or so. SONG: Loud, melodious whistle, *tew-tew - teeeu*; also some mellow whistles, *tyop-tiu* or *tyu-tio*. CALL: Rattling *krrr* or *charrarauk*, said to sound like the shaking of a matchbox containing only a few matches. When feeding, flocks keep up a constant cackling. HABITAT: Mixed or evergreen forest mainly of fir and birch, hemlock or maple.

5 WHITE-WINGED GROSBEAK *Mycerobas carnipes* 22cm FIELD NOTES: Feeds mainly in treetops but also in scrub and undergrowth. Generally in pairs or small flocks; larger flocks in winter. SONG: *add-a-dit - un-di-di-di-dit* or similar. CALL: Squawking *add-a-dit*, *wit* or *wet*; a nasal *shwenk* contact note. HABITAT: Fir and mixed forest, also juniper and scrub near or above the tree line.

6 YELLOW-BILLED GROSBEAK (CHINESE GROSBEAK) *Eophona migratoria* 18cm FIELD NOTES: Feeds in trees, often hidden in foliage, and on ground. Usually in pairs; bigger floc during migration. SONG: Various whistles and trills, said to be Linnet-like. CALL: Loud *tek-tek*. HABITAT: Woodlands, mainly oak, birch, alder and beech, also orchards, parks and gardens.

7 JAPANESE GROSBEAK *Eophona personata* 20cm FIELD NOTES: Secretive. Feeds in the treetops, in pairs or small flocks. Juvenile browner than adults and lacks black cap. SONG: Series of 4 or 5 fluty, whistled notes. CALL: Hard *tak-tak*. HABITAT: Mature deciduous and mixe woods in valleys and on hillsides, also parks and gardens.

8 HAWFINCH *Coccothraustes coccothraustes* 17cm FIELD NOTES: Wary. Feeds in trees, or o ground below tall trees, in pairs or small groups; sometimes in large flocks in E of range. SONG Seldom heard, bunting-like *deek-waree-ree-ree* or *tchee-tchee-turr-wee-wee*. CALL: Abrupt *tick c tzik*, also a thin *seep* or *sreee*. HABITAT: Deciduous and mixed woodlands, orchards and parks; h a fondness for hornbeams. More open areas with bushes in winter.

9 EVENING GROSBEAK *Hesperiphona vespertina* 20cm (Vagrant) FIELD NOTES: Usually gregarious. Feeds in trees and frequently visits garden feeding stations, especially in winter. SONG: Rambling, erratic warble ending with a whistle. CALL: Loud *clee-ip* or *cleer*. HABITAT: In native N America: coniferous and mixed forests, woods and copses; in winter, often visits parks and suburban gardens.

73 AMERICAN WOOD-WARBLERS

1 YELLOW WARBLER *Dendroica petechia* 13cm (Vagrant) FIELD NOTES: Agile active feeder in trees and bushes, and on ground. SONG: High-pitched *sweet-sweet-sweet-I'm-so-swee* CALL: Musical *tship* and a high, buzzy *zzee* flight note. HABITAT: In native N America: thickets, especially willow and alder near water, bushy areas including gardens.

2 CHESTNUT-SIDED WARBLER *Dendroica pensylvanica* 13cm (Vagrant) FIELD NOTES: Agile feeder at low to medium levels in shrubs and lower branches of trees. SONG: Transcribe as *pleased-pleased-pleased-to-meecha*. CALL: Husky *tchip*; a rough *zeet* flight note. HABITAT: In native N America: bushy undergrowth, thickets, woodland edge.

3 BLACK-THROATED GREEN WARBLER *Dendroica virens* 13cm (Vagrant) FIELD NOTES: Actions typical of genus. Usually feeds in tree canopy. SONG: Husky *zeee-zeee-zee-zo-ze* CALL: High, thin *sit*, often repeated. HABITAT: In native N America: open coniferous and mixe woodland, woodland edge and thickets.

4 BLACK-THROATED BLUE WARBLER *Dendroica caerulescens* 13cm (Vagrant) FIELD NOTES: Active feeder, from understorey to canopy. SONG: Wheezy *zweea-zweea-zweea-zwee*. CALL: A dull *stip*; a metallic *twik* in flight. HABITAT: In native N America: mature deciduous and mixed woodland with rich understorey.

5 CAPE MAY WARBLER *Dendroica tigrina* 13cm (Vagrant) FIELD NOTES: Active forager treetops. SONG: High *seet-seet-seet-seet*. CALL: Thin, very high *tsip* and a slightly descending *ts tsee*, often given in flight. HABITAT: In native N America: coniferous and mixed forest; all type of woodland frequented on migration.

6 BLACKBURNIAN WARBLER *Dendroica fusca* 13cm (Vagrant) FIELD NOTES: Forages actively, mainly high in canopy. SONG: High and thin, ending in an ascending trill. CALL: Sha *tsip* and a buzzy *seet* flight note. HABITAT: In native N America: coniferous and mixed forest; o migration, found in all types of woodland and tall bushes.

7 YELLOW-RUMPED WARBLER (MYRTLE WARBLER) *Dendroica coronata* 14cm (Vagrant) FIELD NOTES: Typical actions of genus. Feeds in low vegetation and bushes as well as treetops. SONG: Slow trill, *uwee-tuwee-tuwee-tuwee-tuwee…*, which often changes pitch at the end. CALL: Sharp *chek* and a thin *tsee* flight note. HABITAT: In native N America: open conifer and mixed woodland; out of breeding season frequents hedgerows, thickets and gardens.

8 MAGNOLIA WARBLER *Dendroica magnolia* 13cm (Vagrant) FIELD NOTES: Active and agile feeder in tree foliage at low to mid-levels. SONG: Short, musical *weety-weety-wee* or *weet weety-weety-wee*; last note is occasionally higher. CALL: Full *tship* or *dzip*, also a harsh *tshekk*; a buzzy *zee* in flight. HABITAT: In native N America: young conifer stands; on migration, found other woodland, thickets and tall scrub.

9 PALM WARBLER *Dendroica palmarum* 14cm (Vagrant) FIELD NOTES: Mainly ground feeder. Hops, does not run or walk. SONG: Series of buzzy *tsee* notes. CALL: Sharp *chek*, *tick* or su a high *seep* flight note. HABITAT: In native N America: spruce and larch bogs; in non-breeding season inhabits woodland, hedgerows, thickets, gardens, etc.

10 BLACKPOLL WARBLER *Dendroica striata* 14cm (Vagrant) FIELD NOTES: Constantly on move. SONG: High-pitched *sit-sit-sit-sit-sit-sit…*; notes are on one pitch with the middle or more emphasised. CALL: Loud *smack* and high *seet*. HABITAT: In native N America: coniferous forest; in non-breeding season frequents a wider range of woodland, also thickets and scrubb or bushy areas.

11 BAY-BREASTED WARBLER *Dendroica castanea* 14cm (Vagrant) FIELD NOTES: Feeds from middle to high levels. SONG: Series of high *si* notes on one pitch. CALL: High-pitched *sip see*. Sometimes gives a loud *chip*. HABITAT: In native N America: open conifer, mixed forests with birch and maple; after breeding, uses any type of woodland.

♀

♂

♂ n-br

2

♂ br

♀

3

♂

♀

4

♂

n-br

5

♂ br

♂ n-br

6

♂ br

n-br

7

♂ br

♂ n-br

8

♂ br

-br

9

♂ br

♂ n-br

10

♂ br

♀ br

♂ n-br

NA

11

♂ br

74 AMERICAN WOOD-WARBLERS

1 CERULEAN WARBLER *Dendroica cerulea* 12cm (Vagrant) FIELD NOTES: Active and agile, feeds mainly in tree canopy. SONG: Short, accelerating series of buzzy notes ending in a high buzzy trill. CALL: Sharp *chip*; loud *zzee* flight note. HABITAT: In native N America: mature, open deciduous or mixed forest, often near swamps.

2 NORTHERN PARULA (PARULA WARBLER) *Parula americana* 11cm (Vagrant) FIELD NOTES: Very agile, often hanging upside-down; forages in tree canopy. SONG: Ascending, buzzing trill, ending with abrupt *tship*. CALL: Abrupt *chip*; weak *tsif* flight note. HABITAT: In native N America: all woodland types, usually near water.

3 GOLDEN-WINGED WARBLER *Vermivora chrysoptera* 12cm (Vagrant) FIELD NOTES: Very agile, often feeding tit-like in bushes and trees. Probes dead leaf clumps for insects. SONG: Soft, buzzy *zee-bee-bee-bee*, occasionally more trilling. CALL: Short *tchip*. HABITAT: In native N America: bushy pastures, woodland edge and clearings, also thickets close to water.

4 TENNESSEE WARBLER *Vermivora peregrina* 12cm (Vagrant) FIELD NOTES: Usually forages high in tree canopy. Active and agile. SONG: Loud, staccato series of double and single notes ending in a trill. CALL: Sharp *tsit* and a thin *see*. HABITAT: In native N America: coniferous and mixed woodland; on migration occurs in open woodland, thickets and scrubby areas.

5 YELLOWTHROAT (COMMON YELLOWTHROAT) *Geothlypis trichas* 13cm (Vagrant) FIELD NOTES: Skulking forager in thick vegetation, usually in damp areas. Often cocks tail. SONG: Loud *wichity-wichity-wichity-wich* or softer *wee-too - wee-too - wee-too - wee-too*. CALL: Dry *chep* or *tchuk*. HABITAT: In native N America: thick waterside vegetation, also dry bushy pastures, woodland edge and regenerating woodland.

6 AMERICAN REDSTART *Setophaga ruticilla* 13cm (Vagrant) FIELD NOTES: Very active, regularly makes fly-catching sallies after flying insects. SONG: Variable *tsee-tsee-tsee-tsee-sir*, the last note of which can be up- or down-slurred; also a *teetsy-teetsy*. CALL: *chip*, *tsip* or *chick*, and a thin *tzit*; a *sweet* flight note. HABITAT: In native N America: open deciduous and mixed woodland, especially second growth, woodland edge, clearings, tall bush and thickets.

7 WILSON'S WARBLER *Wilsonia pusilla* 12cm (Vagrant) FIELD NOTES: Active, constantly flicks wings and tail. SONG: Staccato *chi-chi-chi-chi-chi-chet-chet* that drops in pitch at end. CALL: Sharp *chip* or *chet*; a hard *tlik* or *tsip* in flight. HABITAT: In native N America: waterside thickets, open coniferous woodland with bogs, mountainside woods and alpine meadow edge.

8 HOODED WARBLER *Wilsonia citrina* 13cm (Vagrant) FIELD NOTES: Active feeder in low bushes, constantly flicks wings and tail. SONG: Loud *too-ee - too-ee - too-ee - tee-chu*. CALL: Sharp *tchip* or *tchink*; soft *zrrt* flight note. HABITAT: In native N America: dense understorey in mature deciduous woodland, often near streams.

9 CANADA WARBLER *Wilsonia canadensis* 13cm (Vagrant) FIELD NOTES: Feeds actively, in bushes and low trees. Often cocks tail. SONG: A burst of staccato notes. CALL: *tchip*, *chick* or *check*. HABITAT: In native N America: forest undergrowth and waterside thickets.

10 BLACK-AND-WHITE WARBLER *Mniotilta varia* 13cm (Vagrant) FIELD NOTES: Feeds nuthatch-like, probing bark for insects. SONG: Thin, high-pitched *see - wee-see - wee-see - wee-see - wee-see*. CALL: Sharp *tick* and a thin *tzeet* or *tsip*. HABITAT: In native N America: various types of deciduous and mixed woodlands, with a liking for those in moist areas.

11 OVENBIRD *Seiurus aurocapilla* 15cm (Vagrant) FIELD NOTES: Bobs head and flicks up tail. SONG: Emphatic *teecher - teecher - teecher - teecher*, rising in pitch and volume. CALL: *chuk* or *tsuk*, often repeated. HABITAT: In native N America: closed-canopy woodland with dense undergrowth.

12 NORTHERN WATERTHRUSH *Seiurus noveboracensis* 15cm (Vagrant) FIELD NOTES: Constantly bobs its rear end. SONG: *swee-swee-chit-chit-weedleoo*, last note down-slurred. CALL: Loud, metallic *chink*. HABITAT: In native N America: thickets and woodland near water.

75 VIREOS, BOBOLINK, AMERICAN BLACKBIRDS, AMERICAN ORIOLE AND TANAGERS

1 YELLOW-THROATED VIREO *Vireo flavifrons* 14cm (Vagrant) FIELD NOTES: Arboreal. More sluggish than American wood-warblers. SONG: Often transcribed as *three-eight* or *ee-yay*. CALL: A low *heh-heh-heh*. HABITAT: In native N America: deciduous woodlands.

2 PHILADELPHIA WARBLER *Vireo philadelphicus* 13cm (Vagrant) FIELD NOTES: Actions and habits typical of genus. SONG/CALL: Like Red-eyed Vireo but slower and higher. HABITAT: In native N America: broadleaf forest, especially edge and clearings, also thickets and parkland.

3 RED-EYED VIREO *Vireo olivaceus* 15cm (Vagrant) FIELD NOTES: Active, but with heavy movements. Feeds mainly in tree canopy. SONG: Rambling warble that often ends abruptly, e.g. *teeduee-tueedee-tuee-teeudeeu….* CALL: Nasal, whining *chway* or *tshay*. HABITAT: In native N America: broadleaf and mixed woodlands, parkland and gardens.

4 BOBOLINK *Dolichonyx oryzivorus* 18cm (Vagrant) FIELD NOTES: Mainly ground feeder. SONG: Bubbling *bobolink-bobolink-bobolink…*, often given during display-flight. CALL: Clear *pink*, often in flight. HABITAT: In native N America: pastures, arable fields and open grassland.

5 BROWN-HEADED COWBIRD *Molothrus ater* 19cm (Vagrant) FIELD NOTES: Mainly ground feeder. Juveniles paler than females and with faint darker breast streaks, also attain variable dark patches as they moult into adult plumage. SONG: Bubbly *glug-glug-gleeee*. CALL: Harsh *chuk* and squeaky *weee-titi*, often given in flight. HABITAT: In native N America: farmland, pastures, open woodland, parks and gardens.

6 RUSTY BLACKBIRD *Euphagus carolinus* 23cm (Vagrant) FIELD NOTES: Often feeds along shores of woodland pools. SONG: Creaky *kush-a lee*. CALL: Loud *chack*. HABITAT: In native N America: wooded swamps.

7 YELLOW-HEADED BLACKBIRD *Xanthocephalus xanthocephalus* 24cm (Vagrant) FIELD NOTES: Mainly ground feeder. SONG: Low, hoarse and rasping notes ending with a buzz. CALL: Croaking *kruck*, *kack* or *ktuk*. HABITAT: In native N America: freshwater marshes and reed-beds, farmland and pastures.

8 COMMON GRACKLE *Quiscalus quiscula* 32cm (Vagrant) FIELD NOTES: Mainly ground feeder. SONG: Wheezing *tssh-shkleet*. CALL: Loud, hoarse *chuk* or *chak*. HABITAT: In native N America: open grassland, farmland, parks, gardens and towns.

9 BALTIMORE ORIOLE (NORTHERN ORIOLE) *Icterus galbula* 22cm (Vagrant) FIELD NOTES: Forages in foliage of tree canopy, often hard to locate. SONG: Series of *hew-li* call notes. CALL: Fluty *hew-li*; rattling *cher-r-r-r-r* when alarmed. HABITAT: In native N America: open woodland, orchards and parks.

10 SCARLET TANAGER *Piranga olivacea* 18cm (Vagrant) FIELD NOTES: Forages mainly in treetops but will descend to feed on ground. SONG: Raspy *querit-queer-query-querit-queer*. CALL: Hoarse *chip-burr*. HABITAT: In native N America: mature deciduous woodland.

11 SUMMER TANAGER *Piranga rubra* 19cm (Vagrant) FIELD NOTES: Mainly arboreal. Has been noted making fly-catching sallies after bees and wasps. SONG: Thrush-like series of sweet, clear notes. CALL: *chick* or a chattering *pit-a-chuck*, *piki-i-tuck* or *piki-i-tuck-i-tuck*. HABITAT: In native N America: oak or mixed pine and oak woodland.

76 BUNTINGS

1 CINEREOUS BUNTING *Emberiza cineracea* 16cm FIELD NOTES: Wary. Migrants often join with Ortolan and Cretzschmar's buntings. SONG: Rapid, ringing *drip-drip-drip-drip-drie-drieh, dzuu-zuu-zuu-zuu-zee-uie* or similar. CALL: Soft *tsik* and a descending *tieu.* HABITAT: Rocky slopes with scattered bushes and scrub. In winter, also in dry lowland areas, including stubble fields. RACES: *E. c. semenowi* (fig 1b) SE Turkey.

2 JAPANESE YELLOW BUNTING *Emberiza sulphurata* 14cm FIELD NOTES: Unobtrusive. Forms small flocks in non-breeding season. SONG: Alternating twittering phrases, e.g. *twee-twee-tsit-prewprew-zrii, ziriritt-zee-zee* and *psew-zereret-zeetew.* CALL: *tsip-tsip.* HABITAT: Deciduous and mixed forest edge in foothills and lower slopes of high mountains. Winters in weedy and bushy areas.

3 YELLOWHAMMER *Emberiza citrinella* 16cm FIELD NOTES: Conspicuous, often perches in the open on bush tops or wires. Winters in small flocks alongside finches and sparrows. SONG: *zi-zi-zi-zi-zi-zi-zrii-zreeeee,* often written as *little-bit-of-bread-and-no-cheese.* CALL: Metallic *tsit,* a thin *see* and a clicking *tit-tit-tit-tit.* HABITAT: All types of open country.

4 CIRL BUNTING *Emberiza cirlus* 16cm FIELD NOTES: Less conspicuous, unless singing, than Yellowhammer. SONG: Rattled trill, *sre'sre'sre'sre'sre…,* or similar. CALL: Sharp *zitt,* a descending *zeee* and a rapid clicking. HABITAT: Lightly wooded country, farmland with tall hedgerows, orchards, vineyards and large gardens. In non-breeding season, in stubble or weedy fields

5 CHESTNUT-EARED BUNTING *Emberiza fucata* 16cm FIELD NOTES: Actions typical of genus. SONG: More rapid and twittering than most buntings, *zwee-zwizwezwizizi-triip-triip* or similar. CALL: Explosive *pzick,* also used alongside a high-pitched *zii* or *zii-zii;* also a lower-pitched *chutt.* HABITAT: Scrubby vegetation on hillsides, marshland and meadows, also cultivated areas and rice stubble in winter.

6 YELLOW-BREASTED BUNTING *Emberiza aureola* 15cm FIELD NOTES: Gregarious, especially in east, where very large winter flocks are formed. Race *ornata* (Japan, E Russia; not shown) differs mainly in having black forehead that extends to above eye. SONG: Variable, basic form transcribed as *do-do-dee-dee-do-de* or *tru-tru-tree-tree-tri-tri-iih-tiu.* CALL: Sharp *tsik;* abrupt *chup* when flushed. HABITAT: Meadows, wet or dry, with scattered bushes, also riverside thickets, forest clearings, birch-forest edge and burnt areas.

7 RED-HEADED BUNTING *Emberiza bruniceps* 16cm FIELD NOTES: Conspicuous, especially when singing. In Caspian region, often hybridises with Black-headed Bunting. SONG: Harsh, monotonous *zrit-zrit-zrit-chri-chri-cheuh-cheuh-ah* or similar. CALL: Sharp *zrip,* a *chip* and a harsh *cheu.* HABITAT: Dry, open country, steppe, semi-desert with bushy areas, also hill- and mountainsides with scattered bushes.

8 BLACK-HEADED BUNTING *Emberiza melanocephala* 16.5cm FIELD NOTES: Actions similar to Red-headed Bunting (*see* notes above on hybrids etc). SONG/CALL: Generally very similar to Red-headed Bunting. HABITAT: Open country with scattered trees and bushes, also thickets, wooded steppe, maquis, olive groves and vineyards.

9 CHESTNUT BUNTING *Emberiza rutila* 14cm FIELD NOTES: Unobtrusive, sings from relatively concealed perch. SONG: Variable, short, rapid jingle. CALL: *zick,* often repeated. HABITAT: Open deciduous (alder or birch) and coniferous (pine or larch) forest with rich ground cover. On migration said to feed in grain fields.

10 LITTLE BUNTING *Emberiza pusilla* 13cm FIELD NOTES: Mainly ground feeder; during non-breeding season often associates with other ground feeders, e.g. pipits and finches. Sings from exposed treetop perch. SONG: Metallic, variable, combining clear, harsh and rolling notes transcribed as *tzrü-tzrü-tzrü-zee-zee-zee-zee-zriiiiiru* or *tserererere-chu-chu-chu-chu;* also *tserererere-tswee-tswee-chu-teee.* CALL: Hard *tzik* or *pwick.* HABITAT: Moist open taiga with dwarf birch and willow undergrowth. Winters in various open areas.

164

77 BUNTINGS

1 MEADOW BUNTING *Emberiza cioides* 16cm FIELD NOTES: Forms small to medium winter flocks. Usually sings from bush tops. SONG: Transcribed as *chi-hu - chee - tswee-tsweetuee*. CALL: Sharp *zit-zit-zit*. HABITAT: Wide range of dry, open, grassy, scrubby, lightly wooded areas, forest edge in hill or mountain country. RACES: *E. c. ciopsis* (fig 1b) S Sakhalin, Japan.

2 JANKOWSKI'S BUNTING *Emberiza jankowskii* 16cm FIELD NOTES: Little recorded. Forages on ground. Sings from tops of small bushes. SONG: Simple *chu-chu-cha-cha-chee* or *hsuii-dzja-dzja-dzjeee*. CALL: Various, including *tsiit* or *tsiit-tsiit*; explosive *sstlitt* or thin *hsiu* when alarmed. HABITAT: Dry, overgrown sand-dunes with little ground cover and low bushes, also adapted to poplar and pine plantations.

3 HOUSE BUNTING *Emberiza striolata* 14cm FIELD NOTES: After breeding forms parties with other buntings, Desert Larks and Trumpeter Finches. SONG: Simple, repetitive *chippy-chiwy-chiwy-chiwy*. CALL: Nasal *dschu*; sparrow-like *tchiele* flight note. HABITAT: Dry, desolate, rocky hills; race *sahari* has adapted to human habitations. RACES: *E. s. sahari* (fig 3b) NW Africa.

4 CINNAMON-BREASTED BUNTING *Emberiza tahapisi* 14cm FIELD NOTES: Usually occurs singly, in pairs or in small parties, sometimes in larger flocks in winter. SONG: Short *dzit-dzit-dzirera* or *try-tri - tve-rerir*, the last 2 notes higher in pitch. Occasionally ends with some scratchy notes. CALL: Subdued *dwee*, a thin *tsiii-i* and a nasal *per-we-e*. HABITAT: Dry, rocky and stony hillsides with scattered vegetation.

5 ROCK BUNTING *Emberiza cia* 16cm FIELD NOTES: Usually in pairs or small parties. SONG: Series of rapid, rising and falling, high-pitched notes, transcribed as *seut-wit-tell-tell-wit-drr-weeay-sit-seeay*. CALL: Sharp, weak *tzi* or *tzit*, a fuller *tewp*; thin *seeee* when alarmed; rattling *si-tititi* or *zi-dididi* in flight. HABITAT: Rocky hill and mountain slopes, usually with bushes and scattered trees, small mountain fields, sparse upland forest clearings and edge.

6 GODLEWSKI'S BUNTING *Emberiza godlewskii* 17cm FIELD NOTES: Often considered conspecific with Rock Bunting. Frequently found in small flocks in non-breeding season. SONG: Similar to Rock Bunting but beginning with higher-pitched notes. CALL: Thin *tzii* and a hard *pett-pett*. HABITAT: Bushy, rocky mountainsides, often near forests. Often visits fields in winter.

7 WHITE-CAPPED BUNTING *Emberiza stewarti* 15cm FIELD NOTES: Gregarious in winter, often with other buntings. SONG: Given from exposed perch; similar to Yellowhammer but lacking the final drawn-out note. CALL: Sharp *tit*; a twittered *tjuriritt* in flight. HABITAT: Mainly grassy and rocky slopes, with or without bushes and trees.

8 GREY-NECKED BUNTING *Emberiza buchanani* 15cm FIELD NOTES: Gregarious on migration and in winter. SONG: Variable, *dzeee-zeee-zeee-zee-zee-deo* or, from eastern populations, *ti-ti-ti-tiu-tiu-tiuu-u*. CALL: *tcheup* or *chep*; a soft *tsip* given in flight. HABITAT: Bare mountain slopes and foothills with sparse vegetation.

9 CRETZSCHMAR'S BUNTING *Emberiza caesia* 16cm FIELD NOTES: Terrestrial, normally only perches in bushes when alarmed or singing. SONG: Variable, may be thin, low-pitched or buzzy with a drawn-out final note, e.g. *dzree-dzree-dzreee*, *ziii-ziii-ziii-ziiiii* or *zwiie-zwiie-zwiie-ziüüüüü*. CALL: *tchipp*, *plet* and *tchu*. HABITAT: Dry rocky hillsides with scattered bushes.

10 PINE BUNTING *Emberiza leucocephalos* 16.5cm FIELD NOTES: Occasionally hybridises with closely related Yellowhammer. SONG: Similar to Yellowhammer, perhaps softer, *ze-ze-ze-ze-ze-ze-ziiiii*. CALL: Very similar to Yellowhammer. HABITAT: Open, mainly coniferous, forests, forest edge and clearings; winters on arable fields, waste ground, orchards, etc.

11 ORTOLAN BUNTING *Emberiza hortulana* 16cm FIELD NOTES: Feeds on the ground and in trees. Gregarious. SONG: Variable, *dzii-dzii-dzii-dzii-hüü-hüü*, *witt-witt-witt-witt-hüü-hüü* or *zree-zree-zree-züü*. CALL: Dry *plet*, a clear, metallic *ziie*, often followed by a short *tew*, which may be given separately. HABITAT: Open cultivated country with scattered trees and bushes; in south of range favours bare mountainsides and gullies with scattered trees and bushes.

78 BUNTINGS

1 KOSLOV'S BUNTING (TIBETAN BUNTING) *Emberiza koslowi* 16cm FIELD NOTES: Forms small flocks in non-breeding season. Little else recorded, presumably actions similar to other buntings? SONG: Twittering *cheep-chüüp-tererep-cheechûû* or *chep-chip-chip-chiriree-chip-chee*. CALL: Thin *seee*; a *tsip-tsip* in flight. HABITAT: High-altitude cotoneaster and other low bushes on rocky slopes and ridges.

2 YELLOW-THROATED BUNTING *Emberiza elegans* 15cm FIELD NOTES: Actions and habits much as others of genus. SONG: Monotonous twitter, *tswit-tsu-ri-tu-tswee-witt-tsuri-wee-dee-tswit-tsuri-tu*. CALL: Repeated *tzik*. HABITAT: Open, dry, deciduous forest on hills and ridge sides.

3 YELLOW-BROWED BUNTING *Emberiza chrysophrys* 15cm FIELD NOTES: Secretive. Actions typical of genus. SONG: *chuee-swii-swii-chew-chew* or *chuee-tzrrii-tzrrii-wee-wee-wee-tueei*. CALL: Short *ziit* contact note. HABITAT: Mixed forests with a decent proportion of low conifers, especially along rivers; prefers clearings and margins.

4 TRISTRAM'S BUNTING *Emberiza tristrami* 15cm FIELD NOTES: Actions typical of genus. SONG: Variable, *hsiee-swee-swee-swee-tsirririri* or *hsiee-swiii-chew-chew-chew* or similar. CALL: Explosive *tzick*. HABITAT: Mixed or pine forest, spruce taiga, all with dense understorey.

5 RUSTIC BUNTING *Emberiza rustica* 14cm FIELD NOTES: Actions as others of genus. Forms small to large flocks in winter. SONG: Hurried, mellow warble, *deduleu-dewee-deweea-weeu*. CALL: Sharp *tzik*, often repeated. Also a high-pitched *tsiee*. HABITAT: Margins between damp coniferous or birch forest, willow scrub alongside rivers and fens, also boggy areas. Out of breeding season frequents woodland, cultivation and open country.

6 REED BUNTING (COMMON REED BUNTING) *Emberiza schoeniclus* 14.5cm FIELD NOTES: Unobtrusive, except when singing from reed stem or bush top. Forms small winter flocks. SONG: Short, simple series, e.g. *zritt-zreet-zreet-zreet-zritt-zriüüü* or similar. CALL: *seeoo* used as contact note or when alarmed; migrating birds often give a hoarse *brzee*. HABITAT: Marshy areas with scrub, reeds or other tall herbage. In non-breeding season often resorts to fields, woodland clearings, etc., not necessarily near water. RACES: *E. s. pyrrhuloides* (fig 6b) Caspian Sea through C Asia to S Kazakhstan.

7 PALLAS'S REED BUNTING *Emberiza pallasi* 14cm FIELD NOTES: Actions and habits very similar to Reed Bunting. SONG: Plain series of monotonous, rasping notes, *srih-srih-srih-srih*. CALL: Sparrow-like *tschialp* and a slightly rasping *tschirp*. HABITAT: Arctic and mountain tundra and steppe. Willow, alder and dwarf birch scrub near rivers, lakes or bogs.

8 JAPANESE REED BUNTING (OCHRE-RUMPED BUNTING) *Emberiza yessoensis* 14.5cm FIELD NOTES: Actions similar to Reed Bunting. SONG: Brief twittering, transcribed as *chuwi-chiwu-sii-psere-dsee* or *chui-tsui-chirin*. CALL: Short *tick*; a *bschet* flight note. HABITAT: Reed-beds, shrubby marshland and wet meadows in highlands. Winters in coastal marshes.

9 BLACK-FACED BUNTING *Emberiza spodocephala* 14cm FIELD NOTES: Actions typical of genus. Continually twitches tail, revealing white outer feathers. SONG: Lively chirps and trills, *chi-chi-chu - chirri-chu - chi-zeee-chu - chi-chi*, given from hidden perch inside tree or bush. CALL: Sharp *tzii*. HABITAT: Moist shrubby undergrowth along watercourses; in Japan, often in broadleaf mountain forest and subalpine birch forest. RACES: *E. s. personata* (fig 9b) Japan, Sakhalin and S Kuril Islands; *E. s. sordida* (fig 9c) C China.

10 GREY BUNTING *Emberiza variabilis* 17cm FIELD NOTES: Secretive. Ground feeder. SONG: Simple *hsüüü - twis-twis-twis* or similar. CALL: Sharp *zhii*. HABITAT: Bamboo and dense undergrowth in mountain forests.

79 BUNTINGS, AMERICAN GROSBEAKS, JUNCO AND TOWHEE

1 SNOW BUNTING *Plectrophenax nivalis* 16.5cm FIELD NOTES: In winter forms small flock often mixed with larks, pipits and other buntings. Ground feeder. SONG: Variable series of repeated phrases, e.g. *terere-dziüü-weewa-tererere-dziüü-tsee-tsee…*, often given during display-flight. CALL: Harsh *djee*; flight notes are a rippling *tirirririt* often followed by a ringing *pyu*. HABITAT: Barren tundra, rocky mountain tops, scree, sea cliffs and, locally, human settlements. Winters in open country and on beaches and coastal marshes.

2 SLATY BUNTING *Latoucheornis siemsseni* 13cm FIELD NOTES: Ground feeder. In winter forms loose flocks. Said to be attracted to heaps of kitchen refuse. SONG: Variable, high-pitched and tit-like, e.g. *ziiii-ziiiu-tzitzitzitzi-hee, ze-ze-ze-ze-swee-twitwit* or similar. CALL: Sharp *zick*, often repeated. HABITAT: Bamboo, secondary growth and semi-open degraded areas, 1500–2100m. Winters lower, in forests, city parks and near human habitations.

3 LAPLAND BUNTING (LAPLAND LONGSPUR) *Calcarius lapponicus* 15cm FIELD NOTES: Gregarious outside breeding season, often in mixed flocks with larks, pipits and Snow Buntings. Ground feeder. SONG: Short, jangling warble, *djüü-tiiah-preeyu-chirio-twi-trii-tri-leeoh* or *towii-chü - dowewichidow-e - djüü-chürü-triiahli*, often given during display flight. CALL: Melodious *tee-uu* and in flight a high *jeeb*; also a rattled *prrt*, often followed by a clear *chu*. HABITAT: Tundra, mountains with low shrubbery, willow bushes near wet areas. Winters in pastures, stubble fields, steppe and coastal marshes.

4 CORN BUNTING *Miliaria calandra* 17.5cm FIELD NOTES: Sings from exposed perch, with a liking for overhead wires. Gregarious in winter, often mixes with other buntings and larks. SONG: Series of chipping notes followed by harsh jangling, e.g. *teuk-teuk-teuk-zik-zee-zrrissississ*. CALL: Hard, dry *tuk* or *bitt*, often rapidly repeated. HABITAT: Steppe, cereal crops, downland, coastal dunes and other rough ground with grass cover.

5 ROSE-BREASTED GROSBEAK *Pheucticus ludovicianus* 19cm (Vagrant) FIELD NOTES: Arboreal, sluggish. Feeds in bushes and tree canopy. SONG: Thrush-like rising and falling passages. CALL: Metallic *kink* or *eek*. HABITAT: In native N America: open woodland, woodland edge, hedgerows, orchards and large gardens.

6 BLUE GROSBEAK *Passerina caerulea* 17cm (Vagrant) FIELD NOTES: Shy, feeds in dense cover. Flares tail when perched. SONG: Rapid warble with short, rising and falling phrases. CALL: Sharp *spink* or *chink* and a rolling *preet*. HABITAT: In native N America: bushy areas, streamside thickets and hedgerows.

7 INDIGO BUNTING *Passerina cyanea* 14cm (Vagrant) FIELD NOTES: Skulking, except when singing. Feeds in trees and bushes or on ground. SONG: High-pitched *sweet-sweet - where where - here-here - see-it-see-it*. CALL: Sharp *tsick* or *spit*. HABITAT: In native N America: bushy pastures, thickets, often near water, woodland clearings and edge.

8 LAZULI BUNTING *Passerina amoena* 14cm (Vagrant) FIELD NOTES: Keeps in cover. Feeds on or near the ground. SONG: Rapid *see-see-sweert-sweert-sweert-zee-sweet-zeer-see-see*. CALL: Sharp *tzip* or *pit* and a dry buzz. HABITAT: In native N America: open woodland, thickets, especially near water, also overgrown fields and cultivation.

9 DARK-EYED JUNCO (SLATE-COLOURED JUNCO) *Junco hyemalis* 15cm (Vagrant) FIELD NOTES: Ground feeder, in leaf litter and weedy vegetation. SONG: Rapid loose trill. CALL: Liquid *chek*, sharp *dit* and a dry, twittering flight note. HABITAT: In native N America coniferous and mixed woods; in winter, frequents farmland, scrub, parks and gardens.

10 RUFOUS-SIDED TOWHEE (EASTERN TOWHEE) *Pipilo erythrophthalmus* 20cm (Vagrant) FIELD NOTES: Ground feeder, usually under cover of bushes. SONG: Often rendered as *drink-your-tea-ee-ee-ee-ee*. CALL: Rising *tow-whee* or *chee-wink*, also a soft *hew* and sharp *sit*. HABITAT: In native N America: undergrowth, thickets, woodland edge and gardens.

80 DICKCISSEL AND AMERICAN SPARROWS

1 DICKCISSEL *Spiza americana* 16cm (Vagrant) FIELD NOTES: Ground feeder, perches on wires and fences. Gregarious, often mixes with sparrows. SONG: Staccato *dik-dik-serrr-si-si, dick ciss-ciss-ciss* or *chup-chup-klip-klip-klip*. CALL: Buzzing *dzzrrrt*, often given in flight. HABITAT: In native N America: open country, especially cereal fields and grassland with weedy areas.

2 AMERICAN TREE SPARROW *Spizella arborea* 16cm (Vagrant) FIELD NOTES: Mainly terrestrial. Gregarious in winter areas. SONG: Begins with several clear *seet* notes followed by a rapid, variable warble. CALL: *tseet* and a musical *teedle-eet-teedle-eet*. HABITAT: In native N America: tundra edge, in open areas with scattered trees and bushes. Winters in weedy fields near woods, also hedges and marshes.

3 SAVANNAH SPARROW *Passerculus sandwichensis* 14cm (Vagrant) FIELD NOTES: Groun feeder. Actions often pipit-like. SONG: Lisping *tsit-tsit-tsit-tseeee-tsaaay*. CALL: Light *tsip* and a thin *tsi* or *seep*, often given in flight. HABITAT: In native N America: open fields, salt marshes, dunes and shorelines. RACES: *P. s. princeps* (Ipswich Sparrow) (fig 3b) Sable Island, Nova Scoti

4 LARK SPARROW *Chondestes grammacus* 17cm (Vagrant) FIELD NOTES: Ground feeder. Perches on low vegetation. SONG: 2 loud notes followed by a series of rich, melodious phrases, trills and unmusical buzzes. CALL: Sharp *tsip*, often rapidly repeated. HABITAT: In native N Americ open country with bushes and trees, farmland and waste ground with weedy vegetation.

5 FOX SPARROW *Passerella iliaca* 17cm (Vagrant) FIELD NOTES: Shy and skulking. Groun feeder amongst leaf litter, usually under cover of undergrowth. SONG: Loud, clear, melodious notes, slowly rising then falling away, often interspersed with some buzzy trills. CALL: Drawn-out *stsssp* and various *chips*. HABITAT: In native N America: dense undergrowth in coniferous and deciduous woodland, streamside thickets and tall scrub. RACES: *P. i. unalaschcensis* (fig 5b Alaska, Aleutian Islands.

6 SONG SPARROW *Melospiza melodia* 16cm (Vagrant) FIELD NOTES: Skulking ground feeder, usually under cover. Hops with tail slightly raised. Pumps tail in flight. SONG: Series of clear notes followed by a buzzing rattle and a trill. CALL: Nasal *tchep* and a thin *tsee*. HABITAT: In native N America: thickets, waterside undergrowth, hedgerows and woodland edge.

7 WHITE-CROWNED SPARROW *Zonotrichia leucophrys* 16cm (Vagrant) FIELD NOTES: Ground feeder, both in undergrowth cover and in open. Perches on bushes. Raises crown feathers when agitated. SONG: Sad *more-wet-wetter-chee-zee*. CALL: Metallic *pink* or *chink*, also a thin *tseep*. HABITAT: In native N America: various bushy areas, e.g. woodland edge, thickets, stunted conifers, mountain shrubbery, parks and gardens.

8 WHITE-THROATED SPARROW *Zonotrichia albicollis* 16cm (Vagrant) FIELD NOTES: Ground feeder, but never far from cover. Perches on bushes. SONG: Series of clear whistles, often transcribed as *pure-sweet-Canada-Canada-Canada*, *Old-Sam-Peabody-Peabody-Peabody Sow-wheat-Peverly-Peverly-Peverly*. CALL: Thin, high *tseet*, a sharp *chink* or *pink* similar to White-crowned Sparrow. HABITAT: In native N America: open coniferous or mixed woodland woodland edge and clearings, birch and alder scrub. Often found in parks and gardens in winte

9 GOLDEN-CROWNED SPARROW *Zonotrichia atricapilla* 16cm (Vagrant) FIELD NOTES Shy. Ground feeder, usually near cover. SONG: 3 melancholy, flute-like notes, transcribed as *I'm-so-weary* or *oh-dear-me - three-bind-mice*. CALL: Sharp, loud *chink* and a thin *seet*. HABITAT: In native N America: mountain and tundra, alpine meadows with bushes or small trees, scrubby hillsides and waterside scrub.

FURTHER READING

Ali, S. & Ripley, S.D. (1987) *Compact Handbook of the Birds of India and Pakistan*, 2nd edn. Oxford University Press.

Alström, P. & Mild, K. (2003) *Pipits and Wagtails of Europe, Asia and North America*. Helm.

Baker, K. (1997) *Warblers of Europe, Asia and North Africa*. Helm.

Beaman, M. (1994) *Palearctic Birds*. Harrier.

Beaman, M. & Madge, S. (1998) *The Handbook of Bird Identification for Europe and the Western Palearctic*. Helm.

Brazil, M.A. (1991) *The Birds of Japan*. Helm.

Brown, L.H., Urban, E.K., Newman, K., Fry, C.H. & Keith, G.S. (eds) (1982–2004) *The Birds of Africa, vols 1–7*. Academic Press.

Byers, C., Olsson, U. & Curson, J. (1995) *Buntings and Sparrows*. Helm.

Clement, P., Harris, A. & Davis, J. (1993) *Finches and Sparrows*. Helm.

Clement, P. & Hathway, R. (2000) *Thrushes*. Helm.

Cramp, S., Simmons, K.E.L. & Perrins, C.M. (eds) (1977–94) *The Birds of the Western Palearctic, vols 1–9*. Oxford University Press.

Curson, J., Quinn, D. & Beadle, D. (1994) *New World Warblers*. Helm.

Feare, F. & Craig, A. (1998) *Starlings and Mynas*. Helm.

Harrop, S. & Quinn, D. (1996) *Tits, Nuthatches and Treecreepers*. Helm.

Hollom, P.A.D., Porter, R.F., Christensen, S. & Willis, I. (1988) *Birds of the Middle East and North Africa*. Poyser.

del Hoyo, J., Elliott, A. & Sargatal, J. (eds) (1992–2005) *Handbook of the Birds of the World, vols 1–10*. Lynx.

Lefranc, N. & Worfolk, T. (1997) *Shrikes*. Pica.

MacKinnon, J. & Phillipps, K. (2000) *A Field Guide to the Birds of China*. Oxford University Press.

Madge, S. & Burn, H. (1991) *Crows and Jays*. Helm.

Mullarney, K., Svensson, L., Zetterström, D. & Grant, P.J. (1999) *Collins Bird Guide*. HarperCollins.

Palmer, R.S. (ed.) (1962–88) *Handbook of North American Birds, vols 1–5*. Yale University Press.

Porter, R.F., Christensen, S. & Schiermacker-Hansen, P. (1996) *Birds of the Middle East*. Helm.

Terres, J.K. (1980) *The Audubon Society Encyclopedia of North American Birds*. Alfred A. Knopf.

Turner, A. & Rose, C. (1989) *Swallows and Martins of the World*. Helm.

Vinicombe, K., Harris, A. & Tucker, L. (1989) *The Macmillan Field Guide to Bird Identification*. Macmillan.

SPECIES DISTRIBUTION MAPS

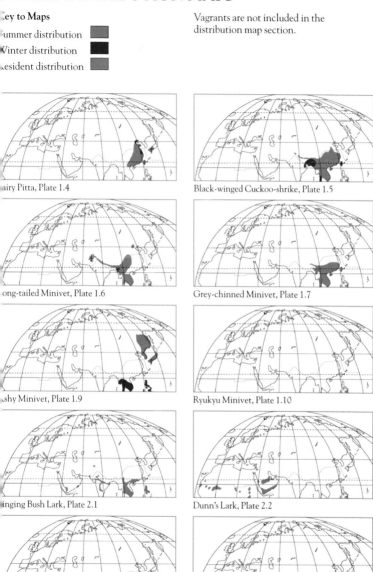

Fairy Pitta, Plate 1.4

Black-winged Cuckoo-shrike, Plate 1.5

Long-tailed Minivet, Plate 1.6

Grey-chinned Minivet, Plate 1.7

Ashy Minivet, Plate 1.9

Ryukyu Minivet, Plate 1.10

Singing Bush Lark, Plate 2.1

Dunn's Lark, Plate 2.2

Kordofan Bush Lark, Plate 2.3

Black-crowned Sparrow-lark, Plate 2.4

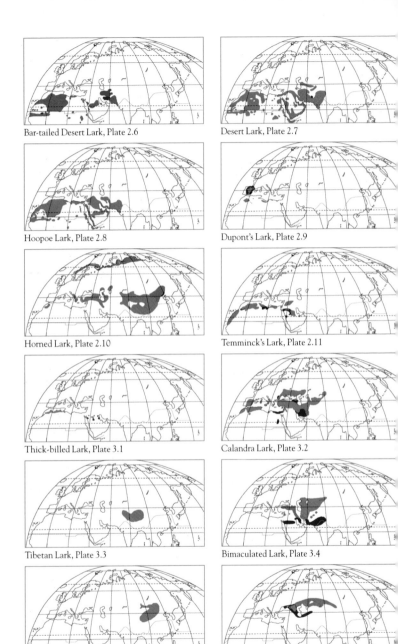

Bar-tailed Desert Lark, Plate 2.6

Desert Lark, Plate 2.7

Hoopoe Lark, Plate 2.8

Dupont's Lark, Plate 2.9

Horned Lark, Plate 2.10

Temminck's Lark, Plate 2.11

Thick-billed Lark, Plate 3.1

Calandra Lark, Plate 3.2

Tibetan Lark, Plate 3.3

Bimaculated Lark, Plate 3.4

Mongolian Lark, Plate 3.5

White-winged Lark, Plate 3.6

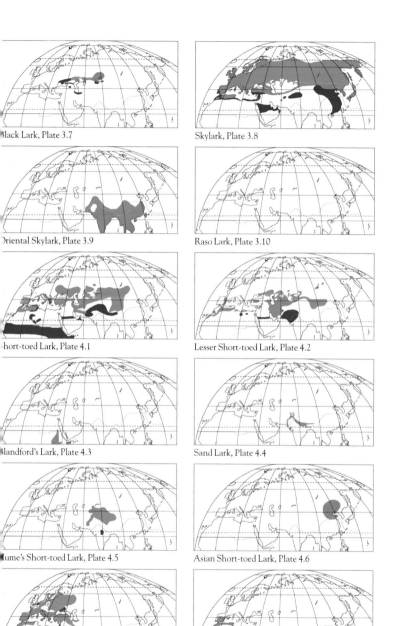

Black Lark, Plate 3.7

Skylark, Plate 3.8

Oriental Skylark, Plate 3.9

Raso Lark, Plate 3.10

Short-toed Lark, Plate 4.1

Lesser Short-toed Lark, Plate 4.2

Blandford's Lark, Plate 4.3

Sand Lark, Plate 4.4

Hume's Short-toed Lark, Plate 4.5

Asian Short-toed Lark, Plate 4.6

Woodlark, Plate 4.7

Thekla Lark, Plate 4.8

177

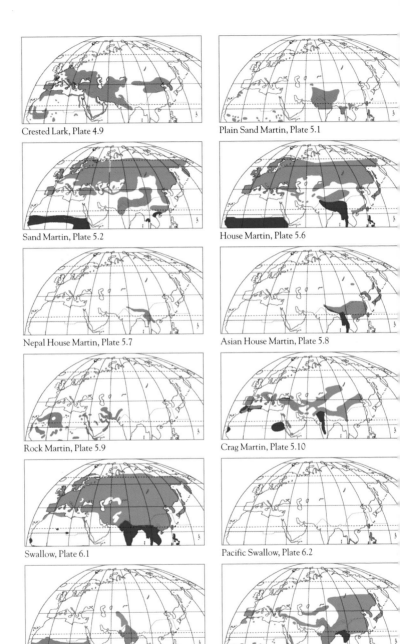

Crested Lark, Plate 4.9

Plain Sand Martin, Plate 5.1

Sand Martin, Plate 5.2

House Martin, Plate 5.6

Nepal House Martin, Plate 5.7

Asian House Martin, Plate 5.8

Rock Martin, Plate 5.9

Crag Martin, Plate 5.10

Swallow, Plate 6.1

Pacific Swallow, Plate 6.2

Wire-tailed Swallow, Plate 6.4

Red-rumped Swallow, Plate 6.5

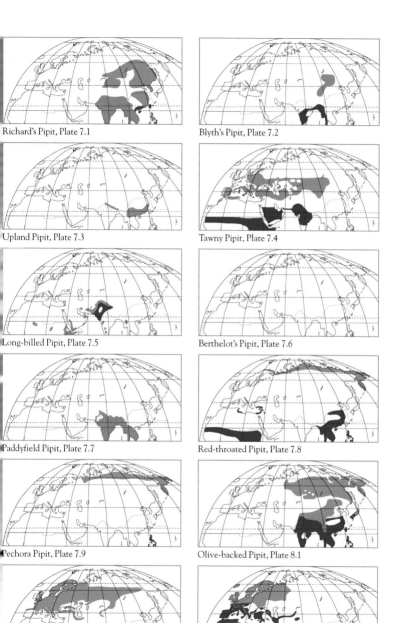

Richard's Pipit, Plate 7.1

Blyth's Pipit, Plate 7.2

Upland Pipit, Plate 7.3

Tawny Pipit, Plate 7.4

Long-billed Pipit, Plate 7.5

Berthelot's Pipit, Plate 7.6

Paddyfield Pipit, Plate 7.7

Red-throated Pipit, Plate 7.8

Pechora Pipit, Plate 7.9

Olive-backed Pipit, Plate 8.1

Tree Pipit, Plate 8.2

Meadow Pipit, Plate 8.3

179

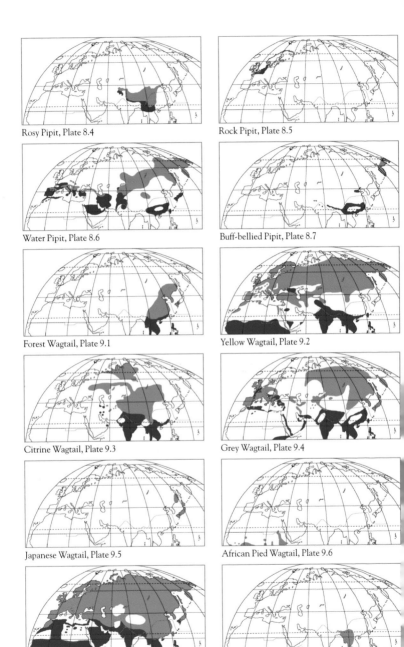

Rosy Pipit, Plate 8.4

Rock Pipit, Plate 8.5

Water Pipit, Plate 8.6

Buff-bellied Pipit, Plate 8.7

Forest Wagtail, Plate 9.1

Yellow Wagtail, Plate 9.2

Citrine Wagtail, Plate 9.3

Grey Wagtail, Plate 9.4

Japanese Wagtail, Plate 9.5

African Pied Wagtail, Plate 9.6

White Wagtail, Plate 9.7

Crested Finchbill, Plate 10.1

180

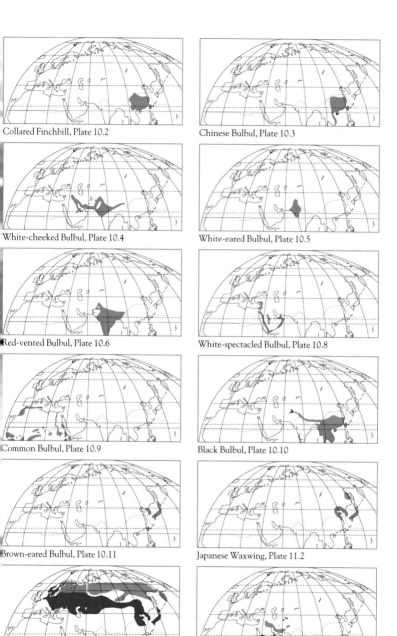

Collared Finchbill, Plate 10.2

Chinese Bulbul, Plate 10.3

White-cheeked Bulbul, Plate 10.4

White-eared Bulbul, Plate 10.5

Red-vented Bulbul, Plate 10.6

White-spectacled Bulbul, Plate 10.8

Common Bulbul, Plate 10.9

Black Bulbul, Plate 10.10

Brown-eared Bulbul, Plate 10.11

Japanese Waxwing, Plate 11.2

Waxwing, Plate 11.3

Grey Hypocolius, Plate 11.4

181

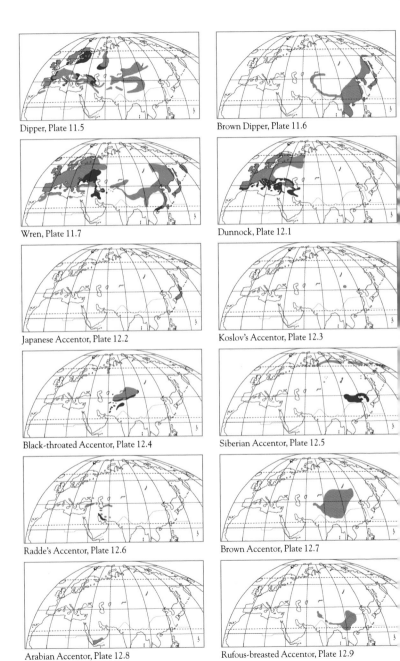

Dipper, Plate 11.5

Brown Dipper, Plate 11.6

Wren, Plate 11.7

Dunnock, Plate 12.1

Japanese Accentor, Plate 12.2

Koslov's Accentor, Plate 12.3

Black-throated Accentor, Plate 12.4

Siberian Accentor, Plate 12.5

Radde's Accentor, Plate 12.6

Brown Accentor, Plate 12.7

Arabian Accentor, Plate 12.8

Rufous-breasted Accentor, Plate 12.9

182

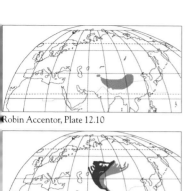

Robin Accentor, Plate 12.10

Maroon-backed Accentor, Plate 12.11

Altai Accentor, Plate 12.12

Alpine Accentor, Plate 12.13

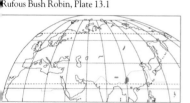

Rufous Bush Robin, Plate 13.1

Black Bush Robin, Plate 13.2

Gould's Shortwing, Plate 13.3

Rusty-bellied Shortwing, Plate 13.4

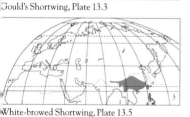

White-browed Shortwing, Plate 13.5

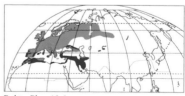

Robin, Plate 13.6

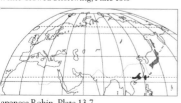

Japanese Robin, Plate 13.7

Ryukyu Robin, Plate 13.8

183

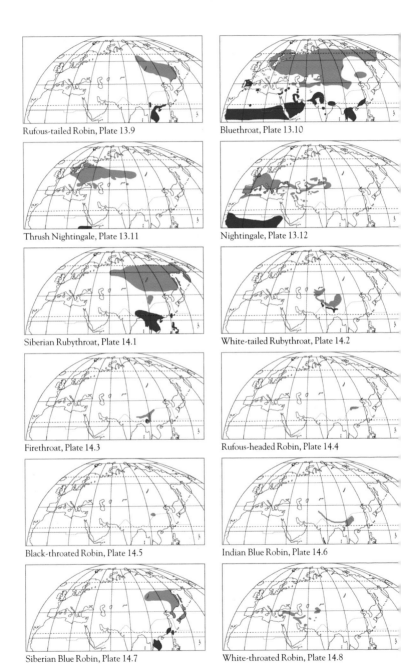

Rufous-tailed Robin, Plate 13.9

Bluethroat, Plate 13.10

Thrush Nightingale, Plate 13.11

Nightingale, Plate 13.12

Siberian Rubythroat, Plate 14.1

White-tailed Rubythroat, Plate 14.2

Firethroat, Plate 14.3

Rufous-headed Robin, Plate 14.4

Black-throated Robin, Plate 14.5

Indian Blue Robin, Plate 14.6

Siberian Blue Robin, Plate 14.7

White-throated Robin, Plate 14.8

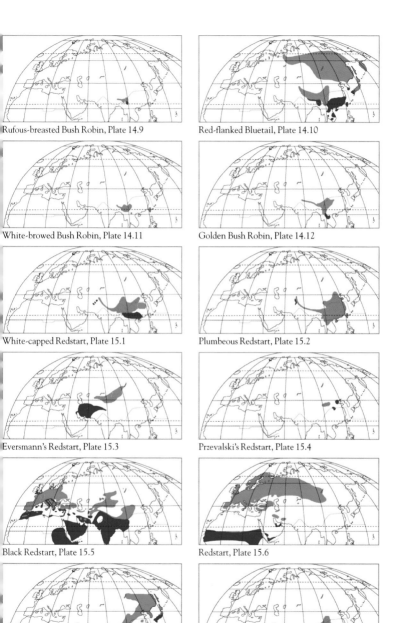

Rufous-breasted Bush Robin, Plate 14.9

Red-flanked Bluetail, Plate 14.10

White-browed Bush Robin, Plate 14.11

Golden Bush Robin, Plate 14.12

White-capped Redstart, Plate 15.1

Plumbeous Redstart, Plate 15.2

Eversmann's Redstart, Plate 15.3

Przevalski's Redstart, Plate 15.4

Black Redstart, Plate 15.5

Redstart, Plate 15.6

Daurian Redstart, Plate 15.7

Hodgson's Redstart, Plate 15.8

185

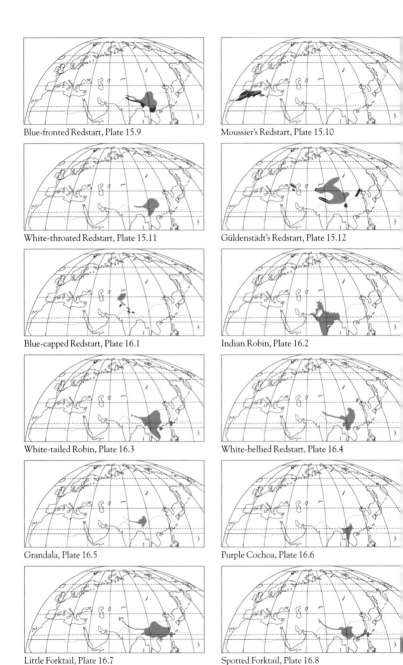

Blue-fronted Redstart, Plate 15.9

Moussier's Redstart, Plate 15.10

White-throated Redstart, Plate 15.11

Güldenstädt's Redstart, Plate 15.12

Blue-capped Redstart, Plate 16.1

Indian Robin, Plate 16.2

White-tailed Robin, Plate 16.3

White-bellied Redstart, Plate 16.4

Grandala, Plate 16.5

Purple Cochoa, Plate 16.6

Little Forktail, Plate 16.7

Spotted Forktail, Plate 16.8

White-crowned Forktail, Plate 16.9

Oriental Magpie Robin, Plate 16.10

Fuerteventura Stonechat, Plate 17.2

Whinchat, Plate 17.3

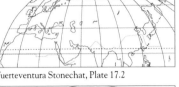

Stonechat, Plate 17.4

Hodgson's Bushchat, Plate 17.5

Pied Stonechat, Plate 17.6

Grey Bushchat, Plate 17.7

Red-breasted Wheatear, Plate 18.1

Isabelline Wheatear, Plate 18.2

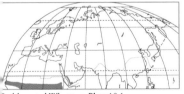

Wheatear, Plate 18.3

Black-eared Wheatear, Plate 18.4

187

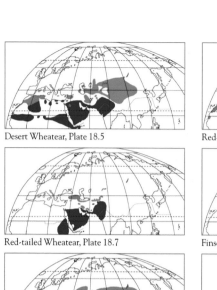

Desert Wheatear, Plate 18.5

Red-rumped Wheatear, Plate 18.6

Red-tailed Wheatear, Plate 18.7

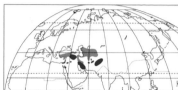

Finsch's Wheatear, Plate 19.1

Pied Wheatear, Plate 19.2

Cyprus Wheatear, Plate 19.3

Eastern Pied Wheatear, Plate 19.4

Arabian Wheatear, Plate 19.5

Mourning Wheatear, Plate 19.6

Hume's Wheatear, Plate 19.7

Black Wheatear, Plate 19.8

Hooded Wheatear, Plate 19.9

'hite-crowned Black Wheatear, Plate 19.10

Blackstart, Plate 20.2

ttle Rock Thrush, Plate 20.3

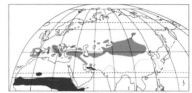

Rock Thrush, Plate 20.4

ue-capped Rock Thrush, Plate 20.5

White-throated Rock Thrush, Plate 20.6

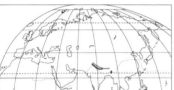

hestnut-bellied Rock Thrush, Plate 20.7

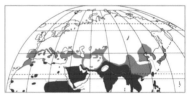

Blue Rock Thrush, Plate 20.8

lue Whistling Thrush, Plate 20.9

Plain-backed Thrush, Plate 21.1

ong-tailed Thrush, Plate 21.2

Scaly Thrush, Plate 21.3

189

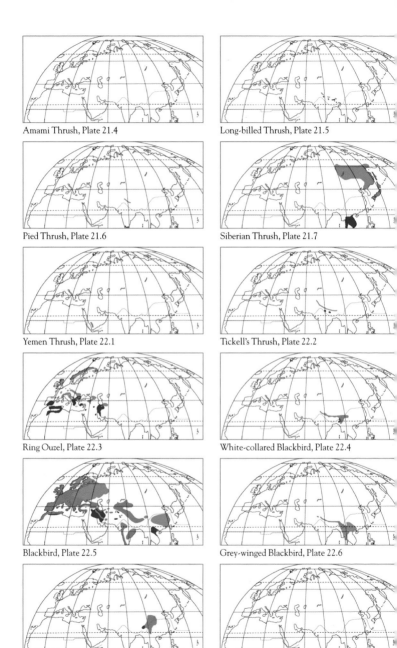

Amami Thrush, Plate 21.4

Long-billed Thrush, Plate 21.5

Pied Thrush, Plate 21.6

Siberian Thrush, Plate 21.7

Yemen Thrush, Plate 22.1

Tickell's Thrush, Plate 22.2

Ring Ouzel, Plate 22.3

White-collared Blackbird, Plate 22.4

Blackbird, Plate 22.5

Grey-winged Blackbird, Plate 22.6

Kessler's Thrush, Plate 22.8

Izu Thrush, Plate 22.9

190

Brown-headed Thrush, Plate 22.10

Chestnut Thrush, Plate 23.1

Grey-sided Thrush, Plate 23.2

Pale Thrush, Plate 23.3

Grey-backed Thrush, Plate 23.4

Eyebrowed Thrush, Plate 23.5

Naumann's Thrush, Plate 23.6

Red-throated Thrush, Plate 23.7

Japanese Thrush, Plate 23.8

Mistle Thrush, Plate 24.1

Chinese Thrush, Plate 24.2

Song Thrush, Plate 24.3

191

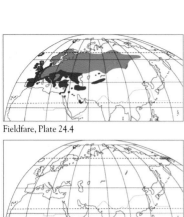

Fieldfare, Plate 24.4

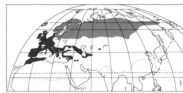

Redwing, Plate 24.5

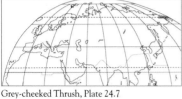

Grey-cheeked Thrush, Plate 24.7

Asian Stubtail, Plate 25.1

Japanese Bush Warbler, Plate 25.2

Brownish-flanked Bush Warbler, Plate 25.3

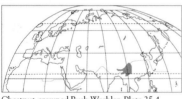

Chestnut-crowned Bush Warbler, Plate 25.4

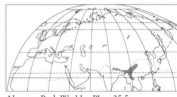

Aberrant Bush Warbler, Plate 25.5

Yellowish-bellied Bush Warbler, Plate 25.6

Grey-sided Bush Warbler, Plate 25.7

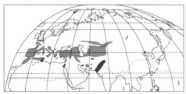

Cetti's Warbler, Plate 25.8

Spotted Bush Warbler, Plate 25.9

192

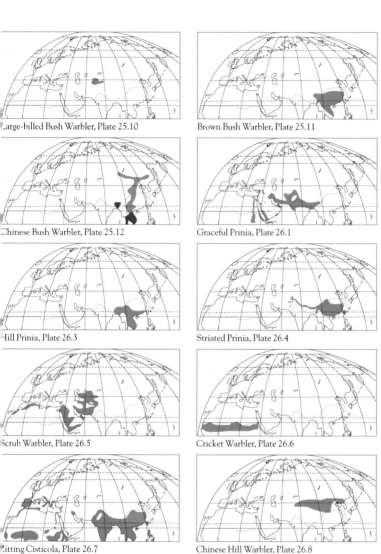

Large-billed Bush Warbler, Plate 25.10

Brown Bush Warbler, Plate 25.11

Chinese Bush Warbler, Plate 25.12

Graceful Prinia, Plate 26.1

Hill Prinia, Plate 26.3

Striated Prinia, Plate 26.4

Scrub Warbler, Plate 26.5

Cricket Warbler, Plate 26.6

Zitting Cisticola, Plate 26.7

Chinese Hill Warbler, Plate 26.8

Pallas's Grasshopper Warbler, Plate 26.9

Lanceolated Warbler, Plate 26.10

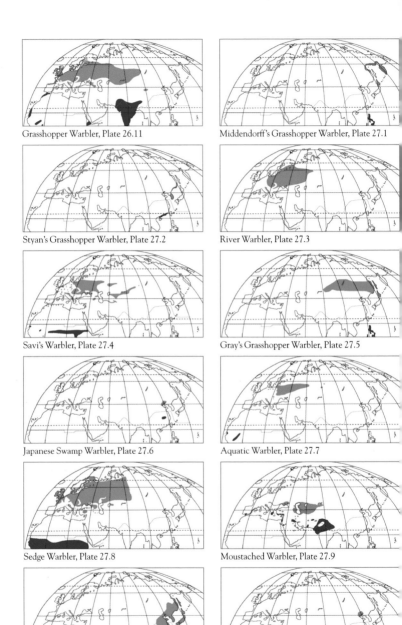

Grasshopper Warbler, Plate 26.11

Middendorff's Grasshopper Warbler, Plate 27.1

Styan's Grasshopper Warbler, Plate 27.2

River Warbler, Plate 27.3

Savi's Warbler, Plate 27.4

Gray's Grasshopper Warbler, Plate 27.5

Japanese Swamp Warbler, Plate 27.6

Aquatic Warbler, Plate 27.7

Sedge Warbler, Plate 27.8

Moustached Warbler, Plate 27.9

Black-browed Reed Warbler, Plate 27.10

Speckled Reed Warbler, Plate 27.11

Blunt-winged Warbler, Plate 28.1

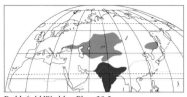
Paddyfield Warbler, Plate 28.2

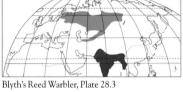
Blyth's Reed Warbler, Plate 28.3

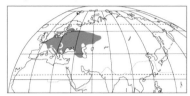
Marsh Warbler, Plate 28.4

Cape Verde Warbler, Plate 28.5

African Reed Warbler, Plate 28.6

Reed Warbler, Plate 28.7

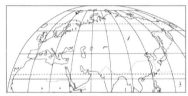
Clamorous Reed Warbler, Plate 28.8

Oriental Reed Warbler, Plate 28.9

Great Reed Warbler, Plate 28.10

Basra Reed Warbler, Plate 28.11

Thick-billed Warbler, Plate 28.12

195

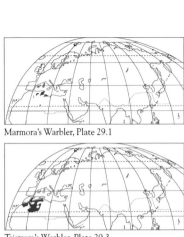

Marmora's Warbler, Plate 29.1

Dartford Warbler, Plate 29.2

Tristram's Warbler, Plate 29.3

Subalpine Warbler, Plate 29.4

Spectacled Warbler, Plate 29.5

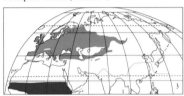

Whitethroat, Plate 29.6

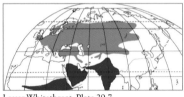

Lesser Whitethroat, Plate 29.7

Desert Warbler, Plate 29.8

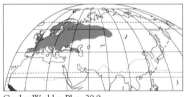

Garden Warbler, Plate 29.9

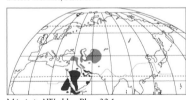

Ménétries' Warbler, Plate 30.1

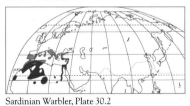

Sardinian Warbler, Plate 30.2

Rüppell's Warbler, Plate 30.3

196

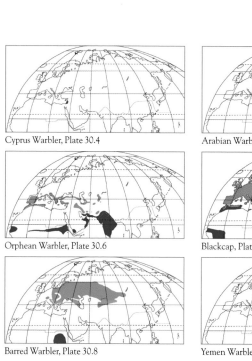

Cyprus Warbler, Plate 30.4

Arabian Warbler, Plate 30.5

Orphean Warbler, Plate 30.6

Blackcap, Plate 30.7

Barred Warbler, Plate 30.8

Yemen Warbler, Plate 30.9

Olivaceous Warbler, Plate 31.1

Booted Warbler, Plate 31.2

Upcher's Warbler, Plate 31.3

Olive-tree Warbler, Plate 31.4

Icterine Warbler, Plate 31.5

Melodious Warbler, Plate 31.6

197

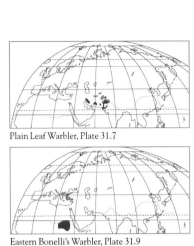

Plain Leaf Warbler, Plate 31.7

Wood Warbler, Plate 31.8

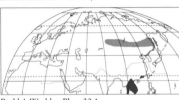

Eastern Bonelli's Warbler, Plate 31.9

Western Bonelli's Warbler, Plate 31.10

Radde's Warbler, Plate 32.1

Yellow-streaked Warbler, Plate 32.2

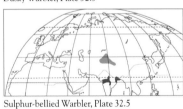

Dusky Warbler, Plate 32.3

Smoky Warbler, Plate 32.4

Sulphur-bellied Warbler, Plate 32.5

Tytler's Leaf Warbler, Plate 32.6

Buff-throated Warbler, Plate 32.7

Chiffchaff, Plate 32.8

198

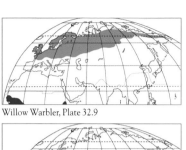

Willow Warbler, Plate 32.9

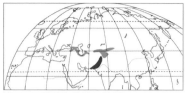

Mountain Chiffchaff, Plate 32.10

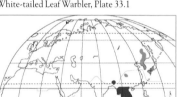

White-tailed Leaf Warbler, Plate 33.1

Blyth's Leaf Warbler, Plate 33.2

Eastern Crowned Warbler, Plate 33.3

Western Crowned Warbler, Plate 33.4

Ijima's Leaf Warbler, Plate 33.5

Ashy-throated Warbler, Plate 33.6

Pallas's Warbler, Plate 33.7

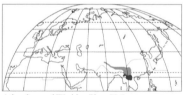

Lemon-rumped Warbler, Plate 33.8

Chinese Leaf Warbler, Plate 33.9

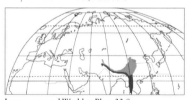

Brooks's Leaf Warbler, Plate 33.10

199

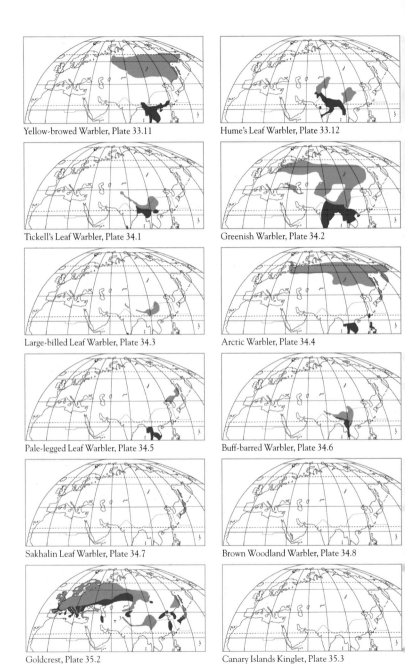

Yellow-browed Warbler, Plate 33.11

Hume's Leaf Warbler, Plate 33.12

Tickell's Leaf Warbler, Plate 34.1

Greenish Warbler, Plate 34.2

Large-billed Leaf Warbler, Plate 34.3

Arctic Warbler, Plate 34.4

Pale-legged Leaf Warbler, Plate 34.5

Buff-barred Warbler, Plate 34.6

Sakhalin Leaf Warbler, Plate 34.7

Brown Woodland Warbler, Plate 34.8

Goldcrest, Plate 35.2

Canary Islands Kinglet, Plate 35.3

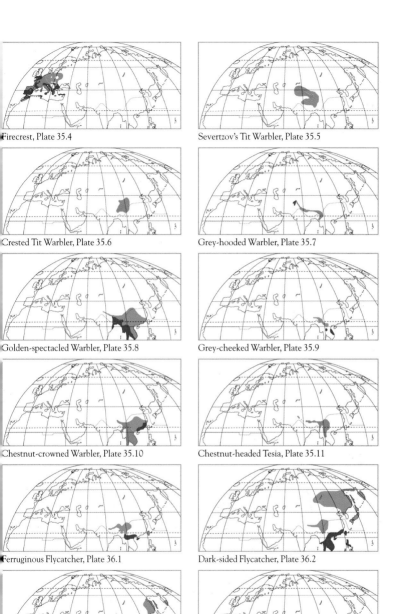

Firecrest, Plate 35.4

Severtzov's Tit Warbler, Plate 35.5

Crested Tit Warbler, Plate 35.6

Grey-hooded Warbler, Plate 35.7

Golden-spectacled Warbler, Plate 35.8

Grey-cheeked Warbler, Plate 35.9

Chestnut-crowned Warbler, Plate 35.10

Chestnut-headed Tesia, Plate 35.11

Ferruginous Flycatcher, Plate 36.1

Dark-sided Flycatcher, Plate 36.2

Grey-streaked Flycatcher, Plate 36.3

Rusty-tailed Flycatcher, Plate 36.4

201

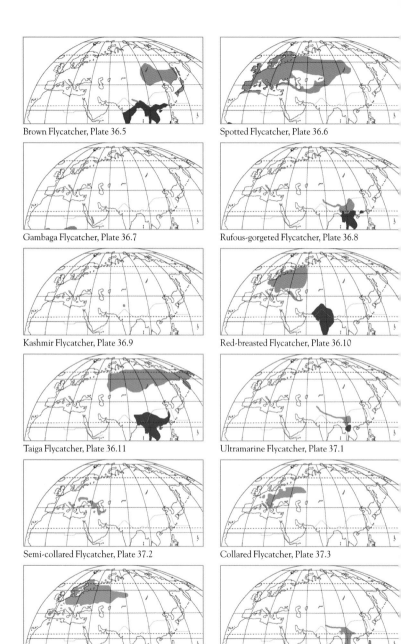

Brown Flycatcher, Plate 36.5

Spotted Flycatcher, Plate 36.6

Gambaga Flycatcher, Plate 36.7

Rufous-gorgeted Flycatcher, Plate 36.8

Kashmir Flycatcher, Plate 36.9

Red-breasted Flycatcher, Plate 36.10

Taiga Flycatcher, Plate 36.11

Ultramarine Flycatcher, Plate 37.1

Semi-collared Flycatcher, Plate 37.2

Collared Flycatcher, Plate 37.3

Pied Flycatcher, Plate 37.4

Little Pied Flycatcher, Plate 37.5

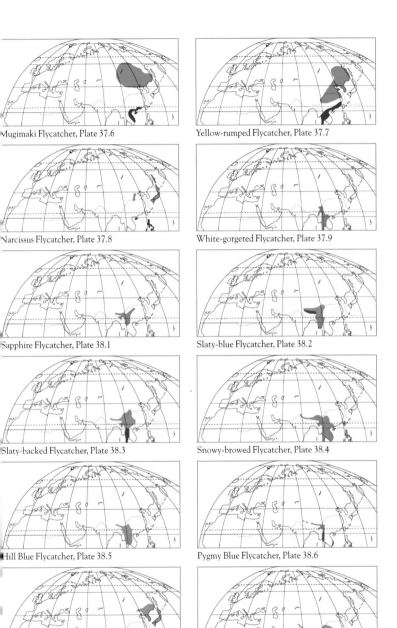

Mugimaki Flycatcher, Plate 37.6

Yellow-rumped Flycatcher, Plate 37.7

Narcissus Flycatcher, Plate 37.8

White-gorgeted Flycatcher, Plate 37.9

Sapphire Flycatcher, Plate 38.1

Slaty-blue Flycatcher, Plate 38.2

Slaty-backed Flycatcher, Plate 38.3

Snowy-browed Flycatcher, Plate 38.4

Hill Blue Flycatcher, Plate 38.5

Pygmy Blue Flycatcher, Plate 38.6

Blue-and-white Flycatcher, Plate 38.7

Verditer Flycatcher, Plate 38.8

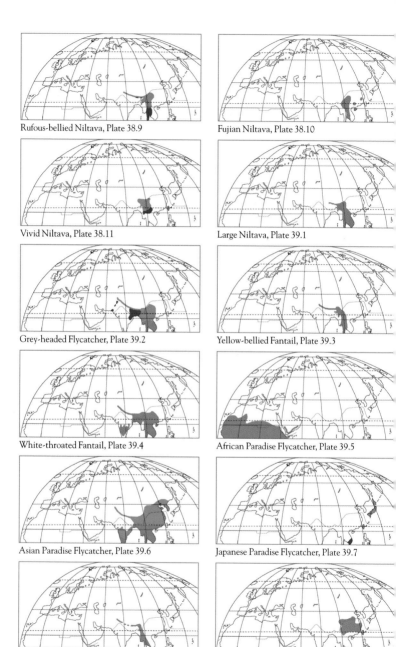

Rufous-bellied Niltava, Plate 38.9

Fujian Niltava, Plate 38.10

Vivid Niltava, Plate 38.11

Large Niltava, Plate 39.1

Grey-headed Flycatcher, Plate 39.2

Yellow-bellied Fantail, Plate 39.3

White-throated Fantail, Plate 39.4

African Paradise Flycatcher, Plate 39.5

Asian Paradise Flycatcher, Plate 39.6

Japanese Paradise Flycatcher, Plate 39.7

Rusty-cheeked Scimitar Babbler, Plate 40.1

Spot-breasted Scimitar Babbler, Plate 40.2

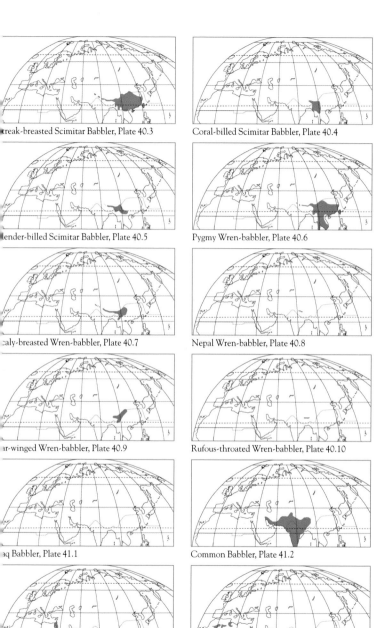

reak-breasted Scimitar Babbler, Plate 40.3

Coral-billed Scimitar Babbler, Plate 40.4

lender-billed Scimitar Babbler, Plate 40.5

Pygmy Wren-babbler, Plate 40.6

caly-breasted Wren-babbler, Plate 40.7

Nepal Wren-babbler, Plate 40.8

ar-winged Wren-babbler, Plate 40.9

Rufous-throated Wren-babbler, Plate 40.10

aq Babbler, Plate 41.1

Common Babbler, Plate 41.2

rabian Babbler, Plate 41.3

Fulvous Babbler, Plate 41.4

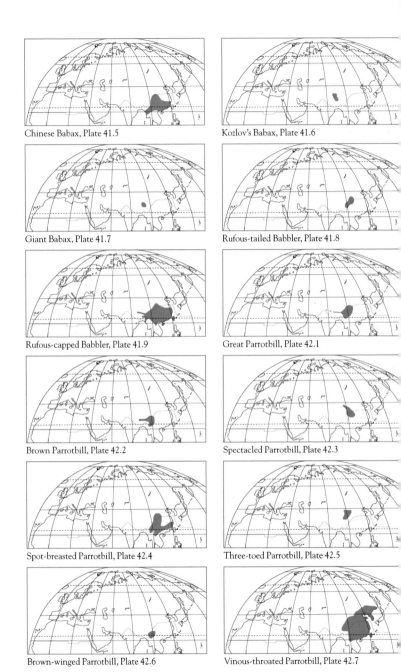

Chinese Babax, Plate 41.5

Kozlov's Babax, Plate 41.6

Giant Babax, Plate 41.7

Rufous-tailed Babbler, Plate 41.8

Rufous-capped Babbler, Plate 41.9

Great Parrotbill, Plate 42.1

Brown Parrotbill, Plate 42.2

Spectacled Parrotbill, Plate 42.3

Spot-breasted Parrotbill, Plate 42.4

Three-toed Parrotbill, Plate 42.5

Brown-winged Parrotbill, Plate 42.6

Vinous-throated Parrotbill, Plate 42.7

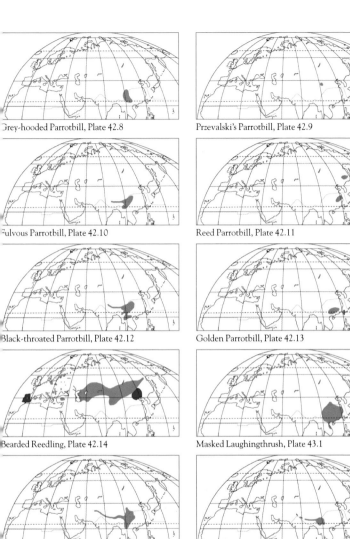

Grey-hooded Parrotbill, Plate 42.8

Przevalski's Parrotbill, Plate 42.9

Fulvous Parrotbill, Plate 42.10

Reed Parrotbill, Plate 42.11

Black-throated Parrotbill, Plate 42.12

Golden Parrotbill, Plate 42.13

Bearded Reedling, Plate 42.14

Masked Laughingthrush, Plate 43.1

White-throated Laughingthrush, Plate 43.2

Striated Laughingthrush, Plate 43.3

Variegated Laughingthrush, Plate 43.4

Père David's Laughingthrush, Plate 43.5

Sukatschev's Laughingthrush, Plate 43.6

Rufous-chinned Laughingthrush, Plate 43.7

Moustached Laughingthrush, Plate 43.8

Biet's Laughingthrush, Plate 43.9

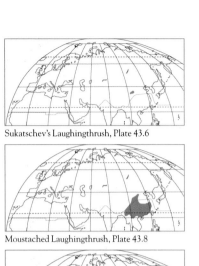
Hwamei, Plate 43.10

Giant Laughingthrush, Plate 44.1

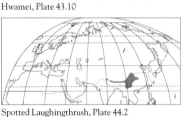
Spotted Laughingthrush, Plate 44.2

Barred Laughingthrush, Plate 44.3

Streaked Laughingthrush, Plate 44.4

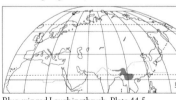
Blue-winged Laughingthrush, Plate 44.5

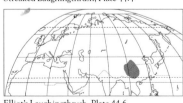
Elliot's Laughingthrush, Plate 44.6

Scaly Laughingthrush, Plate 44.7

208

Prince Henri's Laughingthrush, Plate 44.8

Black-faced Laughingthrush, Plate 44.9

Chestnut-crowned Laughingthrush, Plate 44.10

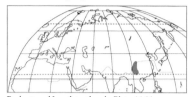

Red-winged Laughingthrush, Plate 44.11

Emei Shan Liocichla, Plate 45.1

Fire-tailed Myzornis, Plate 45.2

Red-billed Leiothrix, Plate 45.3

White-browed Shrike-babbler, Plate 45.4

Black-headed Shrike-babbler, Plate 45.5

Green Shrike-babbler, Plate 45.6

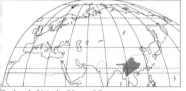

Red-tailed Minla, Plate 45.7

Chestnut-tailed Minla, Plate 45.8

209

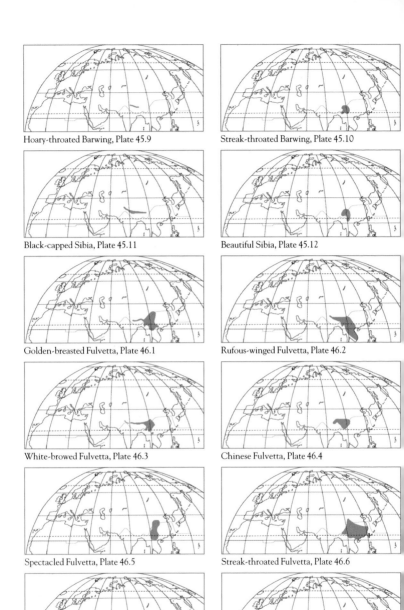

Hoary-throated Barwing, Plate 45.9

Streak-throated Barwing, Plate 45.10

Black-capped Sibia, Plate 45.11

Beautiful Sibia, Plate 45.12

Golden-breasted Fulvetta, Plate 46.1

Rufous-winged Fulvetta, Plate 46.2

White-browed Fulvetta, Plate 46.3

Chinese Fulvetta, Plate 46.4

Spectacled Fulvetta, Plate 46.5

Streak-throated Fulvetta, Plate 46.6

Ludlow's Fulvetta, Plate 46.7

Whiskered Yuhina, Plate 46.8

Stripe-throated Yuhina, Plate 46.9

White-collared Yuhina, Plate 46.10

Rufous-vented Yuhina, Plate 46.11

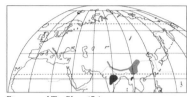

Fire-capped Tit, Plate 47.1

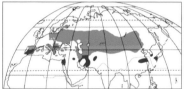

Penduline Tit, Plate 47.2

Sooty Tit, Plate 47.3

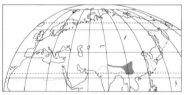

Black-browed Tit, Plate 47.4

White-throated Tit, Plate 47.5

White-cheeked Tit, Plate 47.6

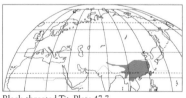

Black-throated Tit, Plate 47.7

Long-tailed Tit, Plate 47.8

Marsh Tit, Plate 48.1

211

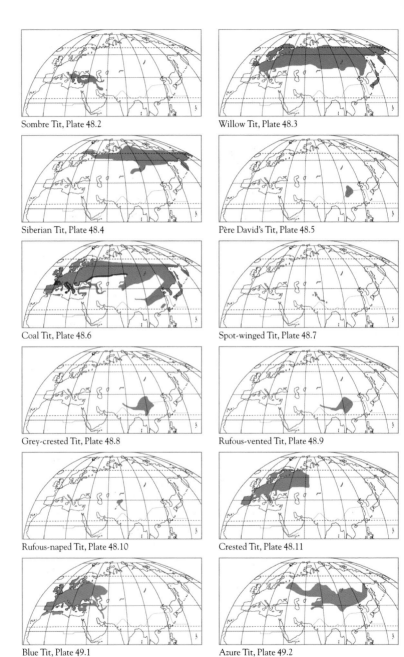

Sombre Tit, Plate 48.2

Willow Tit, Plate 48.3

Siberian Tit, Plate 48.4

Père David's Tit, Plate 48.5

Coal Tit, Plate 48.6

Spot-winged Tit, Plate 48.7

Grey-crested Tit, Plate 48.8

Rufous-vented Tit, Plate 48.9

Rufous-naped Tit, Plate 48.10

Crested Tit, Plate 48.11

Blue Tit, Plate 49.1

Azure Tit, Plate 49.2

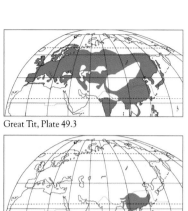

Great Tit, Plate 49.3

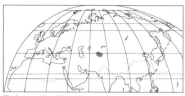

Turkestan Tit, Plate 49.4

Yellow-cheeked Tit, Plate 49.5

Black-lored Tit, Plate 49.6

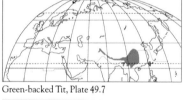

Green-backed Tit, Plate 49.7

Yellow-bellied Tit, Plate 49.8

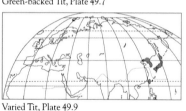

Varied Tit, Plate 49.9

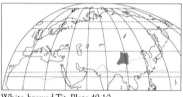

White-browed Tit, Plate 49.10

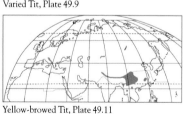

Yellow-browed Tit, Plate 49.11

Yunnan Nuthatch, Plate 50.1

Chinese Nuthatch, Plate 50.2

Krüper's Nuthatch, Plate 50.3

213

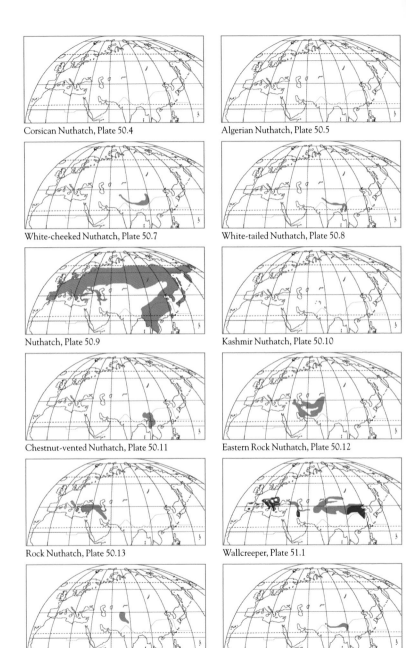

Corsican Nuthatch, Plate 50.4

Algerian Nuthatch, Plate 50.5

White-cheeked Nuthatch, Plate 50.7

White-tailed Nuthatch, Plate 50.8

Nuthatch, Plate 50.9

Kashmir Nuthatch, Plate 50.10

Chestnut-vented Nuthatch, Plate 50.11

Eastern Rock Nuthatch, Plate 50.12

Rock Nuthatch, Plate 50.13

Wallcreeper, Plate 51.1

Bar-tailed Treecreeper, Plate 51.2

Rusty-flanked Treecreeper, Plate 51.3

Brown-throated Treecreeper, Plate 51.4

Sichuan Treecreeper, Plate 51.5

Treecreeper, Plate 51.6

Short-toed Treecreeper, Plate 51.7

Bonin Honeyeater, Plate 51.8

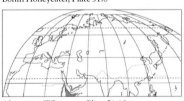

Japanese White-eye, Plate 51.9

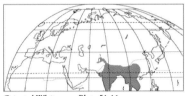

Abyssinian White-eye, Plate 51.10

Oriental White-eye, Plate 51.11

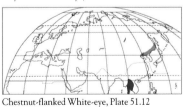

Chestnut-flanked White-eye, Plate 51.12

Pygmy Sunbird, Plate 52.1

Nile Valley Sunbird, Plate 52.2

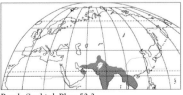

Purple Sunbird, Plate 52.3

215

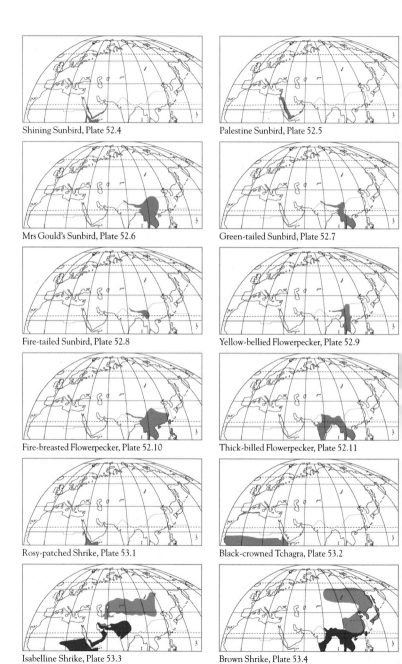

Shining Sunbird, Plate 52.4

Palestine Sunbird, Plate 52.5

Mrs Gould's Sunbird, Plate 52.6

Green-tailed Sunbird, Plate 52.7

Fire-tailed Sunbird, Plate 52.8

Yellow-bellied Flowerpecker, Plate 52.9

Fire-breasted Flowerpecker, Plate 52.10

Thick-billed Flowerpecker, Plate 52.11

Rosy-patched Shrike, Plate 53.1

Black-crowned Tchagra, Plate 53.2

Isabelline Shrike, Plate 53.3

Brown Shrike, Plate 53.4

Tiger Shrike, Plate 53.5

Red-backed Shrike, Plate 53.6

Bay-backed Shrike, Plate 53.7

Bull-headed Shrike, Plate 53.8

Long-tailed Shrike, Plate 54.1

Grey-backed Shrike, Plate 54.2

Grey-backed Fiscal Shrike, Plate 54.3

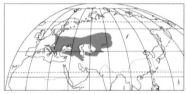

Lesser Grey Shrike, Plate 54.4

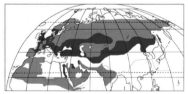

Great Grey Shrike, Plate 54.5

Chinese Grey Shrike, Plate 54.6

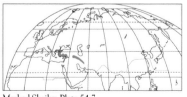

Masked Shrike, Plate 54.7

Woodchat Shrike, Plate 54.8

217

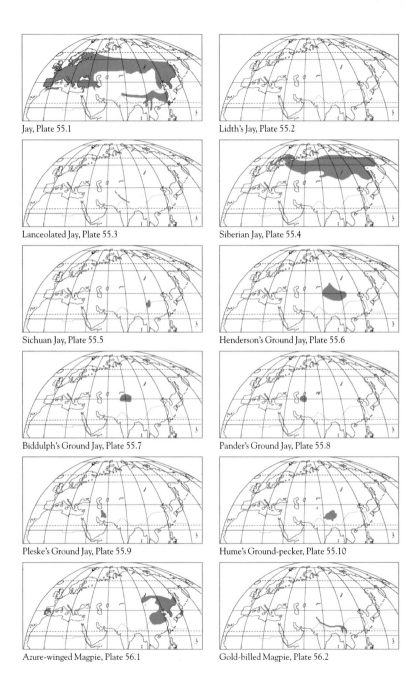

Jay, Plate 55.1

Lidth's Jay, Plate 55.2

Lanceolated Jay, Plate 55.3

Siberian Jay, Plate 55.4

Sichuan Jay, Plate 55.5

Henderson's Ground Jay, Plate 55.6

Biddulph's Ground Jay, Plate 55.7

Pander's Ground Jay, Plate 55.8

Pleske's Ground Jay, Plate 55.9

Hume's Ground-pecker, Plate 55.10

Azure-winged Magpie, Plate 56.1

Gold-billed Magpie, Plate 56.2

218

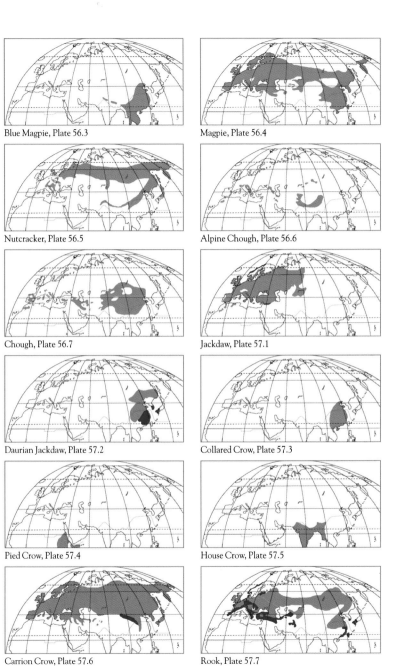

Blue Magpie, Plate 56.3

Magpie, Plate 56.4

Nutcracker, Plate 56.5

Alpine Chough, Plate 56.6

Chough, Plate 56.7

Jackdaw, Plate 57.1

Daurian Jackdaw, Plate 57.2

Collared Crow, Plate 57.3

Pied Crow, Plate 57.4

House Crow, Plate 57.5

Carrion Crow, Plate 57.6

Rook, Plate 57.7

219

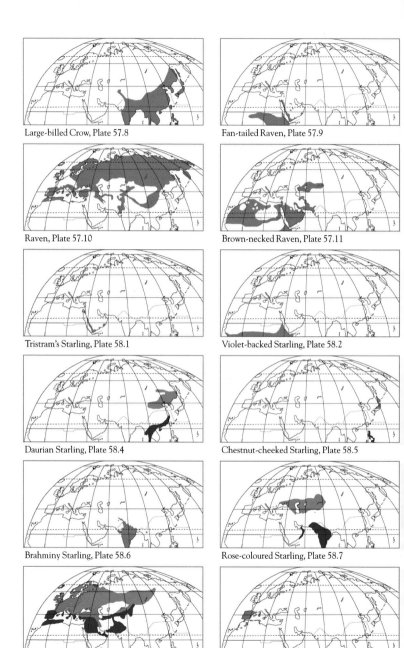

Large-billed Crow, Plate 57.8

Fan-tailed Raven, Plate 57.9

Raven, Plate 57.10

Brown-necked Raven, Plate 57.11

Tristram's Starling, Plate 58.1

Violet-backed Starling, Plate 58.2

Daurian Starling, Plate 58.4

Chestnut-cheeked Starling, Plate 58.5

Brahminy Starling, Plate 58.6

Rose-coloured Starling, Plate 58.7

Starling, Plate 58.9

Spotless Starling, Plate 58.10

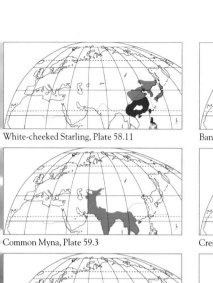

White-cheeked Starling, Plate 58.11

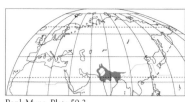

Bank Myna, Plate 59.2

Common Myna, Plate 59.3

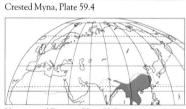

Crested Myna, Plate 59.4

Black Drongo, Plate 59.7

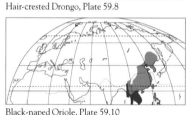

Hair-crested Drongo, Plate 59.8

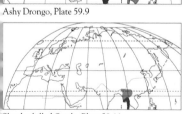

Ashy Drongo, Plate 59.9

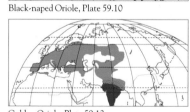

Black-naped Oriole, Plate 59.10

Slender-billed Oriole, Plate 59.11

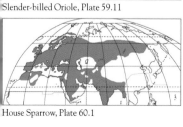

Golden Oriole, Plate 59.12

House Sparrow, Plate 60.1

Spanish Sparrow, Plate 60.2

221

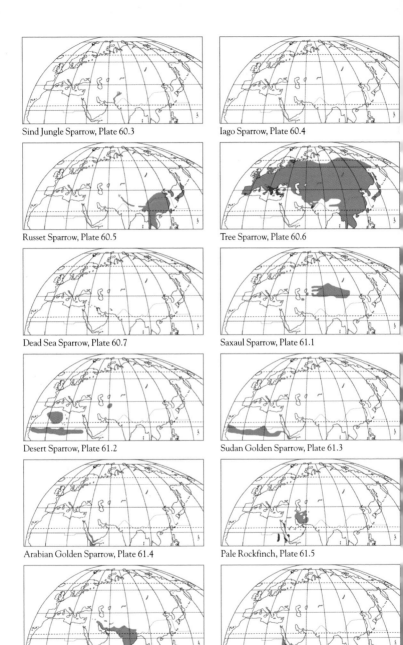

Sind Jungle Sparrow, Plate 60.3

Iago Sparrow, Plate 60.4

Russet Sparrow, Plate 60.5

Tree Sparrow, Plate 60.6

Dead Sea Sparrow, Plate 60.7

Saxaul Sparrow, Plate 61.1

Desert Sparrow, Plate 61.2

Sudan Golden Sparrow, Plate 61.3

Arabian Golden Sparrow, Plate 61.4

Pale Rockfinch, Plate 61.5

Chestnut-shouldered Petronia, Plate 61.6

Bush Petronia, Plate 61.7

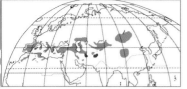

Rock Sparrow, Plate 61.8

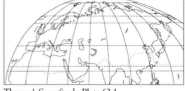

Theresa's Snowfinch, Plate 62.1

Blanford's Snowfinch, Plate 62.2

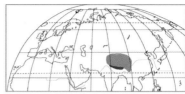

Rufous-necked Snowfinch, Plate 62.3

Père David's Snowfinch, Plate 62.4

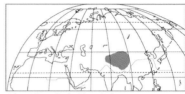

Adams' Snowfinch, Plate 62.5

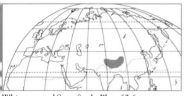

White-rumped Snowfinch, Plate 62.6

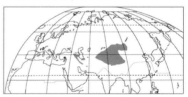

Snowfinch, Plate 62.7

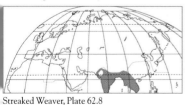

Streaked Weaver, Plate 62.8

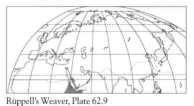

Rüppell's Weaver, Plate 62.9

Common Waxbill, Plate 63.1

Arabian Waxbill, Plate 63.2

223

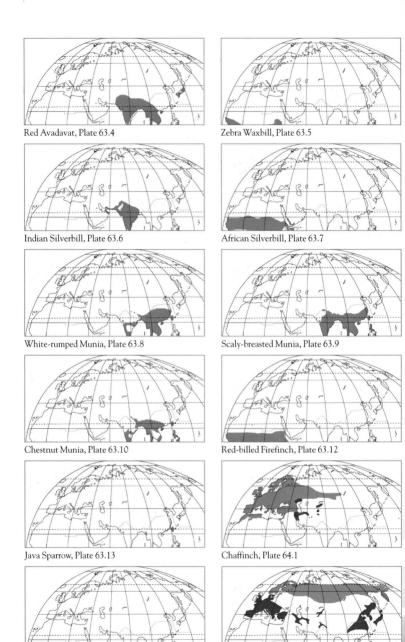

Red Avadavat, Plate 63.4

Zebra Waxbill, Plate 63.5

Indian Silverbill, Plate 63.6

African Silverbill, Plate 63.7

White-rumped Munia, Plate 63.8

Scaly-breasted Munia, Plate 63.9

Chestnut Munia, Plate 63.10

Red-billed Firefinch, Plate 63.12

Java Sparrow, Plate 63.13

Chaffinch, Plate 64.1

Blue Chaffinch, Plate 64.2

Brambling, Plate 64.3

224

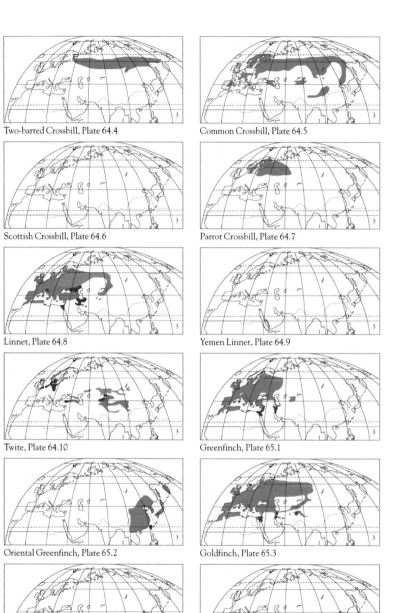

Two-barred Crossbill, Plate 64.4

Common Crossbill, Plate 64.5

Scottish Crossbill, Plate 64.6

Parrot Crossbill, Plate 64.7

Linnet, Plate 64.8

Yemen Linnet, Plate 64.9

Twite, Plate 64.10

Greenfinch, Plate 65.1

Oriental Greenfinch, Plate 65.2

Goldfinch, Plate 65.3

Black-headed Greenfinch, Plate 65.4

Yellow-breasted Greenfinch, Plate 65.5

225

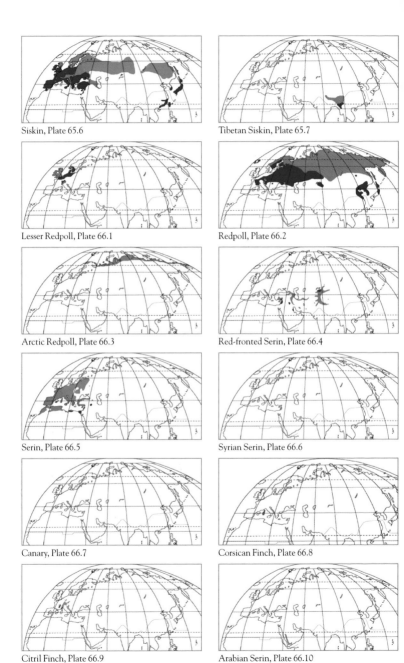

Siskin, Plate 65.6

Tibetan Siskin, Plate 65.7

Lesser Redpoll, Plate 66.1

Redpoll, Plate 66.2

Arctic Redpoll, Plate 66.3

Red-fronted Serin, Plate 66.4

Serin, Plate 66.5

Syrian Serin, Plate 66.6

Canary, Plate 66.7

Corsican Finch, Plate 66.8

Citril Finch, Plate 66.9

Arabian Serin, Plate 66.10

226

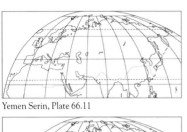

Yemen Serin, Plate 66.11

Plain Mountain Finch, Plate 67.1

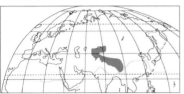

Brandt's Mountain Finch, Plate 67.2

Sillem's Mountain Finch, Plate 67.3

Asian Rosy Finch, Plate 67.4

Grey-crowned Rosy Finch, Plate 67.5

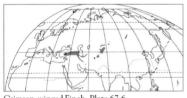

Crimson-winged Finch, Plate 67.6

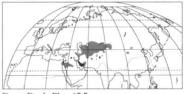

Desert Finch, Plate 67.7

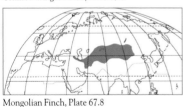

Mongolian Finch, Plate 67.8

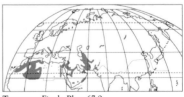

Trumpeter Finch, Plate 67.9

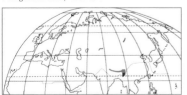

Scarlet Finch, Plate 68.1

Roborovski's Rosefinch, Plate 68.2

227

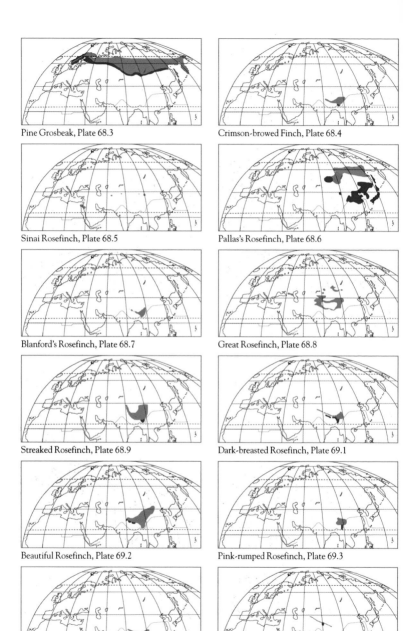

Pine Grosbeak, Plate 68.3

Crimson-browed Finch, Plate 68.4

Sinai Rosefinch, Plate 68.5

Pallas's Rosefinch, Plate 68.6

Blanford's Rosefinch, Plate 68.7

Great Rosefinch, Plate 68.8

Streaked Rosefinch, Plate 68.9

Dark-breasted Rosefinch, Plate 69.1

Beautiful Rosefinch, Plate 69.2

Pink-rumped Rosefinch, Plate 69.3

Spot-winged Rosefinch, Plate 69.4

Pink-browed Rosefinch, Plate 69.5

Vinaceous Rosefinch, Plate 69.6

Dark-rumped Rosefinch, Plate 69.7

Red-mantled Rosefinch, Plate 69.8

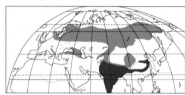

Common Rosefinch, Plate 70.1

White-browed Rosefinch, Plate 70.2

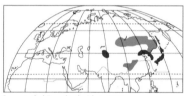

Three-banded Rosefinch, Plate 70.3

Red-breasted Rosefinch, Plate 70.4

Long-tailed Rosefinch, Plate 70.5

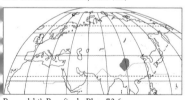

Przewalski's Rosefinch, Plate 70.6

Spectacled Finch, Plate 70.7

Golden-naped Finch, Plate 70.8

Brown Bullfinch, Plate 71.1

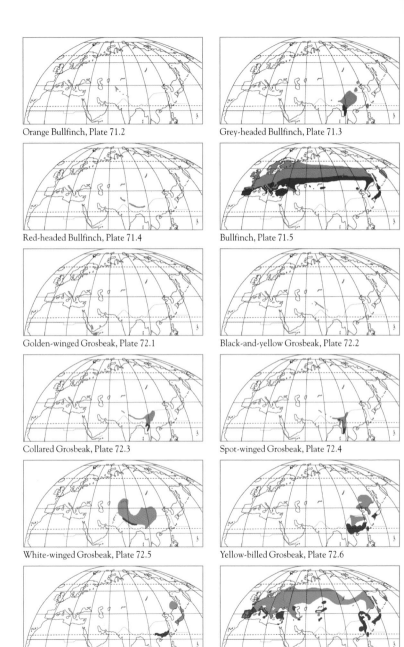

Orange Bullfinch, Plate 71.2

Grey-headed Bullfinch, Plate 71.3

Red-headed Bullfinch, Plate 71.4

Bullfinch, Plate 71.5

Golden-winged Grosbeak, Plate 72.1

Black-and-yellow Grosbeak, Plate 72.2

Collared Grosbeak, Plate 72.3

Spot-winged Grosbeak, Plate 72.4

White-winged Grosbeak, Plate 72.5

Yellow-billed Grosbeak, Plate 72.6

Japanese Grosbeak, Plate 72.7

Hawfinch, Plate 72.8

230

Cinereous Bunting, Plate 76.1

Japanese Yellow Bunting, Plate 76.2

Yellowhammer, Plate 76.3

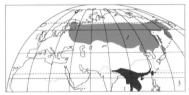

Cirl Bunting, Plate 76.4

Chestnut-eared Bunting, Plate 76.5

Yellow-breasted Bunting, Plate 76.6

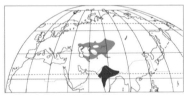

Red-headed Bunting, Plate 76.7

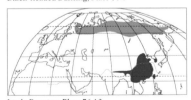

Black-headed Bunting, Plate 76.8

Chestnut Bunting, Plate 76.9

Little Bunting, Plate 76.10

Meadow Bunting, Plate 77.1

Jankowski's Bunting, Plate 77.2

231

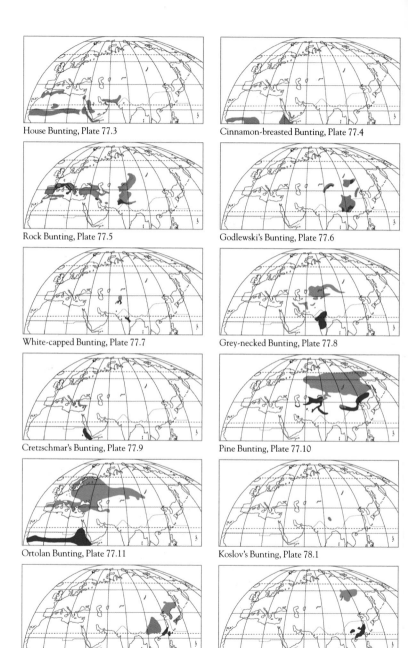

House Bunting, Plate 77.3

Cinnamon-breasted Bunting, Plate 77.4

Rock Bunting, Plate 77.5

Godlewski's Bunting, Plate 77.6

White-capped Bunting, Plate 77.7

Grey-necked Bunting, Plate 77.8

Cretzschmar's Bunting, Plate 77.9

Pine Bunting, Plate 77.10

Ortolan Bunting, Plate 77.11

Koslov's Bunting, Plate 78.1

Yellow-throated Bunting, Plate 78.2

Yellow-browed Bunting, Plate 78.3

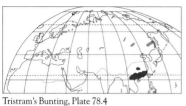

Tristram's Bunting, Plate 78.4

Rustic Bunting, Plate 78.5

Reed Bunting, Plate 78.6

Pallas's Reed Bunting, Plate 78.7

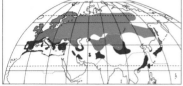

Japanese Reed Bunting, Plate 78.8

Black-faced Bunting, Plate 78.9

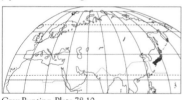

Grey Bunting, Plate 78.10

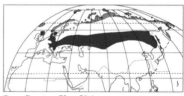

Snow Bunting, Plate 79.1

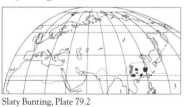

Slaty Bunting, Plate 79.2

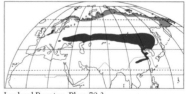

Lapland Bunting, Plate 79.3

Corn Bunting, Plate 79.4

233

237

238

239